Responsive States

The US Constitution did not establish a clear division of responsibilities between the national government and state governments, so the distribution of policymaking authority is subject to constant renegotiation and debate. When national lawmakers introduce policy initiatives that implicate the states in important ways, why do state leaders sometimes respond with strong support and at other times with indifference or outright hostility? Moving beyond the conventional story that state officials simply want money and autonomy from their national counterparts, this book explains how the states' responses over the short, medium, and long term are shaped by policy design, timing, and the interaction between the two. Reaching across different historical eras with in-depth case studies of policies such as Superfund, the No Child Left Behind Act, and the Patient Protection and Affordable Care Act, this book shows how federalism has influenced, and continues to influence, the evolution of American public policy.

Andrew Karch is Arleen C. Carlson Professor in the Department of Political Science at the University of Minnesota. He is the author of *Early Start: Preschool Politics in the United States* (2013) and *Democratic Laboratories: Policy Diffusion among the American States* (2007).

Shanna Rose is Associate Professor of Government at Claremont McKenna College. She is the author of *Financing Medicaid: Federalism and the Growth of America's Health Care Safety Net* (2013).

Responsive States

Federalism and American Public Policy

ANDREW KARCH
University of Minnesota

SHANNA ROSE
Claremont McKenna College

CAMBRIDGE
UNIVERSITY PRESS

CAMBRIDGE
UNIVERSITY PRESS

University Printing House, Cambridge CB2 8BS, United Kingdom

One Liberty Plaza, 20th Floor, New York, NY 10006, USA

477 Williamstown Road, Port Melbourne, VIC 3207, Australia

314–321, 3rd Floor, Plot 3, Splendor Forum, Jasola District Centre, New Delhi – 110025, India

79 Anson Road, #06–04/06, Singapore 079906

Cambridge University Press is part of the University of Cambridge.

It furthers the University's mission by disseminating knowledge in the pursuit of education, learning, and research at the highest international levels of excellence.

www.cambridge.org
Information on this title: www.cambridge.org/9781108485173
DOI: 10.1017/9781108750264

© Cambridge University Press 2019

First published 2019

Printed and bound in Great Britain by Clays Ltd, Elcograf S.p.A.

A catalogue record for this publication is available from the British Library.

ISBN 978-1-108-48517-3 Hardback
ISBN 978-1-108-71923-0 Paperback

To Kaori, Dahlia, Jonah, and Annabelle,
and
Peter, Lulu, and Stellan

Contents

Tables

Figures

Acknowledgments

This project began several years ago as a conference paper. At the conference we were asked whether the paper was part of a longer book manuscript. We mulled it over for a while and then decided that the answer to that question should be yes. Today, after various modifications and multiple drafts, as well as one cross-country move and the addition of one new member to each of our respective families, we are thrilled to see the project finally come to fruition.

We are very grateful for the generous guidance and support we received from numerous individuals throughout the course of the project. We would like to thank Kimberley Johnson, Carol Weissert, and Alan Jacobs for the thoughtful and constructive feedback they provided on the conference papers that laid the foundation for the book. We appreciate the opportunities we received to present our research at Indiana University, the University of Colorado Boulder, the Southern California Law and Social Science Forum, and the University of Minnesota. Engaged audiences at each of these seminars helped us sharpen our thinking and improved the quality of our work. We owe an especially large debt to the anonymous reviewers who generously read the entire manuscript and provided many helpful suggestions that greatly improved it. Of course, none of these individuals or audiences should be faulted for the weaknesses that remain in the finished product.

Several institutions provided support that made the project possible. Andy Karch thanks the Center for the Study of Federalism as well as the College of Liberal Arts and the Department of Political Science at the University of Minnesota for their financial support, especially during the sabbatical year during which much of the book was drafted. Shanna Rose thanks Claremont McKenna College for an enhanced yearlong sabbatical. We appreciate the opportunity to work with Cambridge University Press. Our editor, Sara Doskow, offers a combination of knowledge, calm, and patience that makes working with her a pleasure. Finally, we also would like to acknowledge permission to use material that appeared in our previously published article: "States as Stakeholders: Federalism, Policy Feedback, and Government

Elites," *Studies in American Political Development* 31, Number 1 (April 2017):47–67.

This book is dedicated to our families, without whom this project would have been completed several years earlier, but for whom we are nonetheless extremely grateful.

Introduction

States as Stakeholders

After the November 2016 elections gave the Republican Party unified control over the presidency and both chambers of Congress, its longstanding goal of "repealing and replacing" the Patient Protection and Affordable Care Act (ACA) seemed to be well within its reach. The House of Representatives voted to eradicate the central domestic policy accomplishment of the Obama administration in early May 2017, at which point all eyes turned to the Senate. Since Senate Republicans were using the reconciliation process to circumvent the possibility of a Democratic filibuster and held only a 52–48 majority in the chamber, media attention focused on the handful of GOP senators viewed as capable of bucking the party line.

Senator Dean Heller of Nevada, generally described as the most electorally vulnerable Republican up for reelection in 2018, was watched especially closely. As one version of "repeal and replace" made its way through the upper chamber, Heller held a dramatic press conference in June 2017 at which he argued that the Senate bill was "simply not the answer." He explained that the proposed measure would lead to major losses of insurance coverage and would do nothing to lower the cost of insurance premiums. The senator made clear, however, that he was particularly troubled by the bill's treatment of the so-called "Medicaid expansion" through which millions of Americans, including 200,000 Nevadans, had acquired health insurance. He stated, "This is all about the Medicaid expansion ... You have to protect Medicaid expansion states. That's what I want." Heller wanted any rollback of national government financial support for the expansion to be accompanied by a boost in payment rates for states like Nevada, and his position put him at odds with many of his Republican colleagues (Haberkorn and Pradhan 2017; Sullivan 2017).

Brian Sandoval, the very popular Republican governor of Nevada, stood next to Heller at the press conference. The senator made clear that his stance on any health care measure would be influenced strongly, if not necessarily determined, by the views of his state's chief executive. "If you want my support [on repealing Obamacare]," Heller explained, "you better make sure that the Republican governors that have expanded Medicaid sign off on it ... I've been saying that for months ... Where is Governor Sandoval? What does he think?" (Cohn 2017). The governor had defied party orthodoxy to expand Medicaid and set up a state-run Obamacare exchange through which small companies and individuals without health insurance gained access to a government-regulated marketplace with different levels of coverage. These changes had lowered the state's uninsured rate considerably, and the governor made it very clear that he opposed rolling back the state's policy shifts: "Until I am satisfied and convinced that it's going to protect those 300,000 plus people, I won't be signed on to it" (Snyder 2017). Moreover, Sandoval had been one of seven governors to sign on to a letter that urged Congress to prioritize stabilizing the individual market rather than making major changes to Medicaid (Messerly 2017).[1] The press conference and the seemingly tight relationship between Heller and Sandoval led a journalist to characterize the governor as "the most important person in the Senate health care debate" (Scott 2017).

The initial Senate effort to repeal and replace the ACA failed later that summer,[2] but in early September another proposal gained unexpected momentum. Sponsored by Bill Cassidy (R-LA), Lindsey Graham (R-SC), Heller, and Ron Johnson (R-WI), the bill called for a combination of changes that would have affected the states dramatically. It proposed giving the states control over billions of dollars in health spending while imposing deep Medicaid cuts and preventing the states from taxing health care providers in order to fund Medicaid. This time a bipartisan group of ten governors "dealt a major blow" to the proposal by coming out against it. Alaska governor Bill Walker, an independent, was a member of the group, and one journalistic account described his opposition as "particularly notable" because he "holds some sway over" Lisa Murkowski, the Alaska Republican who was undecided on the measure (Sullivan, Snell, and Eilperin 2017). The Senate effort to enact health care legislation stalled yet again, and gubernatorial opposition was one of several reasons why it failed.

---

[1] The other governors who signed the letter were John Kasich (R-OH), Charles Baker (R-MA), John Hickenlooper (D-CO), Steve Bullock (D-MT), Tom Wolf (D-PA), and John Bel Edwards (D-LA).

[2] Ironically, Heller defied the wishes of the governor and voted for the "skinny repeal" proposal that came within a vote of clearing the Senate. The three Republican senators who opposed it were Susan Collins of Maine, John McCain of Arizona, and Lisa Murkowski of Alaska. The Nevada senator ultimately lost his bid for reelection, and his defeat by Democrat Jacky Rosen was interpreted by political observers as "a message about Heller's health care vote and sudden embrace of President Donald Trump" (Nilsen 2018).

In an era of intense partisan polarization where a "defining feature of American politics [is] a vast and growing gap between liberals and conservatives, Republicans and Democrats,"[3] intraparty disputes between Republican governors and their fellow partisans in Congress might seem surprising. Yet the summer of 2017 was not the first time that the governors had mobilized to defend Medicaid; such spirited defenses have been a prominent feature of the program's history nearly since its creation in 1965 (Rose 2013; Thompson 2012).[4] Moreover, intergovernmental tensions of the sort that helped derail the Senate attempt to "repeal and replace" the ACA seem to be a defining feature of the contemporary era. In recent years, disputes between the national government and the states have cut across an astonishingly wide array of issues that include education, immigration, gun control, climate change, marijuana legalization, and many others. Their ubiquity leads some observers to characterize the current state of affairs as "fragmented federalism" (Bowling and Pickerill 2013). The willingness of state leaders to challenge the national government is part and parcel of what has also been labeled "a fend for yourself and activist form of bottom-up federalism" (Gamkhar and Pickerill 2012).

The framers of the US Constitution might not have predicted the specific policy content of these disputes, yet they would not be surprised by their existence. As the fledgling country considered whether to adopt the new governmental framework during the ratification campaign of the late 1780s, the appropriate balance of power between the national government and the states was one of the primary lines of division between those who endorsed the Constitution and those who did not. Anti-Federalists claimed that the proposed document put the civil liberties of states and citizens at risk due to its excessive centralization of power. James Madison responded that the possible mobilization of state governments rendered such concerns irrelevant or at least overwrought:

But ambitious encroachments of the federal government on the authority of the State governments would not excite the opposition of a single State, or of a few States only. They would be signals of general alarm. Every government would espouse the common cause. A correspondence would be opened. Plans of resistance would be concerted. One spirit would animate and conduct the whole. (Rossiter 1961, 266)

The dynamic Madison described in his essay, invoking the possibility of a "trial of force," is no doubt more melodramatic than a bipartisan group of governors sending a letter to Congress in opposition to a proposed policy change. However, its relevance lies in its recognition that state officials track and react

---

[3] Pew Research Center, "Political Polarization," accessed March 9, 2018 (www.pewresearch.org /packages/political-polarization).

[4] Chapter 4 of this book examines state officials' impact on the political resilience and unexpected expansion of Medicaid in more detail.

to national government activities and that these officials are capable of engaging in collective action to defend what they view as their prerogatives.

National leaders have enacted policies with profound intergovernmental implications for over a century (Johnson 2007; Clemens 2006), and their efforts in recent decades include several prominent initiatives. The Personal Responsibility and Work Opportunity Reconciliation Act of 1996 (PRWORA) fundamentally reformulated American income support policy by ending the individual entitlement to welfare benefits, imposing strict and escalating work requirements, and granting considerable administrative and fiscal discretion to the states. The No Child Left Behind Act of 2002 (NCLB), the subject of Chapter 7 of this book, relied heavily on the states to implement an accountability-based approach to education reform (Manna 2011). Some of the most significant national initiatives of recent years – such as PRWORA, NCLB, and the ACA – implicate the states in critical ways. National lawmakers have been drawn to intergovernmental initiatives for several reasons. In a political system where representation is based on geography, this approach appeals to members of Congress who want to please the constituents and elected officials they serve. It also can allow subnational officials to customize policy templates to the needs and preferences of their specific jurisdictions. Moreover, implicating state governments in the implementation of national policies holds special appeal in a political environment, like that of recent decades, characterized by intense resistance to increased national taxation.

State officials have greeted these intergovernmental initiatives with responses that range from enthusiasm to indifference to hostility, and this contemporary variation resonates with the historical record. State leaders have responded enthusiastically to some programs, making far-reaching policy changes in line with national government objectives. President Barack Obama's "Race to the Top" initiative, for example, stimulated major state-level education policy reforms through a competitive grant program (Howell and Magazinnik 2017). Similarly, sometimes state officials have mobilized to defend national policies. When the Federal Communications Commission (FCC) moved to roll back net neutrality rules in 2017, nearly two dozen state attorneys general signed on to a lawsuit challenging the policy change, five governors signed executive orders to preserve the rules, and legislators in about thirty states introduced proposals to get around the repeal (Lecher 2018). In other cases, such as the Sheppard–Towner Act that this book examines in more detail in Chapter 3, state officials have barely reacted at all to national policies with intergovernmental implications. Finally, in other cases state leaders have greeted national programs with the antagonism that might be expected in an era of fragmented federalism. When President Donald Trump issued an executive order in January 2017 that restricted travel and suspended the admission of refugees from seven majority-Muslim countries, the state of Washington (later joined by Minnesota) filed suit and seventeen other states filed an amicus brief outlining the undesirable effects of the order (Goelzhauser and Rose 2017, 294). Moreover, sometimes state officials' reactions over the medium and long term do not match the original position they took while a statute was debated, shifting from enthusiasm to indifference or from opposition to support. What explains this varied reception? That question motivates the rest of this book, and it is particularly significant at a historical moment when numerous key issues in American domestic policy invoke long-standing concerns about the appropriate distribution of authority between the national government and the states.

STATES AS STAKEHOLDERS

In outlining the factors that help explain whether and how state officials react to national initiatives, this book builds on the intellectual foundation provided by three lines of study that lie at the intersection of political science and history. The first relevant scholarly literature is the study of American political development (APD). A central feature of APD scholarship is its combination of ambitious scope and historical depth; research in this tradition utilizes a "wide-angle lens" to exploit the possibilities of a regime-level and longitudinal treatment of American politics (Mettler and Valelly 2016, 2–3). This developmental approach has had a profound impact on the study of public policy, where it requires both careful attention to social processes that play out over considerable periods of time and systematic thinking about exactly how those processes unfold (Pierson 2005, 34).[5] In contrast to analytical approaches that focus on individual behavior, whether those individuals are members of Congress or of the American electorate, scholarship in the APD tradition offers a macro-level perspective which prioritizes the emergence and relative durability of existing arrangements. The present study, with its focus on the many different ways in which intergovernmental policy initiatives distribute governing authority and the long-term implications of this variation, applies the insights and methods of developmental scholars to the relationship between the national government and the states. Other scholars have documented the impact of federalism on American political development, yet their insights generally have not been applied to contemporary work on intergovernmental relations (Robertson 2016, 345).

The multifaceted scholarly literature on American federalism is the second line of study on which the book builds. One prominent strand of this literature seeks to characterize the nature of intergovernmental relations in the United States, paying especially close attention to how this relationship has changed over time. Most observers agree that massive shifts occurred in the mid-

---

[5] In the words of Karen Orren and Stephen Skowronek (2004, 9, emphasis in original), "APD research indicates movement *through* time rather than a polity bounded in time and highlights connections *between* politics in the past and politics in the present rather than the separateness and foreignness of past politics."

twentieth century as various forces transformed the federal relationship from "dual federalism" to "cooperative federalism." Under dual federalism, state and national officials operated largely independently of one another, each sovereign in their own issue domains. The transition to cooperative federalism, however, turned state governments into friendly servants charged with carrying out national policy initiatives (Corwin 1950; Elazar 1962; Grodzins 1966). The nature of the federal relationship changed again in the late twentieth century, occasionally fostering heightened intergovernmental tensions. National laws imposed increasingly restrictive administrative constraints on the autonomy of state governments, occasionally even preempting their authority to take action (Zimmerman 2005, 2007). John Kincaid (1990) famously described this change as the shift from cooperative to "coercive" federalism. It fostered a perception among state officials that the national government viewed the states as its administrative outposts. Some legal scholars therefore characterize the contemporary era as one of "uncooperative federalism," portraying a relationship in which the national government seeks cooperation from the states but state leaders increasingly resist and challenge the authority of the national government (Bulman-Pozen and Gerken 2009).

Understanding the changing nature of the relationship between the states and the national government is a valuable scholarly enterprise, yet its ability to account for state officials' diverse responses to national laws is rather limited. The shift from dual to cooperative to uncooperative federalism cannot explain why similar policies adopted at different times, or different policies enacted around the same time, have divergent developmental trajectories. Consider Medicaid and general revenue sharing, two programs that later chapters will examine in greater detail. Enacted in 1965 and 1972, respectively, they sparked opposing reactions among state officials. Although state leaders expressed mild opposition to Medicaid as it navigated the legislative process, they quickly emerged as some of the program's staunchest defenders. These self-reinforcing feedback effects helped prevent members of Congress from retrenching the program during its early years. In contrast, state officials enthusiastically lobbied for the passage of general revenue sharing but did surprisingly little to forestall its elimination only a few years later. The striking difference in the politics of two federalism-related policies adopted during the same time period suggests that it is essential to be attentive to policy content. Specific features of federalism-related initiatives shape their fiscal and administrative implications. Those implications shape how state officials react to the policy in question, determining whether intergovernmental relations are best characterized as autonomous, cooperative, coercive, or uncooperative. A more nuanced view of state officials and how they respond to national laws can bridge and move beyond the well-known generalizations about broad historical eras.

Another branch of the scholarly literature on federalism provides the foundation on which such an account can be built. It focuses on the political mobilization of state and local officials as an interest group, seeking to trace the origins of this "intergovernmental lobby" and to isolate the conditions under which it successfully influences national policy (Cammisa 1995; Haider 1974; Herian 2011; Marbach and Leckrone 2002). The activities of broad professional associations like the National Governors Association (NGA), the Council of State Governments (CSG), and the National Conference of State Legislatures (NCSL) are the modern manifestation of the collective action to which James Madison referred. Similarly, more specialized groups like the National Association of Medicaid Directors (NAMD) and the Association of State and Territorial Solid Waste Management Officials (ASTSWMO) bring together state officials who share a professional focus and a common set of policy concerns. The organizations that make up the intergovernmental lobby are a vital force in national politics, testifying at congressional hearings and lobbying the executive branch in their efforts to shape national policy.[6]

When investigating whether and how state leaders react to national policy initiatives with federalism-related implications, the activities – or inactivity – of the intergovernmental lobby can serve as a critical source of evidence. How involved were these groups in crafting national laws? What role, if any, did they play as these policies were implemented and revisited? Most scholarly analyses of the intergovernmental lobby engage primarily, often even exclusively, with the first of these questions. They focus on the dramatic moment of policy adoption and the occasionally heated battles that lead up to it. Understanding why programs are established, and the respective roles of various political actors in their creation, is an important endeavor. Yet it presents an incomplete view of the policy process. Some reforms succeed after they become law, whereas others unravel (Patashnik 2008). Moreover, as the earlier comparison of Medicaid and general revenue sharing suggests, constituencies might modify their positions as a program changes from an idea into a reality. Existing research on the intergovernmental lobby, by and large, pays little attention to what happens after major policy changes occur. As a result, scholars working in this tradition fail to recognize that the lobbying activities of state and local officials are both an input into the policy process and a reaction to the specific provisions of national policies. In addition, state and local officials do not work in isolation from the other stakeholders in a particular policy arena. They build coalitions in support of their goals, and the specific nature of those goals and their capacity to achieve them depends on the economic, political, and administrative context in which they operate.

Questions of policy durability and sustainability require thinking about state officials as stakeholders in specific programs rather than as a lobby or an interest group. Reframing the issue in this way blends the insights produced by the study of state officials' collective activities with a third body of research, namely, the

---

[6] In addition to attempting to influence national politics, the organizations that comprise the intergovernmental lobby also disseminate information about emerging policy trends across the country (Clark and Little 2002; Karch 2007).

growing literature on policy feedback. This concept suggests that public policies are not only the products of political processes; they also serve as determinants of subsequent political dynamics (Pierson 1993; Jenkins and Patashnik 2012). As E. E. Schattschneider (1935) observed, there are many ways in which "new policies create a new politics." Public policies can generate feedback effects by changing the payoffs associated with alternative strategies, thereby altering political actors' incentives. They can also confer resources on particular individuals or groups, creating privileged positions from which beneficiaries can work to perpetuate those policies. Finally, public policies can have interpretive effects, changing political actors' perceptions of what their interests are or who their allies might be. The adoption of a public policy therefore has the potential to reconfigure political dynamics in profound ways.

With its emphasis on the mechanisms through which the mere existence of a program can reconfigure the political dynamics surrounding a particular issue, research on policy feedback can help scholars understand why national policies with intergovernmental consequences spark such a wide range of reactions from subnational officials. If the state officials affected by a national policy become its staunch defenders, energetically applying it in their own jurisdictions or lobbying at the national level for its preservation or expansion, then the policy has generated self-reinforcing feedback effects. Alternatively, if state officials' response is to drag their heels during the implementation process or they converge on the nation's capital to try to undercut or eliminate the policy initiative, then the policy has generated self-undermining feedback effects. Finally, if the affected state officials make minimal programmatic changes or engage in few lobbying activities related to a national policy, then that policy has generated negligible feedback effects. Thus the policy decisions that state leaders make at home and the lobbying efforts they undertake in Washington, DC serve as empirical indicators of policy feedback.

In addition to providing a conceptual lens through which the varied responses generated by intergovernmental policy initiatives can be viewed, the policy feedback framework offers the critical insight that policies' internal features can reconfigure the political dynamics surrounding their post-enactment trajectories. It is primarily an endogenous account of political change. As a result, a feedback-based approach makes it possible to understand why not all programs enacted at the same historical moment proceed along similar developmental paths. Some will thrive and others will unravel. To be sure, the precise nature of the political and economic context in which a policy is adopted is relevant. However, its relevance lies mainly in the interaction between that environment and key features of the intergovernmental initiative itself. Building on the insights produced by recent research on policy feedback, the central argument of this book is that a combination of policy design, timing, and their interaction helps explain why national laws with intergovernmental implications generate self-reinforcing, self-undermining, or negligible feedback effects. The next section outlines the specific policy design features and contextual factors that influence state officials' reactions, and Chapter 1 develops this analytical framework in more detail.

While the analytical framework that guides the remainder of the book owes a large intellectual debt to existing policy feedback research, it also represents an attempt to reorient and expand this body of work in order to address two limitations. The first limitation of existing research pertains to the range of policies studied. Many accounts offer persuasive illustrations of self-reinforcing feedback effects, highlighting how specific features of a policy contributed to its expansion over the long term. Instances where policy feedback did not materialize tend to receive little attention, and the identification of self-undermining feedback effects has occurred only recently (Oberlander and Weaver 2015; Jacobs and Weaver 2015; Weaver 2010). Moreover, these insightful studies generally examine a single policy or policy sector. Their depth and attention to detail is one of the features that makes them so compelling. However, it also limits scholars' ability to isolate the factors that are conducive to feedback effects. Only by studying a range of outcomes will we be able to better understand when policy feedback effects are most – and least – likely to occur (Patashnik and Zelizer 2013; Campbell 2012; Patashnik 2008). This book therefore investigates seven national laws with intergovernmental implications. The laws provoked a wide range of responses from state officials, thus providing the variation necessary to assess the analytical framework described in the next section.

The second limitation of existing research pertains to the political actors studied. By delegating authority to certain public officials, policies can spur those actors to mobilize to preserve or expand their prerogatives. Although government elites played a central role in early feedback-related studies (Heclo 1974; Skocpol 1992), they have largely been supplanted by a focus on mass publics and, to a lesser extent, interest groups (Mettler and Soss 2004; Campbell 2012; Goss 2013; Anzia and Moe 2016; Hertel-Fernandez and Skocpol 2015). Returning to elite feedback therefore promises to offer a more balanced view of how policies remake politics while simultaneously providing an opportunity to extend the insights of existing research.

POLICY DESIGN, TIMING, AND FEEDBACK EFFECTS

When the US Constitution was ratified, it did not settle the key question of how policymaking prerogatives should be distributed between the national government and the states. Some of its provisions seem to imply a centralization of authority at the national level, whereas others seem to grant discretion to the states. The policy boundaries of American federalism are therefore fluid and contestable, subject to seemingly continuous debate and renegotiation. In the early twenty-first century, the tensions implicit in this arrangement are alive and well, leading to pitched intergovernmental battles over diverse issues like gun control, so-called sanctuary cities, and net neutrality. Understanding why state officials react in divergent ways to various national initiatives is therefore a topic of considerable importance. Specific features of a program can lead state officials to view themselves as having a vested interest in its preservation or expansion or as being placed in an untenable situation, while features of the environment in which the program is established can also influence their reactions.

Policy design profoundly influences how state officials respond to national initiatives. It is sometimes said that state leaders simply want money from their national counterparts, but the history of intergovernmental relations in the United States is littered with grant programs that received a tepid response from state officials. The precise terms on which funds are distributed, including their generosity, the conditions on their use, and the authority they bestow, affect their attractiveness. Grants that match state government spending on generous terms or that represent an open-ended commitment from the national government tend to generate a different response than less generous or capped grants. Similarly, state officials will react differently to policies that grant them considerable fiscal and administrative discretion and programs that impose numerous inflexible requirements. The level of administrative control can affect the extent to which state officials see themselves as having turf to defend, leading them to be more or less invested in the continuation of a policy. Another influential feature of a program is whether its authorization is temporary or permanent. In addition to shaping the reaction of state officials, the extent to which a program is subject to periodic review can make it vulnerable to contextual changes (Lieberman 1998). Finally, programs with intergovernmental implications can impact constituencies beyond state officials, enhancing or decreasing their coalition potential. Policies that provide resources or financial incentives for private-sector actors and government elites alike can create new alliances that did not exist prior to their adoption.

The timing of policy adoption affects the economic, political, and administrative context in which national and state lawmakers operate. It therefore also shapes how state officials react to national policies. The ups and downs of the economic cycle have a profound effect on state government finances, influencing the states' ability to respond to the financial incentives that are embedded in intergovernmental initiatives. Broader economic trends, such as the transition in the United States from an expansionist fiscal regime to a regime of austerity in the 1970s (Pierson 2001), are also key features of the economic context. Patterns of partisan control at the national and state levels, as well as shifts in public opinion, affect the political appeal of specific policies. Institutional changes, such as the dramatic increase in state governments' administrative capacity during the twentieth century, can augment state leaders' expertise and professionalism, thereby leaving them better suited for policy development.

Crucially, specific attributes of a policy can interact with its environment to influence its evolution over the medium to long term. Consider the duration for which a policy is authorized. Temporary authorization can lead to a situation in which a policy is reevaluated in a context that differs from the one in which it was adopted. For instance, the vulnerability of a relatively liberal policy innovation adopted at the outset of a conservative political era will be greater if it comes up for renewal than if it is permanently authorized. Policy updating is a common element of the congressional agenda (Adler and Wilkerson 2012), and it offers both supporters and opponents an opportunity to press for changes. Similarly, intergovernmental policies that require state governments to make substantial financial investments might be especially unlikely to take root and flourish if their enactment occurs during a recession, as even enthusiastic state officials may be unable to allocate the necessary funds.

Thus policy design, timing, and their interaction can help explain whether and how state officials respond to national laws with intergovernmental implications. Chapter 1 articulates this analytical framework in more detail, spelling out how significant features of national policy initiatives (financial generosity, state administrative discretion, duration of authorization, and coalition potential) and the timing of their adoption can spur state-level responses that influence political struggles years or even decades later. The existence, nature, and intensity of these policy feedback effects illuminate the ways in which the interactive relationship between the national government and the states affects policy development. In addition, Chapter 1 offers broader lessons about the durability and sustainability of public policies, identifying factors that help explain why some policies become entrenched and seemingly impervious to reform while others become vulnerable to retrenchment or even to outright elimination. The book's remaining chapters apply this analytical framework to various national policy initiatives, probing both its strengths and its limitations and identifying fruitful directions for future research on intergovernmental relations and policy feedback.

The book's empirical foundation is therefore seven in-depth case studies of national laws with intergovernmental implications. Selected to provide variation along the key dimensions of policy design and timing, they illustrate the myriad ways in which state officials can react to national initiatives that affect their fiscal situations and administrative prerogatives. Unemployment insurance (UI) and Medicaid, examined in Chapters 2 and 4, respectively, generated self-reinforcing feedback effects as state officials joined forces with other stakeholders to preserve the status quo. In the case of Medicaid, these self-reinforcing feedback effects led to programmatic expansion. In contrast, state officials and the business community sought to preserve the UI program so as to curb its generosity. Chapters 3 and 5 investigate the developmental trajectories of the Sheppard–Towner Act and general revenue sharing, two policy initiatives with intergovernmental implications that generated negligible feedback. As Congress considered the termination of both programs, state and local officials barely responded. Their muted reaction was especially surprising in the context of general revenue sharing, a program that the intergovernmental lobby energetically endorsed during its creation. Superfund and the No Child Left Behind Act, the subjects of Chapters 6 and 7, respectively, illustrate how national laws with federalism-related implications can generate self-undermining feedback effects. In both cases, state officials took actions in their own jurisdictions that ran counter to the goals of the national initiative while also working energetically at the national level on behalf of major programmatic changes. Finally, Chapter 8 examines the early trajectory of the ACA, focusing on the two provisions that directly implicated the states; whereas the Medicaid expansion lent itself to self-reinforcing feedback effects, the law's health insurance exchanges did not. This wide variation in outcomes, which represents a change from the single-policy focus of most research on feedback effects, provides the empirical foundation on which to build a better understanding of the factors that influence state officials' reactions to national policy initiatives.

1

Federalism and Policy Feedback

The first step in identifying the factors that explain why state officials' reactions to national initiatives range from enthusiasm to indifference to antagonism is recognizing that public policies are not only the result of broader social and political processes; they also have the potential to reshape existing political dynamics. In particular, policy decisions made at one moment in time have the potential to influence political struggles years or even decades later, with implications for the policy's long-term stability. These policy feedback effects take two forms. First, self-reinforcing processes can make a policy's developmental trajectory difficult to reverse by hindering the adoption of previously plausible alternatives (Skocpol 1992; Weir 1992; Pierson 2004). Second, public policies can generate self-undermining dynamics that diminish rather than reinforce their own long-term viability (Jacobs and Weaver 2015; Oberlander and Weaver 2015; Weaver 2010).[1]

Recently, political scientists have devoted increasing attention to policy feedback and its implications, and the number of persuasive illustrations has grown. Yet critical questions remain about the frequency of feedback effects and the conditions conducive to their generation (Pierson 2006). As one study explains, "[W]e know what feedback can do – but not as much about *when* feedback will or won't happen" (Patashnik and Zelizer 2013, 1075). Some new programs never manage to become firmly entrenched, whereas others "produce social effects that reinforce their own stability" (Pierson 2005, 37). This chapter

---

[1] Scholars sometimes refer to these self-reinforcing and self-undermining processes as "positive" and "negative" feedback, respectively (Fernandez and Jaime-Castillo 2013; Jordan and Matt 2014). Indeed, some early treatments of policy feedback used positive and self-reinforcing interchangeably (Pierson 2000a). This book avoids the positive and negative labels because they overlap with a related but distinct literature on punctuated equilibrium in policy systems in which those terms are used differently (Baumgartner and Jones 1993). For more on this distinction see Jacobs and Weaver (2015) and Weaver (2015).

develops an analytical framework that attempts to account for these important differences. It builds on recent conceptual and empirical advances in the study of policy feedback, positing that specific features of a policy's design, the timing of its adoption, and interactions between those two factors help determine whether a new policy will generate self-reinforcing effects, self-undermining effects, or neither.[2] Policy design, timing, and their interaction help explain why similar policies adopted at different times, or different policies enacted around the same time, have divergent developmental trajectories.

The rest of the chapter proceeds as follows. It begins by explaining why the concept of policy feedback provides a promising lens through which to investigate state officials' wide-ranging responses to national policy initiatives. There are several features of state governments that seem to lend themselves to feedback effects, and the likelihood that such effects will emerge is enhanced by the innate fluidity and contestability of intergovernmental relations in the United States. The chapter then develops an analytical framework that identifies the conditions under which feedback effects are most likely to emerge, articulating how policy design, timing, and their interaction help explain why some national policies generate self-reinforcing effects, others generate self-undermining effects, and still others generate negligible feedback effects. The final section of the chapter briefly describes the seven case studies around which the rest of the book is organized and the evidentiary standards that will be used to assess the relative strengths and weaknesses of its analytical framework.

THE POLITICAL MOBILIZATION OF STATE OFFICIALS

Policy feedback effects can shape the political behavior of individual citizens, motivate the formation and activities of interest groups, and transform the administrative and financial resources of government elites (Pierson 1993). Sometimes public policies generate interpretive effects, providing information that reshapes existing political dynamics. Government action may redefine an issue, changing individuals' and groups' perceptions of what their interests are and who their allies might be. The "impact of previous policy itself" can also serve as an important input into the policy process because it represents an informational resource for policymakers; this dynamic is known as "political learning" (Heclo 1974, 315; see also Hall 1993). Lawmakers can draw lessons

---

[2] In their theory of endogenous institutional change, Greif and Laitin (2004, 648) allow for three possibilities that lead to "neutral, positive, and negative self-reinforcement (undermining)." Similarly, our conceptualization of policy feedback proposes three potential outcomes. Policies may generate self-reinforcing effects through which affected parties lobby for the preservation or expansion of existing programs. They may also spur self-undermining effects through which affected parties work to retrench or to eliminate the policy. Finally, policies may generate negligible political effects, producing a tepid reaction among affected parties that does not influence their mobilization.

that lead them to view programs as successful and worthy of expansion, as in the case of Social Security (Derthick 1979), while perceived policy failures can produce a trial-and-error dynamic during which government elites discard unsuccessful initiatives until they find policy tools that government can employ effectively (Ikenberry 1988).

Public policies also generate feedback effects through two additional mechanisms. They can alter the incentives faced by individuals, interest groups, and government elites, and they can confer resources on (or take resources away from) those same constituencies. Government action can influence individuals' decisions about purchasing a home, pursuing additional education, and saving for retirement. Similarly, if a policy confers benefits or costs on a latent group, including government officials, it can encourage members of the group to mobilize collectively to defend or challenge the status quo. Finally, the adoption decision is crucial not only because it creates the policy itself but also because it establishes a bureaucratic structure to administer it. Policies can endow government elites with resources like specialized knowledge, managerial experience, or decision-making prerogatives, in the process creating privileged positions from which those same elites can work to perpetuate or expand the policies (Pierson 1993; see also Moe 1989). For more than two decades, these mechanisms – interpretive effects, incentives, and resources – have represented the foundation of a lively and informative literature on how policies create politics.

The policy feedback framework provides a useful lens through which to investigate why state officials' responses to national policy initiatives vary so widely. Their responses represent a form of policy feedback among government elites – governors, state legislators, state attorneys general, and executive branch agency officials at the state level, all of whom have an immense stake in national policy. Their administrative discretion, their access to resources, and the policy actions they take within their states can be shaped profoundly by decisions that are made in the nation's capital. Moreover, state officials can and do mobilize collectively, attempting to influence national policymaking in ways that they view as desirable.

What motivates state officials? In addition to their personal ambitions to increase their own power, win reelection, or make sound public policy, state officials "also develop broader institutional interests stemming from their roles as temporary stewards of their respective institutions," much as James Madison articulated in his discussion of ambition in *Federalist 51* (Nugent 2009, 21). Despite partisan, ideological, and regional differences among state officials, these common institutional interests yield substantial areas of agreement on several important federalism-related matters. They generally fall into two broad categories – administrative and fiscal. The creation of a new national policy that bestows administrative prerogatives on state actors or distributes funds to the states has the potential to reshape state officials' resources and incentives and promote their political mobilization, either as individuals or through professional associations like the National Governors Association (NGA), the National Conference of State Legislatures (NCSL), or the National Association of Medicaid Directors (NAMD). These types of organizations are known as the intergovernmental lobby, and they bring together state officials who share a professional focus and a common set of policy concerns (Cammisa 1995; Haider 1974; Herian 2011; Marbach and Leckrone 2002).

Conventional wisdom holds that when it comes to administrative interests, state officials generally value flexibility. They want discretion to make policy decisions without national government input or interference and the ability to customize national initiatives in response to the particularities of their jurisdictions. As a result, they tend to "prefer being handed broad guidelines and goals rather than prescriptive, detailed instructions from Washington" (Nugent 2009, 45). Bureaucrats and elected officials alike typically want the ability to choose how specific goals will be pursued, set eligibility and benefit levels where relevant, and determine the scope of government activity.[3]

Administrative issues focus on the distribution of policymaking responsibilities between the national government and the states. That balance is contestable, in part, because the policy boundaries of American federalism are extraordinarily fluid. The US Constitution did not articulate "immutable rules that spell out which institutions in society must be charged with making decisions" (Baumgartner and Jones 1993, 31), and it did not create a clear division of authority between the national government and the states (Robertson 2012). Instead it created what James Madison called a "compound republic" with shared policymaking authority across different levels of government (Derthick 2001). As a result, the distribution of policymaking responsibilities is subject to constant debate and renegotiation.

State officials also share a common set of fiscal interests. These fiscal interests usually, but not always, encourage them to press for additional funds from the national government.[4] State governments received approximately $591 billion

---

[3] Although state officials generally want greater autonomy, occasionally there are instances in which they press for less administrative flexibility. Sometimes the nationalization of a policy regime aligns with their ideological goals. For instance, in December 2017 twenty-three conservative state attorneys general signed a letter to congressional leaders backing the Concealed Carry Reciprocity Act, which would have circumscribed state governments' ability to impose regulations on gun ownership. In other policy realms, such as environmental protection, liberal state officials have called for national standards that ensure a level regulatory playing field. These differences of opinion can also depend on the specific institutional positions that state officials hold. Elected officials' viewpoints on Medicaid, for instance, do not always align with those of the National Association of Medicaid Directors.

[4] As the unemployment insurance case study in Chapter 2 of this book illustrates, sometimes state officials' fiscal goal of additional funding is superseded by a desire to preserve their policymaking or administrative discretion in order to limit a program's generosity. Moreover, it is important to recognize that the distribution of national funds can depend on specific formulas or criteria that advantage some states at others' expense. In those situations, state officials may collaborate to make more funds available but compete over the criteria used to distribute them.

in intergovernmental transfers from the national government in 2015, an amount that accounted for 27.3 percent of the revenue they collected that year.[5] Since transfers make up such a substantial proportion of revenue, state officials have "a strong interest in how much federal money flows into state-government coffers, how it gets there, and how states are allowed to spend it" (Nugent 2009, 41).

Multiple structural and institutional features of state government finances heighten the importance of intergovernmental transfers. State governments generate substantial revenue from income taxes, sales taxes, and other sources that are very sensitive to the economic cycle. As a result, their revenues decline at the same time that more state residents seek Medicaid, welfare, and other benefits. Balanced budget rules make it difficult for virtually every state government to run a deficit during economic downturns. Thus state governments face especially acute financial pressures during recessions, and additional national funds offer a potential solution to this stress. In addition, many states operate under restrictive borrowing limitations or tax and expenditure limits (TELs) that confine the growth of government revenues or spending. Intergovernmental transfers can help alleviate the fiscal pressures that stem from these limitations.

In addition to being highly sensitive to the economic cycle, state governments also face the pressures of interstate competition for businesses and taxpayers. Since businesses are usually attracted to states that offer a low ratio of taxes paid to services received, state officials seek to enhance their economic position relative to their peers. For example, states appear to be sensitive to the tax and redistributive policies of their neighbors (Bailey and Rom 2004; Besley and Case 1995; Peterson 1995; Volden 2002). Heightened capital mobility implies that companies are not limited by geographic proximity, meaning that this economic competition also can be national in scope. In a competitive economic context, which is magnified by the structural and institutional constraints outlined in the preceding paragraph, state lawmakers have strong incentives to appeal to national officials for the expansion of intergovernmental transfers and the alleviation of administrative and tax burdens.

Why might national officials respond to the entreaties of state elites? The answer lies in the "electoral connection" created by the geographic basis of representation in the United States (Mayhew 1974). Of course, the states' role differs from that of voters or interest groups. Even so, several features of the Constitution give them a central role in the selection and composition of the

---

[5] State and Local Government Finance Initiative Data Query System. http://slfdqs .taxpolicycenter.org/pages.cfm. The Urban-Brookings Tax Policy Center. Data from US Census Bureau, Annual Survey of State and Local Government Finances, Government Finances, Volume 4, and Census of Governments (1977–2015). Date of access: May 9, 2018. Own-source revenue (72.0 percent) and intergovernmental transfers from local governments (0.7 percent) accounted for the remaining revenue in 2015.

national government. Members of the House of Representatives serve geographically defined districts that are redrawn every ten years by state policymakers, and senators represent the states themselves. The Electoral College gives states a central role in presidential campaigns, since the electoral votes that ultimately determine the victor are awarded on a state-by-state basis. Frayed relations with governors, state legislators, mayors, and other public officials can lead to charges that members of Congress have lost touch with their district or state, and even presidents depend on subnational officials to build a winning coalition.[6] These constitutional features provide what Herbert Wechsler (1954) famously described as the "political safeguards of federalism" (see also Nugent 2009), and they give national elected officials reason to respond to, or at least consider, the preferences of state-level actors.[7]

In sum, state leaders share common fiscal and administrative prerogatives vis-à-vis the national government and, thus, an incentive to defend their preferred jurisdictional and financial arrangements. A few studies showcase how states responded to a new national initiative with the aim of securing additional resources or flexibility. For example, state officials have defended their financial stake in the Medicaid program (Rose 2013; Brown and Sparer 2003; Grogan and Patashnik 2003); they have also mobilized to try to retain their control over workers' compensation (Howard 2002) and early childhood education (Karch 2013). These individual studies are persuasive and compelling, yet they are neither generalizable nor predictive, since each examines a single policy area. The next step in this research tradition is to develop an analytical framework that attempts to identify the specific conditions under which state leaders mobilize to reinforce or undermine federal policies. For guidance, we turn to the literature on policy feedback and mass publics.

THE IMPORTANCE OF POLICY DESIGN AND TIMING

In his seminal review essay on the study of policy feedback, Paul Pierson (1993) argued that feedback effects on mass publics had received insufficient attention.

---

[6] Existing research on distributive politics identifies the electoral benefits that members of the House receive when they "bring home the bacon" to their districts. For example, Bickers and Stein (1996) link lower flows of distributive policy benefits to an increased likelihood that quality challengers will oppose incumbents in primary and/or general elections. Another strand of this literature suggests that presidential decision-making about such issues as domestic spending, military base closures, and trade protections is affected by strategic electoral concerns (Kriner and Reeves 2015; Lowande, Jenkins, and Clarke 2018).

[7] Intergovernmental relations in federal systems like Canada and Germany are governed by distinctive constitutional provisions that establish different sets of political safeguards. A comprehensive comparative analysis of these safeguards and their implications lies beyond the scope of this book, but the concluding chapter will return briefly to the benefits of applying the framework advanced here to the study of other federal systems.

Numerous scholars answered his call, sparking the development of a rich literature "bridging policy studies and mass politics" (Mettler and Soss 2004; see also Campbell 2012). The electorate is the main focus of these studies, which illustrate how policies affect the political behavior of their target populations by providing politically relevant resources, affecting levels of political interest, and modifying their likelihood of political mobilization.

Consider some canonical examples of feedback effects on mass publics. Social Security, the social insurance program that provides governmental pensions to tens of millions of elderly residents of the United States, influences the participatory capacity, political interest, and political participation patterns of seniors (Campbell 2002, 2003a). Moreover, those who are most dependent financially on the program are especially likely to mobilize politically in response to "policy threats" to age-related policy (Campbell 2003b).[8] The GI Bill, through which millions of World War II veterans attended college or gained vocational training, had both interpretive and resource-based effects on its recipients. Veterans' memories of how they were treated by the program, and the extent to which they believed they "owed" something back to the government or American society, increased their political participation over the short term; over the longer term, the resource effects provided by the GI Bill had strong effects on the recipients who had attained the highest levels of education (Mettler and Welch 2004; see also Mettler 2002, 2005).

The preceding examples illustrate how feedback effects on mass publics operate through interpretive effects, incentives, and resources. In addition, these studies make two important and related contributions to our understanding of policy feedback and its implications. First, they begin to address issues of case selection. Second, they start to identify the specific conditions that make feedback effects more or less likely. Even though early studies of policy feedback offered many persuasive illustrations of self-reinforcing feedback effects, generally they were not accompanied by analyses of policies whose provisions either undermined their long-term viability or generated negligible feedback. This case selection strategy limited the inferences that could be drawn about both the frequency and the sources of policy feedback.

In contrast, the scope and range of the literature on mass feedback effects means that, in addition to demonstrating how policies can reshape individual behavior, it has also identified instances where such effects failed to materialize. For example, the Personal Responsibility and Work Opportunity

---

[8] In addition to affecting the political activity of elderly individuals, Social Security and related legislation helped foster the proliferation of interest groups serving the aged. Organizations like the American Association of Retired Persons and the National Council of Senior Citizens did not form until decades after national legislation created the Social Security program (Walker 1991, 29–30). These developments illustrate how feedback effects can motivate the formation and activities of interest groups.

Reconciliation Act (PRWORA), landmark welfare reform legislation signed into law by President Bill Clinton in 1996, produced few changes in mass opinion (Soss and Schram 2007). The impact of program enrollment also can vary. Whereas beneficiaries of Aid to Families with Dependent Children (AFDC) became skeptical about government's responsiveness to their concerns and less likely to participate in politics, recipients of Social Security Disability Insurance (SSDI) did not experience these demobilizing effects (Soss 1999). Important questions about the frequency of policy feedback, and the conditions conducive to it, cannot be answered without examining a range of outcomes. To understand why some public policies produce self-reinforcing effects and others facilitate their own demise or have a limited political impact, it is necessary to investigate episodes where feedback both did and did not occur (Campbell 2012; Patashnik 2008; Patashnik and Zelizer 2013).

Thus the growing literature on "how policy makes mass publics" has begun to identify some of the conditions that make feedback effects more or less likely by incorporating a range of programs with diverse effects on mass publics. This is its second important contribution. Studies in this tradition have increased our understanding of policy feedback by moving beyond simple illustrations of the phenomenon. Specifically, they suggest that policy design and timing affect whether and when a policy will generate feedback effects. The analytical framework advanced in this chapter builds on that insight, positing that a similar logic applies to government elites. Just as policy design and timing can influence whether policies will increase, undermine, or have a negligible impact on their beneficiaries' political participation, they also can alter elite behavior. Government elites, including elected officials and the administrators charged with implementing policy initiatives, may or may not mobilize to preserve, eliminate, expand, or retrench a given program. Their calculus will be influenced by the central design features of the policy, the timing of its enactment, and the interaction of these two factors.

Policy Design

The wide range of policies and outcomes investigated in the literature on mass feedback has helped identify several features of policy design that can influence a program's long-term social and political impact. For example, one comparison found that more experience with programs that are "designed according to universal principles (meaning that they are not subject to income limits)" was associated with a greater likelihood of voting, whereas enrollment in means-tested programs had the opposite effect (Mettler and Stonecash 2008, 274). Overall, the study of feedback effects has identified the "size, visibility, and traceability of benefits, the proximity of beneficiaries, and modes of program administration" as influential (Campbell 2012, 333). It is possible to apply these broad lessons to an analysis of government elites: specific provisions of a policy may help determine whether politicians and administrators mobilize to preserve or to challenge the status quo. Four specific dimensions of policy design – financial generosity, duration of authorization, administrative control, and coalition potential – are likely to shape elite reactions.

Financial generosity can influence how mass publics and government elites respond to a program. Initiatives like Social Security and the GI Bill had a profound long-term political effect, in part, because they distributed considerable material and nonmaterial support (Campbell 2003a; Mettler 2005). In general, mass feedback effects tend to be more pronounced when beneficiaries receive larger and more visible benefits over an extended period (Campbell 2012). Even though public officials do not profit personally as the budget of a program increases, a similar dynamic is likely to emerge in an elite context. Politicians and bureaucrats with jurisdiction over a policy may be more inclined to view it as worth defending when the financial stakes are high, whereas programs with a limited budget may be perceived as less important and therefore fail to generate this kind of loyalty.

In the context of American federalism, national initiatives frequently require that state officials respond to the financial incentives embedded in intergovernmental grants (Derthick 1970; Welch and Thompson 1980). The relative strength of those financial incentives can shape state officials' reactions and the extent to which they come to feel invested in the policy. Some grants require states to invest two dollars before receiving a dollar in matching funds from the national government, while others offer up to four dollars for each dollar of state spending. In addition, some grants represent an open-ended commitment by the national government to match state spending regardless of how much the state commits to the program, but more often the grants are capped. Policies are more likely to generate feedback effects when they induce substantial financial investments (Patashnik 2003, 2008; Pierson 2006), and the precise financial incentives embedded in intergovernmental grants can help determine whether such investments will occur. After all, state officials can decline the grants if the ratio of benefits to costs is not high enough to be attractive (Ingram 1977).

A second critical component of policy design is the duration for which a new initiative is authorized. Some policies are authorized on a permanent basis, whereas others are temporary and therefore require periodic reauthorization. Although one might expect members of Congress to establish permanent laws whenever possible, short-term authorizations are common and serve as one of the many "established lawmaking routines that encourage policy updating" (Adler and Wilkerson 2012, xi). Moreover, programs vary in the duration of their authorizations. Temporary authorizations and a reliance on the annual appropriations process render existing arrangements unstable because they open a "window of opportunity" for major policy change. The "scheduled renewal of a program ... creates an opportunity for many participants to push their pet project or concern" (Kingdon 1995, 165). The reauthorization process can facilitate the growth of a program, but it also offers opponents a chance to eliminate it or to make changes that reduce its sustainability. In contrast, permanent authorizations provide a more stable environment for the agencies that implement programs, enhancing their ability to plan, develop policy changes, and accommodate new demands and constituencies (Lieberman 1998, 18–19).[9] Thus the impact of a temporary (as opposed to permanent) authorization can be profound. The potential power of this design feature derives partly from its interaction with other variables, particularly those linked to timing. These potential interactions and their implications, which are discussed in more detail in the next subsection, suggest that duration of authorization often can be the most powerful of the design features that appear in our analytical framework.

Administrative control is a third design feature with the potential to influence how mass publics and government elites respond to policies. The details of public administration produce "structural politics" that affect both the policy's implementation and its ultimate form. Decisions about the type and locus of administrative responsibility affect the political dynamics of conflict and collaboration that then affect how a public policy evolves (Moe 1989). Thus one of the most enduring effects of a new policy is its impact on administrative capacities. This form of feedback can "serve either to promote or to frustrate the further extension of that line of policymaking" (Skocpol 1992, 58). Decisions about which level of government and which agencies will oversee and implement a policy affect its potential to generate feedback effects in multiple ways. At the individual level, beneficiaries' feelings of political efficacy are altered by a program's "routines, organizational cultures, and structures," and these experiences then spill over into the political realm because they "become the clients' indicator of their place in society and government" (Campbell 2012, 231; see also Soss 1999).

Program administration can have an analogous impact on the reactions of elected officials and bureaucrats. For example, the type and locus of administrative control can shape subsequent political dynamics if those who exercise authority over a program mobilize to resist attempts to shift responsibility to other actors or institutional venues. This form of self-reinforcing feedback can lead to the "filling up" or "preemption" of a policy space if government elites mobilize to preserve their administrative prerogatives (Pierson 1995a). In contrast, the administrative design of a policy may be conducive to self-undermining feedback effects if it establishes blurred lines of bureaucratic authority or creates an administrative apparatus that essentially duplicates what already exists. Eric Patashnik (2008, 28) emphasizes the

---

[9] Given the inherent vulnerability of policies with temporary authorizations, one might wonder why lawmakers do not enact permanent laws. Adler and Wilkerson (2012, 207–208) speculate that members of Congress use temporary authorizations because they know that policies rarely work as intended and therefore they believe that the ability to revisit a policy will facilitate experimentation, permit the incorporation of new information, and promote consensus.

importance of "creative destruction" as a prerequisite for durable policy reform, explaining, "Before a reform can create a new order, it must break up the existing one." The existence of parallel programs pursuing the same objective can spark a competitive dynamic that is not conducive to the generation of self-reinforcing feedback effects or to policy durability.

The administrative provisions of a program are especially important in the context of American federalism. The relative balance of authority between the national government and the states is a significant feature of intergovernmental programs, which vary considerably along this dimension (McCann 2016). As discussed earlier, state officials tend to prefer programs that grant them the flexibility they need to customize a policy template to the specific political and social circumstances that prevail in their states. Sometimes national lawmakers are willing to grant this discretion to their state-level counterparts, but in other cases state government autonomy is more restricted. According to some federalism scholars, national policymakers' willingness to impose constraints on the exercise of state government powers has increased over time (Kincaid 1990; Zimmerman 2005). Policies that limit the states' autonomy by treating them as administrative outposts of the national government might provoke self-undermining feedback as state officials mobilize to redesign or terminate them, whereas those same state officials might become loyal defenders of programs that strike a more state-centric balance.

Finally, policy design may also influence coalition formation and maintenance, whereby government elites work in concert with other groups affected by a policy. The scholarly literature on institutional reform is instructive. Major changes to legislative institutions have been called "common carriers" that represent a "confluence of interests ... whereby several groups support the change, but each group believes it will promote a different interest" (Schickler 2001, 13). Public policies also appeal to different groups for different reasons; they serve multiple purposes, can be viewed through various lenses, and are inherently multidimensional. For example, some officials believe that the primary objective of education programs is to promote economic development, while others emphasize their potential impact on equality of opportunity. Coalition-building is an important precursor to program adoption as policy entrepreneurs try to bring together the diverse groups whose support they need.

Once a policy is enacted, coalition formation can also be critical to its consolidation. If a coalition forms to push for a policy but subsequently disintegrates, the new program is unlikely to persist (March 1994). In contrast, self-reinforcing feedback effects are more likely to emerge when a new policy leads previously unaligned groups to coalesce into a unified force. During the mid twentieth century, for instance, some conservatives favored the gradual expansion of Social Security benefits as a bulwark against union demands for more employer-financed pensions, and liberals endorsed the same expansion out of "equalitarian sympathies" (Lindblom 1965, 140). The

Social Security example shows how members of different parties with divergent ideological proclivities can come together to support a program. In other words, it matters "not only whether the interests that originally prompted a reform will endure, but whether a reform sustains the coalitions that brought it about or *causes* new coalitions to emerge *after* enactment" (Patashnik and Zelizer 2013, 1074, emphasis in original; see also Patashnik 2008).

Thus the emergence of an enduring coalition, either during debates over the creation of a policy or during its implementation, influences how a policy evolves. Coalition-building plays a key role in the idea of "picket fence federalism," which posits that program specialists at various levels of government share similar perspectives and work together in ways that transcend their different governmental jurisdictions (Sanford 1967). Yet these sorts of professional links may be insufficient to stabilize intergovernmental relations over the long term. Sometimes program specialists at the state and national levels will compete with one another for scarce funds. In other cases they may share a particular goal but disagree about how best to achieve it. In addition, picket fence federalism advances an overly narrow vision of the coalition-building process. Policies that bring together program specialists, policy generalists like elected officials, and private-sector actors may be especially impactful. The probability that an intergovernmental initiative will generate self-reinforcing feedback effects is enhanced if its provisions draw the support of nongovernmental actors.

Certain features of policy design can lead private-sector actors to work together with government elites in support of a program's preservation or expansion. Public-private coalitions are especially important in the United States, where many programs are delegated to private-sector actors. Several studies of social policy in the United States note that the American public simultaneously identifies limited government as one of its core values and expresses support for social programs. Elected officials sometimes try to resolve this apparent contradiction by enacting policies that are "submerged" or "hidden" (Mettler 2011; Howard 1997). Rather than providing goods and services directly, the government turns to nonstate actors. Tax expenditures that subsidize private-sector activities in fields like health care and pensions are one manifestation of this politically expedient strategy;[10] delegated governance in programs like Medicare is another (Hacker 2002; Howard 1997, 2007; Mettler 2011; Morgan and Campbell 2011). A tax deduction for interest on home mortgages, for example, generates support from builders, realtors, and other members of the real estate industry. Thus policies that provide financial incentives or resources to government elites and private-sector actors might

---

[10] This strategy has been described as politically expedient because it offers "a way to provide social protections in a political environment hostile to direct government" (Morgan and Campbell 2011, 236). The American public would react negatively both to direct government provision of goods and services and to their diminished availability.

generate a powerful coalition in support of the status quo, while initiatives that foster competition between these two constituencies may sow the seeds of their own demise. If a new government program starts to provide goods or services that are already offered in the private marketplace, then the affected groups may mobilize against it.

Coalition potential can have an especially profound impact on public policies with an intergovernmental component. Although the political safeguards of federalism give the president and members of Congress an electoral incentive to respond to requests from their counterparts at the state level, this incentive is even stronger when state officials work in tandem with or have support from key intrastate constituencies that can mobilize voters and contribute financially to campaigns. For instance, state officials repeatedly joined forces with insurance companies, trial attorneys, doctors, and others to fight attempts to give the national government a stronger role in the implementation of workers' compensation. Their efforts were successful, generating a self-reinforcing dynamic that has preserved the status quo for close to a century (Howard 2002). If a policy does not provide the foundation for a coalition between public and private stakeholders, its durability may be questionable over the long term.

Timing

As Andrea Louise Campbell (2012, 346) explains in her superb summary of research on mass feedback effects, "Feedbacks may not emerge because of poor timing; policy change may go with the political or economic stream or run against it."[11] The "political stream" can promote or inhibit the generation of policy feedback through many channels. Policies that are inconsistent with prevailing ideological norms are unlikely to generate strong feedback among mass publics or the government elites who serve them. For example, a liberal policy initiative adopted on the cusp of a conservative era is unlikely to endure and flourish, whereas a conservative policy may be more likely to generate self-reinforcing feedback effects due to its resonance with the general public's "policy mood" (Stimson 1991). Numerous studies have deployed aggregated measures of Americans' preferences to demonstrate a general correspondence between public opinion and public policy in the United States (Erikson, Wright, and McIver 1993; Stimson, MacKuen, and Erikson 1995). In the context of federalism, the general tenor of national lawmaking can affect how state leaders interpret proposals to amend existing programs. Chapter 2's analysis of Unemployment Insurance (UI), for example, illustrates how state officials

---

[11] This emphasis on the "political or economic stream" differs from other treatments of timing that focus on when specific events occur relative to other unfolding historical processes or the order in which particular developments occur (Hacker 2002; Pierson 2000b, 2004; Orren and Skowronek 2004).

interpreted seemingly minor administrative changes to the program as precursors to its nationalization due to the sweeping and expansive programs that had been adopted in other policy arenas around the same time.

Similarly, political turnover can influence the likelihood that a new policy will generate feedback. Stable partisan control of the legislative and executive branches may enhance program durability, especially if the initial congressional vote to create a program was strongly partisan. The debate surrounding the ACA illustrates this dynamic; Republican efforts to "repeal and replace" the landmark health care reform law were unlikely to succeed while Barack Obama, the Democratic president who signed the law, was in office. In contrast, policies become vulnerable to modification, retrenchment, or even elimination when the coalition responsible for their adoption loses power (Berry, Burden, and Howell 2010; Maltzman and Shipan 2008). It is common for enacting coalitions to degrade over time, as the elected officials responsible for the initial decision to adopt a policy either fail to win reelection or retire from office. A study of policy reversals identifies a ten-year "tipping point" where major and minor changes "are more likely than at any point in a policy's lifecycle," and it speculates that at that moment "the normal degradation of enacting coalitions" may reach a threshold that "renders legislative agreements especially vulnerable to reversal" (Ragusa 2010, 1037–1038; see also deLeon 1978).

Changes in the political stream are not limited to short-term ideological fluctuations and shifts in partisan control. They also include broader changes in the American polity, such as the civil rights realignment of the mid twentieth century (Schickler 2016), that distinguish historical eras from one another. For example, the highly polarized partisan politics that characterize the contemporary era differentiate it from earlier periods; this polarization has affected congressional operations (Theriault 2008), intergovernmental relations (Bulman-Pozen 2014), public attitudes (Mason 2018), and various other features of American politics. New initiatives frequently must coexist with the policy residue of earlier eras even when existing programs represent divergent principles. Like institutions, public policies are created "at different times, in light of different experiences, and often for quite contrary purposes" (Orren and Skowronek 2004, 112). These differences are not limited to policies adopted at different historical moments, however. Policies created around the same time may represent different logics or adopt different approaches, and their long-term political fortunes may diverge based on how these logics and approaches interact with broader contextual changes (Finegold and Skocpol 1995; Mettler 1998; Lieberman 1998).

In the "economic stream," the ups and downs of the economic cycle can either help or hinder policy entrenchment. If a new policy is adopted during an economic downturn, actors are unlikely to make large investments that can influence their future preferences and increase their willingness to defend existing programs. Even program supporters may be unable to invest in ways that facilitate policy consolidation when they face economic constraints. If the economy is strong, in contrast, key actors may be more responsive to incentives that strive to induce them to make large financial investments. Such considerations are particularly salient in the context of American federalism, where many policies rely on intergovernmental matching grants and state government finances are vulnerable to the economic cycle, but their implications extend broadly. New initiatives are likely to generate self-reinforcing feedback when they create incentives that induce substantial financial or physical investments (Patashnik 2003, 2008; Pierson 2006). For example, the Airline Deregulation Act of 1978 facilitated major changes in the airline industry, and these "substantial, asset-specific investments" caused key stakeholders to "accommodate themselves" to the law because they had little to gain from its repeal (Patashnik 2008, 177). By either facilitating or discouraging financial investment, the "economic stream" can influence a program's long-term political trajectory.

The potential effect of the "economic stream" is not limited to the cyclical ups and downs of the economy, however. Broader trends and developments are also relevant. The configuration of political interests, institutions, and policy arrangements that structure conflicts over taxes and spending comprise what Paul Pierson (2001) has termed the prevailing "fiscal regime," and this general context can and does change over time. For instance, the expansionist fiscal regime that prevailed in the United States from roughly 1950 to the early 1970s rapidly gave way to a regime of austerity. This transition, which itself was facilitated by various policy changes and political shifts, made it more difficult to introduce new spending initiatives and to expand existing ones. Thus the prevailing fiscal regime can make it more or less likely that relatively generous policies will be established. These financial resources, in turn, are a crucial design feature that influences whether a policy generates self-reinforcing feedback effects.

Key features of a policy can interact with the political or economic environment in which it is established and affect its ability to take root. Policies that require periodic renewal may be especially vulnerable to changing background conditions. If a program is due for reauthorization at a moment when the coalition responsible for its enactment is no longer in power, then its foes might succeed in significantly altering or even reversing or terminating it (Berry, Burden, and Howell 2010; Maltzman and Shipan 2008; Ragusa 2010). Moreover, the likelihood of reversal or termination might be especially high when changes in partisan control occur at moments of high polarization. Similarly, polarization might influence the effectiveness of the financial incentives embedded in intergovernmental grants as state officials prioritize their ideological commitments over financial considerations. Economic changes may have a similar effect, with temporary programs struggling to expand or suffering cutbacks during an economic downturn.

Policies with permanent authorizations will not be impervious to political or economic developments, but they may be less susceptible to them.

Similarly, state officials' responsiveness to policies' financial incentives may depend on both the incentives' generosity and the economic context, which provides another illustration of the interactive relationship between policy design and timing. Consider the early years of Aid to Dependent Children (ADC), the cash assistance program created by the Social Security Act of 1935. ADC was financed through a matching grant in which the national government provided one dollar for every two dollars of state spending. This formula was less generous than those of policies like Old Age Assistance (OAA) and UI that were created at the same time, and it exacerbated the fiscal constraints that state governments faced during the "prolonged fiscal emergency" of the Great Depression (Shipman and Saum 1936, 289; see also Mettler 1998, 314). The grant's limited generosity amidst a challenging economic environment was one factor that contributed to state officials' tepid reaction to ADC.[12] Numerous states either chose not to participate in the program or participated in a token manner, and the early trajectory of ADC illustrates how the interaction of policy design and timing can undercut a policy's ability to take root and flourish. In contrast, generous new initiatives that are established in the context of a strong economy are more likely to generate self-reinforcing feedback effects. Government officials and private actors will be more capable of making the financial investments that will put the policy on stronger footing over the long term.

In addition to the political and economic streams, timing also implicates the institutional and administrative context in which a policy evolves. Relevant institutions are created, reformed, and eliminated at different times for different reasons, and this layering can create opportunities for entrepreneurs to exploit or erect barriers to potential reforms (Orren and Skowronek 2004; Schickler 2001). The transformation of political institutions influences the types of individuals who exercise governing authority and the expertise they bring to their positions, both of which affect a policy's ability to generate self-reinforcing policy feedback effects. In other words, the administrative dimension of timing generally concerns enduring, long-term shifts in governance structures and the evolution of the American state.

---

[12] ADC also operated under several political and economic constraints. It lacked a strong base of public support; by the end of the 1930s, "majorities [of Americans] in polls said that most poor people could get off relief if they tried hard enough" (Patterson 1994, 45–46). In contrast to its predecessor – the mothers' pension policies of the 1910s and 1920s whose rapid spread had been due in part to the active support of widespread federated women's organizations (Skocpol 1992) – ADC was not backed by a strong organized group. Finally, the removal of merit-system provisions from the Social Security Act of 1935, and a general lack of interest among national administrators, meant that ADC lacked a strong base of bureaucratic support (Patterson 1994; Steiner 1965).

Compared to the early twentieth century, the contemporary era is characterized by both a dense infrastructure of governing commitments and the heightened resilience of the institutions defending them (Skowronek 1993, 443). One manifestation of these changes is the expansion of the national government, which has undertaken initiatives in a widening range of policy areas and fostered the creation of a "forbidding terrain of . . . existing policies, agencies, and organized interest groups in Washington" (Patashnik and Zelizer 2013, 1083). These national developments are only one component, however, of a broader trend that Karen Orren and Stephen Skowronek (2017) describe as the emergence of the contemporary Policy State (see also Skowronek 2009). In the contemporary Policy State, more issues are subject to policy discretion and policymaking is no longer the special province of the legislature because the number of actors who routinely exercise policymaking authority has grown to include executive branch officials, the courts, and others. Regardless of their institutional posts, "incumbents in every office have become policy entrepreneurs, advancing programs to secure their positions and enhance their power" (Orren and Skowronek 2017, 17). Policy development occurs in an increasingly broad range of institutional venues that cuts across the traditional branches and levels of American government.[13]

The twentieth-century transformation of American state governments is a critical, albeit often overlooked, part of this transformation. States have long been vibrant political forces, both by defining membership in the American community through decisions about voting rights (Key 1984; Kousser 1974; McConnaughy 2013; Springer 2012, 2014) and by serving as a major locus of social policy innovation (Amenta et al. 1987; Howard 1999; Zackin 2010). The second half of the twentieth century, however, was a period of major institutional and administrative change at the state level.[14] Major reforms of state legislative and executive branch institutions dramatically enhanced the states' capacity for policy development and implementation.

The "resurgence of the states" had an especially significant impact on state agencies and legislatures. Through the first half of the twentieth century, poorly

---

[13] Skowronek (2009, 336) posits that "everything assumes a heightened level of contingency" in the era of the Policy State because the density of preexisting policy commitments and governing institutions has made new programmatic initiatives increasingly difficult to sustain (see also Patashnik and Zelizer 2013; Orren and Skowronek 2017). This plausible speculation is not the primary concern of the framework advanced here, which concentrates instead on the transformed administrative capacity of state governments. The concluding chapter of this book will return briefly to the contemporary implications of governmental expansion.

[14] This emphasis on the late twentieth century does not imply that it was the only period during which institutional and other reforms altered the structure of state governments. Historian Jon C. Teaford (2002) isolates the 1920s and 1930s as another period of major change and notes that, beginning in the 1890s, the states continually adapted to a shifting political and policy environment. That being said, political scientists tend to characterize the era from the 1960s to the 1980s as one of especially profound change (Bowman and Kearney 1986; Rosenthal 1996).

funded state agencies usually attracted patronage and other political appointees who lacked the expertise of their counterparts at the national level, while "[s]tate legislatures were more likely to be controlled by politicians with little interest in policy innovation" (Weir 2005, 169). The state-level decline of patronage was a long-term process that was driven in part by national mandates and grant-in-aid policies that pressured the states to develop professional administrative practices. The reforms' impact varied across both states and policy areas (Johnson 2007; Shefter 1983; Mayhew 1986), but from 1958 to 1975 it led to an especially sharp increase in the number of state employees under merit systems (Sabato 1983, 71–74). Around this time, structural changes transformed the governorship, as a series of institutional and administrative reforms tried to establish a more unified executive branch and enhance governors' ability to manage it (Bowman and Kearney 1986). The reforms helped facilitate the emergence of a new generation of ambitious and policy-oriented governors by the mid 1960s (Sabato 1983).

State legislatures underwent an equally profound transformation during the late twentieth century. Legislative salaries increased, sometimes dramatically, in an effort to encourage a wider range of talented individuals to run for office and as a check on corruption. Legislatures began to meet in longer and more frequent sessions. Only four states held annual sessions in 1960, but by the end of the twentieth century all but a few state legislatures met every year. The total number of days in session also increased, and the number of legislative staffers rose significantly in many states. These changes enhanced the institutional capacities of state legislatures across the country (Bowman and Kearney 1986; Squire 2012). The modernization of state legislative processes and structures in the 1960s and 1970s left individual legislators better equipped to perform their jobs and more likely to identify themselves as full-time public officials (Rosenthal 1996).

The long-term expansion of the national government and the increased professionalism of state governments highlight the potential impact of the administrative dimension of timing. This dimension is especially important in the context of American federalism, where national officials have relied on a similar range of policy tools for over a century but the heightened institutional capacity of the states may have altered the reception those tools received. In the early twentieth century, the "Rube Goldberg state" was constructed through intergovernmental grants and other policy instruments that facilitated or occasionally required the establishment of new state-level agencies and associations (Clemens 2006; see also Johnson 2007). Those policy instruments still predominated in the late twentieth century, a time when state governments possessed stronger institutional and organizational capacities. As a result of their growing interest and expertise in policymaking, key state officials might have been better able to respond quickly to appealing national initiatives and to defend them from attack. This possibility provides another illustration of the potential interaction between policy design and timing. However, it is equally important to look beyond generic notions of the expansion of administrative capacity over time. In any era, intergovernmental programs can require state governments to perform a task that represents a logical extension of their existing activities or, alternatively, ask them to move into unfamiliar administrative terrain. The nontrivial nature of a particular task can affect states' capacity and willingness to perform it.

The broader point is that the generation of self-reinforcing or self-undermining feedback effects may be shaped by timing. When a policy is adopted may be just as important as the fact of its adoption. Policies that are a strong fit with the prevailing ideological environment, that are endorsed by a strong and persistent partisan majority, and that depend for their entrenchment on institutionally powerful and financially secure actors are likely to generate political and social effects that facilitate their long-term stability. In contrast, policies that run counter to the partisan or ideological tenor of their times, whose supporters lose control over the levers of government power, or that require the cooperation of actors with limited administrative or financial capacity are unlikely to become entrenched over the medium to long term. These political, economic, and institutional dimensions of timing merit a central place in the study of policy feedback effects. In addition to assessing their independent impact, it is essential to analyze their interaction with key features of the policy itself. Timing and policy design may act together to place a new program on a strong political foundation, or they may undercut its ability to take root and flourish.

Summary

In recent years, research on policy feedback has moved from the illustration of feedback effects to more careful theorizing about the conditions that are conducive to them. Building on this productive shift, the preceding sections outlined several potential ways that policy design, timing, and their interaction can help shape whether a new government initiative will generate self-reinforcing, self-undermining, or negligible feedback. Design features like financial generosity, duration of authorization, administrative control, and coalition potential affect programs' developmental trajectories. In a similar vein, short-term fluctuations and long-term shifts in the political or economic environment can help or hinder a policy's ability to take root, and long-term changes in governance structures and the American state can determine whether the public officials with jurisdiction over a policy have the resources and capacity to engage in policy development. This framework helps explain why national policy initiatives generate responses from state officials that range from enthusiastic support to indifference to vociferous opposition.

RESEARCH DESIGN AND CASE SELECTION

The remaining chapters examine the developmental trajectories of seven programs. The case studies follow the same basic structure. After describing the origins and central provisions of each national initiative, the cases examine how states reacted to the new program over the short term. In each case, after several years the national government considered major changes to the program, frequently attempting to diminish the states' administrative role, reduce the financial resources available for the program, or eliminate the program altogether. The states' responses to those proposed reforms are critical in determining whether the policy generated policy feedback. Did state leaders mobilize to protect or enhance aspects of the initiative that they perceived as beneficial? Did they view one another – or the private-sector interests affected by the program – as potential allies in this endeavor? Affirmative answers to these questions over the medium to long term offer evidence of self-reinforcing feedback effects, particularly in cases where state officials had not lobbied actively for policy adoption or where their preferences ran counter to those of the general public. In contrast, if state officials lobbied their national counterparts to make major changes to the program or worked to undercut it, possibly in concert with private-sector actors, their activities would constitute evidence of self-undermining feedback effects. Finally, if an intergovernmental program did not spark either of these reactions, its failure to alter state officials' behavior over the medium to long term would illustrate the existence of negligible feedback effects.

The mobilization of state officials takes two broad forms, the first of which is the policy decisions that state politicians and administrators make at home. National government initiatives commonly offer state leaders incentives to establish or expand programs or to undertake specific administrative reforms (Derthick 1970; Johnson 2007; Welch and Thompson 1980). State officials' initial responses to these incentives help determine whether a policy will endure. If state leaders respond expeditiously and uniformly to incentives embedded in a national policy, quickly adopting major policy or administrative changes and taking full advantage of federal funding, that policy is more likely to endure. If, by contrast, state officials decide not to make policy or administrative changes or decline available federal funds, the policy is unlikely to take root and flourish. As a result, the cases pay careful attention to the policy decisions state officials make and how they justify those choices.

State officials' involvement in national politics is the second form of mobilization. Just as individuals can engage in several forms of political participation to support their preferences, and interest groups can press national government officials to take or not to take certain actions, state leaders can take part in lobbying campaigns in the nation's capital. Like other stakeholders, state executive and legislative officials often testify at congressional hearings, on behalf of either their individual states or the various professional associations that bring together state lawmakers who hold similar positions in their respective jurisdictions. The content of their testimony illuminates their perceptions of what is in their interest and whether those perceptions have shifted over time. Moreover, state officials sometimes take advantage of the "political safeguards of federalism" by appealing to their respective congressional delegations or by negotiating directly with the White House when they want to affect national decisions. The case studies therefore focus on whether and how state officials try to influence national politics. In summary, state officials' lobbying efforts in the nation's capital, and the policy decisions they make at home, serve as the primary indicators of mobilization in the case studies that follow.

Case Selection and Limitations

Importantly, the cases vary along the two main conceptual dimensions of policy design and timing. The most important differences are summarized in Table 1.[15] The initiatives vary in terms of policy design. Each altered the states' financial incentives, but in ways that range from tax offset provisions to open-ended matching grants. The administrative conditions attached to the programs also diverge, offering state governments varying degrees of control over provisions such as eligibility and benefit levels. Moreover, Congress made the continuation of some policies conditional on periodic review while granting others permanent authorization. Finally, the seven policies had disparate effects on private-sector actors like employers and health care providers, affecting the political pressures state officials faced and their ability to build coalitions. In terms of timing, the original national initiatives were adopted during different decades, each shaped by distinct political, economic, and administrative environments. Some programs were created in the early twentieth century while others were established later, when states possessed stronger institutional and organizational capabilities. This temporal variation helps account for both the increased professionalism of state governments and the dramatic long-term expansion of the national government.

The cases examined in this book vary in ways that offer an analytical advantage over in-depth accounts of a single program. The multiple aspects of policy design and timing, however, mean that the national initiatives do not exhaust all possible permutations. As a result, they embody some of the trade-offs that are part and parcel of a case study approach. Like other recent studies of feedback effects (Jacobs and Weaver 2015; Patashnik and Zelizer 2013), they identify and closely examine the hypothesized role of certain causal mechanisms

---

[15] Table 1 also reveals that differences in the programs' long-term trajectories should not be attributed to the size of their enacting coalitions. Strong congressional support is associated with policy durability (Maltzman and Shipan 2008), and, with the exception of the ACA, all the policies were enacted with such support.

TABLE 1 *Summary of Case Studies*

Policy Dimension	Unemployment Insurance (1935)	Sheppard–Towner Act (1921)	Medicaid (1965)	General Revenue Sharing (1972)	Superfund (1980)	No Child Left Behind Act (2002)	Affordable Care Act (2010) Medicaid Expansion:	Affordable Care Act (2010) Health Insurance Exchanges:
Policy Design								
Financial Generosity	Federal payroll tax offset	Capped matching grant	Generous, open-ended matching grant	Large, unrestricted grants	Limited trust fund widely viewed as inadequate	Small, temporary funding increase	Generous, open-ended matching grant	Small planning and implementation grants
State Discretion	Broad	Constrained	Broad	Very broad	Constrained	Mixed	Broad (waivers)	Mixed
Authorization	Permanent	Temporary	Permanent	Temporary	Temporary	Temporary	Permanent	Permanent
Coalition Potential	Strong (employers)	Weak (opposition from medical professionals)	Strong (hospitals, nursing homes, insurers, physicians)	Weak	Weak (opposition from business community)	Weak (opposition from education community)	Strong (hospitals, nursing homes, insurers, physicians, business groups)	Weak
Timing								
Political Environment	Mixed	Unfavorable	Favorable	Favorable	Unfavorable	Mixed	Unfavorable	Unfavorable
Economic Cycle	Unfavorable	Favorable	Favorable	Unfavorable	Unfavorable	Unfavorable	Unfavorable	Unfavorable

State Administrative Capacity	Weak	Weak	Strong	Strong	Mixed	Strong	Strong	Mixed
Support at Adoption								
Initial State Position	Weak support	Weak support	Weak opposition	Strong support	Weak support	Weak opposition	Weak opposition	Weak support
Congressional Vote	House: 372–33 Senate: 77–6	House: 279–39 Senate: 63–7	House: 313–115 Senate: 68–21	House: 274–122 Senate: 64–20	House: 274–94 Senate: 78–9	House: 381–41 Senate: 87–10	House: 220–215 Senate: 60–39	House: 220–215 Senate: 60–39
Feedback Potential	Mixed	Weak	Strong	Mixed	Weak	Weak	Mixed	Weak
Feedback Effects	Self-reinforcing	Negligible	Self-reinforcing	Negligible	Self-undermining	Self-undermining	Self-reinforcing	Self-undermining

in the context of individual policies and address causal complexity (George and Bennett 2005). Furthermore, they illustrate how different combinations of causes, or distinct causal pathways, can produce the same outcome (Ragin 2004). Even though the case studies can neither conclusively demonstrate that a particular condition was necessary to the outcome nor uncover the frequency with which specific conditions and outcomes arise, they can advance the "defensible claim that the presence of a variable 'favors' an outcome" (George and Bennett 2005, 27).[16] Although the cases focus on the federalism-related implications of national policy initiatives and their short-, medium-, and long-term effects on state government elites, this emphasis should not be interpreted to suggest that the relationship between the national government and the states completely accounts for the developmental trajectories of these policies. The cases are attentive to other factors because the ultimate goal of the book is to identify "mid-range theories that draw attention to key sources of policy resilience without stripping issues out of their broader context" (Patashnik and Zelizer 2013, 1072). The case studies therefore enhance our understanding of feedback effects and the conditions that promote or inhibit them while remaining cognizant of this broader context.

The preceding section of this chapter developed theoretical intuitions about why and how policy design and timing might prompt or discourage government elites to mobilize to defend existing policies. The cases' variation along these dimensions therefore allows some preliminary speculation about their ability to spark self-reinforcing, self-undermining, or negligible feedback effects. A federal-state program of *unemployment insurance (UI)* was established as part of the Social Security Act of 1935. Specific features of UI seem conducive to self-reinforcing feedback. The policy included a federal tax offset provision that gave states a powerful economic incentive to establish their own programs; a permanent authorization; and broad state government authority over benefits, eligibility, and financing. Moreover, state administration of UI served the interests of employer groups, giving them a powerful incentive to work with state officials to preserve the status quo. In contrast, several features of the timing of UI's creation seem inhospitable to the generation of elite feedback effects, including a political environment that featured congressional opposition and a hostile Supreme Court, the ongoing economic devastation wrought by the Great Depression, and the relative weakness of state administrative institutions. Nonetheless, as Chapter 2 explains in more detail, state lawmakers quickly developed a vested interest in the program and worked successfully with employer groups to resist periodic reform attempts. In sum, the UI program generated strong self-reinforcing feedback effects that can be attributed primarily to key features of its design.

---

[16] McKeown (2004) describes this use of empirical evidence as an "identification" process that isolates the presence of a specific causal mechanism. It does not represent a "test" of the conceptual framework advanced here.

The Promotion of the Welfare and Hygiene of Maternity and Infancy Act, better known as the *Sheppard–Towner Act* after its two primary congressional sponsors,[17] was signed into law in 1921. It provided states with matching funds to pursue activities serving mothers, expectant mothers, and very young children in an effort to reduce infant and maternal mortality rates. Like UI, the Sheppard–Towner Act was enacted at a time of limited state administrative capacity, and it required that state governments establish agencies that would coordinate their health programs with the federal Children's Bureau. The economic context of the early 1920s was favorable, but Sheppard–Towner was a progressive policy adopted at the outset of a conservative political era. In addition, several of its features seemed unlikely to lead state officials to mobilize in support of its preservation or expansion. Its grants were capped at a fairly low level, it was authorized for only five years, and its coalition potential was limited because it was not permitted to provide direct payments to physicians, health care providers, or program beneficiaries. Chapter 3 investigates the brief history of the Sheppard–Towner Act, which generated negligible feedback among powerful state officials and was formally repealed in 1929.

Medicaid, the subject of Chapter 4, was enacted in 1965. It possessed several features that seemed conducive to the generation of self-reinforcing feedback. In order to avoid the limited state participation that characterized other federal-state welfare programs, Medicaid incorporated unprecedentedly generous grants that were open-ended and permanently authorized, and gave the states expansive discretion to determine eligibility and benefits. In addition, Medicaid reimburses medical providers for health care services, which created strong financial incentives for industry leaders to seek its preservation and expansion. Medicaid also benefited from relatively propitious timing. In the mid 1960s, state governments possessed stronger institutional and organizational capacities, and both political and economic conditions were favorable to the entrenchment of the program. For all these reasons, Medicaid generated strong self-reinforcing feedback, helping it withstand repeated congressional retrenchment efforts and enabling its long-term expansion.

Congress enacted a program of *general revenue sharing* with state and local governments in 1972. At the time of its adoption, the five-year, $30 billion program was the largest grant-in-aid ever enacted (Stephens and Wikstrom 2006), and with virtually no strings attached it offered recipient governments an unprecedented degree of spending discretion. These design features contributed to its exceptional popularity with state leaders and seemed to be conducive to self-reinforcing feedback. In addition, general revenue sharing took effect at a time when state governments possessed strong institutional capabilities. General revenue sharing was nonetheless characterized by mixed

---

[17] The law was sponsored by Senator Morris Sheppard (D-TX) and Representative Horace Mann Towner (R-IA).

feedback potential. In terms of timing, its enactment preceded a series of inhospitable political and economic developments including partisan turnover, a growing federal deficit, state budget surpluses, intergovernmental tension over fiscal policy, and the transition to a regime of fiscal austerity. In addition, it was granted only a temporary authorization, and its unprecedented state government discretion proved to be a double-edged sword. While state officials appreciated the autonomy it offered, the diffuse benefits resulted in a notable absence of political pressure from state-level special interest groups. Chapter 5 describes how the factors that were inhospitable to the generation of policy feedback ultimately overpowered the ones that seemed conducive to a self-reinforcing dynamic. When the state component of general revenue sharing was discontinued only eight years after its adoption, governors and other state leaders hardly put up a fight.

The Comprehensive Environmental Response, Compensation and Liability Act (CERCLA), better known as *Superfund*, is the focus of Chapter 6. Signed into law in 1980 in response to the emerging problem of hazardous waste cleanup, the politically unstable Superfund program has never functioned as effectively as its supporters hoped it would. With its temporary authorization that many state officials viewed as insufficient, its centralization of administrative discretion, and its alienation of the business community, Superfund possessed multiple design features that seemed likely to generate self-undermining feedback. Moreover, it encouraged state governments to build their administrative capacities in a way that effectively created a competing state-level hazardous waste removal program. Superfund also suffered from inopportune timing, as it was adopted at an inhospitable economic and political moment. State leaders consequently mobilized politically, working energetically and often successfully to encourage Congress to make major changes to the program. As the states' administrative capacities increased, issues of duplication and intergovernmental conflict caused subnational officials to pursue independent action, leaving the national program in an odd state of legislative limbo. Thus Superfund sowed the seeds of its own political instability.

President George W. Bush signed the *No Child Left Behind Act* (NCLB) into law in 2002. NCLB endorsed an accountability-based approach to education reform that incorporated a strict testing regime and a rigid sequence of interventions for underachieving schools and districts; its supporters believed that it would lead to stronger academic performances by students from diverse backgrounds. Many states had already embraced the general principles embodied in NCLB. This overlap and the states' strong administrative capacity in education policy seemed to suggest that it might generate self-reinforcing feedback effects. However, as Chapter 7 describes in more detail, other features of the law and the environment in which it was adopted placed national and state officials on a "collision course" (Manna 2011). Even though the law included a temporary infusion of additional funds, state officials still characterized NCLB as an "unfunded mandate." Supporters claimed that it offered increased subnational flexibility, but state officials chafed at its requirements and the rigidity with which the Bush administration enforced them. Adopted at an inopportune economic moment that was also characterized by growing partisan polarization, the law's temporary authorization also helps explain why it generated self-undermining feedback. Opposition to the law took various forms, arose in numerous states, and intensified dramatically over time. Eventually this opposition facilitated the passage of the Every Student Succeeds Act (ESSA), a law that was widely viewed as a partial repudiation of NCLB.

Signed into law in March 2010, the *Patient Protection and Affordable Care Act* (ACA) was the defining domestic policy initiative of Barack Obama's presidency. A multifaceted effort to move the United States in the direction of universal health coverage, the ACA incorporated two provisions that directly implicated the states. Although these two provisions were created at the same time, Chapter 8 showcases how differences in their respective designs affected the response they received from state officials. The Medicaid expansion was rendered optional by the Supreme Court's 2012 decision upholding the constitutionality of the ACA, but most states ultimately accepted it. Its generous financial incentives and high coalition potential, in addition to the administrative flexibility offered by the "waiver" process, explain its widespread adoption. In contrast, market-oriented health insurance exchanges faced strong resistance. Very few Republican state officials established their own exchanges, in part because they lacked strong financial incentives and the support of state-level private interests.

CONCLUSION

The study of policy feedback effects has greatly enhanced our understanding of the many ways in which "new policies create a new politics" (Schattschneider 1935). The rest of this book builds on these important insights while simultaneously making two contributions to the growing scholarly literature. First, the case studies strive to identify the conditions that are conducive to feedback effects. While much has been gained through individual illustrations of self-reinforcing feedback at both the mass and elite levels, there have been repeated calls for efforts to determine when it is especially likely or unlikely to occur (Patashnik 2008; Patashnik and Zelizer 2013; Pierson 1993, 2006). In addition, a small but growing literature on self-undermining feedback effects suggests that policies may sow the seeds of their own instability. The framework outlined in this chapter posits that certain features of policy design, the timing of policy adoption, and their interaction shape the nature and extent of feedback. The case studies identify how these factors influenced the developmental trajectory of national policy initiatives with implications for American federalism, but they also offer broader lessons about how these factors contribute generally to the long-term durability or vulnerability of public policies.

Second, the case studies build a case for reorienting the study of policy feedback effects. Although elected officials and bureaucrats initially played a central role in the scholarly literature (Heclo 1974; Derthick 1979; Orloff and Skocpol 1984; Weir and Skocpol 1985; Ikenberry 1988), they have largely been superseded by a concern with mass publics. This analytical turn has been productive, but a more balanced view of how policies remake politics, one that accounts for their possible impact on government elites and interest groups,[18] is long overdue.[19] Public policies can give politicians and administrators strong incentives to mobilize politically by providing pivotal information and by conferring costs or benefits on specific actors. The case studies in the remaining chapters of this book suggest that this mobilization of government elites can have a profound impact on a policy's developmental trajectory.

[18] The revitalization of feedback-oriented research on the formation and activities of interest groups already seems to be under way. Recent studies showcase how the adoption of state public-sector collective bargaining laws fueled the emergence of public-sector unions (Anzia and Moe 2016), how changes to the federal tax code mobilized powerful economic interests (Hertel-Fernandez and Skocpol 2015), and how women's rights policies influenced the rhetorical grounding of women's groups' advocacy and the types of policies they chose to embrace (Goss 2013).

[19] For more on the evolution of feedback-related research on government elites see Pierson (1993), Hall (1993), and Karch and Rose (2017).

2

The Surprising Persistence of Unemployment Insurance

The Social Security Act of 1935 created a federal-state program of unemployment insurance (UI) funded by employer payroll taxes and characterized by extensive state discretion over benefits and employer contributions. In the decades that followed, concerns about UI's inadequacies led federal lawmakers to attempt repeatedly to replace it with a national system of unemployment insurance or, failing that, to establish national benefit standards. Nonetheless, the original federal-state arrangement persists to this day with only minor modifications. Upon the program's creation, a powerful alliance of state officials and business groups developed a vested interest in the status quo and successfully resisted periodic reform efforts. These self-reinforcing feedback effects are especially noteworthy since state officials had not lobbied energetically for UI's creation.

This chapter argues that the surprising persistence of unemployment insurance is largely a product of the program's design. UI's payroll-tax financing mechanism and broad state discretion over benefits and employer contributions gave state leaders powerful incentives to retain control over the program in response to interstate competition and pressure from business groups to keep taxes low. UI's design thus lent itself to coalition-building between state officials and private state-level interest groups. Attempts to increase the federal role have been largely fruitless because such "modifications interfered with the states' prerogatives established by the 1935 Social Security Act, which were strongly defended by business" (Weir 1992, 141–142).

The timing of the program's introduction was also conducive to self-reinforcing feedback. For the better part of two decades following its creation, Presidents Roosevelt and Truman and Democratic majorities in Congress pursued unprecedentedly expansive social policies. In this political context, state officials and business interests associated nationalization with higher taxes and liberalization of benefits, strengthening their stake in keeping the program in state hands. The amplification of federal power that accompanied World War II also stoked state officials' fear of nationalization, and it was another catalyst for their political mobilization to preserve the program's existing structure.

ORIGINS AND ENACTMENT

In 1934, as the nation struggled to recover from the Great Depression, President Franklin Roosevelt appointed a Committee on Economic Security to develop a legislative proposal for social insurance to ameliorate "several of the great disturbing factors in life – especially those which relate to unemployment and old age" (Roosevelt 1938, 293). The subject of unemployment insurance in particular produced a heated debate, and the committee spent the majority of its time developing the program, devoting surprisingly little time to Social Security (Derthick 2001; Eliot 1992).

According to committee chair and Secretary of Labor Frances Perkins, "the committee could not keep its mind made up on this one point: should it be a federal-state system or a federal system?" Several committee members had a strong preference for an exclusively federal system to promote adequacy and uniformity of benefits across states, and to allow the pooling of funds and spreading of risk on a national basis. However, there were several pragmatic arguments for a federal-state system. First, as Perkins noted:

There was one outstanding, and, in my mind, determining factor, at that time in favor of the federal-state system ... We were never quite sure whether a federal system of unemployment insurance would be constitutional ... The Federal Government could tax; that was clear. But could it distribute its funds on a basis of social benefit? (Perkins 1946, 278)

The Supreme Court of the mid 1930s leaned conservative and included a group of justices known as the "battalion of death" for worker-friendly legislation. According to committee member Arthur Altmeyer, previous rulings by this Court "had created considerable doubt as to how far the Constitution of the United States permitted the federal government to go in enacting social legislation" (Altmeyer 1966, 14–15).

Second, the committee had "grave doubt" that Congress would enact a law for a purely federal system as "state jealousies and aspirations were involved" (Perkins 1946, 279). Several states had already begun to consider bills to create their own UI programs and – in the absence of a consensus about the form unemployment insurance should take – were mulling a wide range of provisions. Congress, being comprised of representatives of the states and localities, was predisposed to "faithfully defend decentralizing administrative arrangements where related efforts already existed in the states" (Ikenberry and Skocpol 1987, 409). In particular, Southern Democrats, who chaired key congressional committees at the time, were eager to give states the flexibility to protect regional racist practices and low-cost labor policies (Ikenberry and Skocpol 1987). Moreover, two architects of the Wisconsin system – Arthur Altmeyer and Edwin Witte – occupied key positions on the Committee on Economic Security, and were keenly aware that a federal-state system would give the state more flexibility to retain its own policy design than would a uniform national system (Douglas 1936).

Finally, despite having delegated the decision to the committee, the president had expressed a preference for a federal-state system of unemployment insurance. In a June 1934 message to Congress, he opined that a sound system should be based on a "maximum of cooperation between states and the federal government" (Altmeyer 1966, 17). Two months later, when Roosevelt met with several committee members and learned that certain members felt that unemployment insurance should be a federal function, Roosevelt responded: "Oh no, we've got to leave all that we can to the states. All the power shouldn't be in the hands of the federal government. Look – just think what would happen if all the power *was* concentrated here, and *Huey Long* became president" (Eliot 1992, 98). Roosevelt's commitment to intergovernmental cooperation reflected not only his background as governor of New York but also a deeply-held philosophical belief in the states as laboratories of democracy (Altmeyer 1966; Derthick 2001).

For these reasons, the committee "agreed, reluctantly and with mental reservations, that for the present the wisest thing we could do was to recommend a federal-state system" (Perkins 1946, 279). Thus, the program's overarching structure was largely dictated by circumstances at the time of enactment; it was "a product of the decade, of the people, of the Court, of the state bills that preceded it" (Baicker, Goldin, and Katz 1998, 243).

Once the committee had decided on a federal-state configuration, it turned to conceiving the optimal division of labor. The federal government's somewhat minimal responsibilities were to include covering the program's administrative costs, safeguarding its reserve funds, and providing program standards where uniformity was essential. The most important federal role, however, was solving the states' collective action problem by providing a strong incentive for the creation of state UI plans (Witte 1942). In particular, the committee hoped to "make it easier for the states to act by removing those disadvantages in interstate competition which are always raised against purely state legislation that involves costs to industry."[1] Indeed, although more than half the states had considered unemployment compensation bills by 1935, Wisconsin alone had enacted one. Although there were many reasons for this slow progress, "the factor which overshadowed all others" was the fear of placing "a heavy burden on employers of the state which would handicap them in competition with employers from states not having such a law" (Witte 1936, 158).

---

[1] House Committee on Ways and Means, *Economic Security Act: Hearings on H.R. 4120,* 74th Cong., 1st sess., February 4, 1935, 882–883.

The administration's proposed solution was to induce states to create unemployment insurance programs by imposing a federal payroll tax with a sizeable "tax credit offset" for states with approved UI laws. This type of provision had first been used in the 1926 Federal Estate Tax law and was subsequently upheld as constitutional by the Supreme Court. Compared to the grant-in-aid approach that characterizes many other federal programs, the tax offset "acts less as a carrot than a stick since the main incentive it provides a state is an opportunity to avoid having the state's employers lose credit against the federal tax without any gain to the state" (Rubin 1983, 15). The federal payroll tax rate was initially set at 3 percent, with a tax offset of up to 90 percent thereof; the remaining 10 percent would be set aside to cover administrative costs.[2] So long as their state's unemployment insurance law met federal requirements, employers who had paid their full state unemployment tax obligations would receive a 2.7 percent offset credit – thereby paying a net tax rate of only 0.3 percent. Based on a taxable wage base of $3,000, most employers would pay $9 (0.3 percent of $3,000) per employee.

An "experience rating" (originally known as "merit rating") provision permitted states to offer an additional credit to firms that maintained good employment records. Experience rating can take a number of different forms, but among the most common is the "reserve ratio." The reserve ratio is the difference between taxes paid by a firm and benefits disbursed to its employees, all divided by the firm's payroll. Layoffs and increased benefit payouts cause a firm's reserve ratio to decrease and its tax rate to increase; by contrast, curtailing benefit disbursements causes a firm's reserve ratio to increase and its tax rate to decrease (Baicker, Goldin, and Katz 1998, 245). Advocates of experience rating cited two theoretical rationales: equity and stabilization. They believed that firms that created more unemployment should be taxed more heavily on fairness grounds, and they wanted to give firms an incentive to avoid seasonal layoffs. From a political standpoint, experience rating also made the program more acceptable to employers, who did not want to subsidize other firms' employment challenges (Blaustein, O'Leary, and Wandner 1997). The provision was also popular among some state officials; by 1935, Wisconsin had already adopted experience rating, and several other states were considering following suit. Yet experience rating would also turn out to have an important unintended side effect: it became a tool that states could use to minimize employers' tax burdens, as discussed later in this chapter.

Apart from a few federal eligibility guidelines, the states were to be given "broad freedom" over virtually every other aspect of their plans, including the amount and duration of benefits, waiting periods, and disqualification provisions. The committee's report stated that "all matters in which uniformity is not absolutely essential should be left to the states" in light of

---

[2] The tax phased in gradually, from 1 percent in 1936 to 2 percent in 1937 and 3 percent in 1938 and thereafter.

the "desirability of permitting considerable variation, so that we may learn through demonstration what is best" (Committee on Economic Security 1935, 15). From a pragmatic standpoint, deference to the states would help secure congressional passage and satisfy advocates of the Wisconsin plan. Moreover, "there was a fear that if many standards were imposed upon the states the act would be regarded by the courts as being primarily regulatory in its purposes and hence ... declared unconstitutional" (Douglas 1936, 38).

In giving the states this broad freedom, the committee was keenly aware that competitive pressures might lead state officials to provide insufficient protection for workers. Observing that "state administration may develop marked inadequacies," the committee pointed out that "should these fears expressed by the champions of a federally administered system prove true, it is always possible by subsequent legislation to establish such a system." However, the committee also presciently cautioned that state-level "vested interests preventing modification or repeal" might emerge upon the program's creation (Committee on Economic Security 1935, 16). Like other programs authorized in the Social Security Act of 1935, including old-age insurance and cash assistance, UI was permanently authorized and thus spared from periodic congressional review. This feature of the program provided an advantage for stakeholders who wished to preserve the status quo.

Although the states were heavily implicated in the proposed UI program, state officials played a limited role in 1935 when Congress considered that component of the economic security bill. They represented a small proportion of the witnesses who appeared before the House Ways and Means Committee, and those who testified generally did not address UI. When the Acting State Commissioner of Social Welfare for New York State testified on behalf of the state's governor, for example, his testimony focused solely on sections dealing with old age pensions and assistance for families with dependent children.[3] In his first-hand account of the proceedings, Edwin Witte highlights supportive testimony on UI from "labor union officials, industrialists, and prominent citizens" but does not mention state government leaders (Witte 1936, 166).

In 1935, the Democratic Congress overwhelmingly passed the Social Security Act by a margin of 372–33 in the House and 77–6 in the Senate. Two years later, the Supreme Court upheld the constitutionality of the Act's unemployment insurance provisions in a 5–4 vote. In ruling that Congress's actions were within its constitutional power, the majority observed that "it is too late today for the argument to be heard with tolerance that, in a crisis so extreme, the use of the moneys of the nation to relieve the unemployed and their dependents is a use for any purpose narrower than the promotion of the general welfare."[4]

---

[3] House Committee on Ways and Means, *Economic Security Act: Hearings on H.R. 4120*, 74th Cong., 1st sess., February 4, 1935, 861–871.
[4] *Steward Machine Co. v. Davis* (301 US 548 [1937]).

State governments responded quickly and uniformly to the landmark national legislation. By July 1937, all 48 states, Alaska, Hawaii, and the District of Columbia had passed legislation to create UI plans that met federal requirements. This result was not achieved without some heel-dragging; indeed, several states waited until the last minute in the hopes that the Supreme Court would strike down the law as unconstitutional (Haber and Murray 1966). More noteworthy than this tepid resistance, however, was the remarkably widespread diffusion of state UI plans, which laid the foundation for the generation of self-reinforcing feedback effects.

The programmatic details of the state initiatives were equally significant. Early state UI plans were characterized by conservative provisions reflecting state lawmakers' desire to create "fiscally sound" programs that "would not provide more in benefits than could be prudently financed" (Price 1985, 25). Most states initially established a benefit equal to half the claimant's full-time weekly wage up to a maximum of $15 per week. Benefits in most states were paid, after a two- to four-week waiting period, for a maximum duration of sixteen weeks. The Social Security Act had recommended these benefit policies as financially prudent, and the states largely accepted them without question (Haber and Murray 1966). Similarly, most states initially set the employer contribution rate at the recommended 90 percent of the 3 percent federal payroll tax (i.e. 2.7 percent).

The states' conservative benefit and tax policies were based on the assumption of high sustained rates of unemployment. However, rapidly improving business conditions in the late 1930s meant that employer contributions soon began to outstrip benefit payouts. By the end of 1939, reserve funds had ballooned to $1.5 billion – nearly twice the level of contributions for that year (Blaustein 1993, 171). Unemployment declined further following the onset of World War II, as millions of men left the civilian workforce to join the armed forces and the nation faced a shortage of skilled labor. By 1944, benefit payouts had declined to approximately one-tenth of what they had been in 1940 (Wagenet 1960, 52).

Against this backdrop, business groups pressured state lawmakers to reduce employer contributions in order to maintain a favorable tax climate (Harpham 1986). During the 1940s, virtually every state government took advantage of its administrative discretion by endorsing various business-friendly amendments to their UI plans: "Experience-rating provisions were amended to make it easier for employers to qualify for reduced rates. Minimum and maximum contribution rates were lowered, separate rating schedules were added ... and benefits paid to workers under certain circumstances did not enter into the rating procedures" (Wagenet 1960, 36). As a result, between 1938 and 1948, the average state's unemployment insurance tax rate dropped from 2.7 percent to 1 percent, and the average weekly benefit amount dropped from 43 percent of the weekly wage in 1938 to 33 percent in 1954 (Harpham 1986).

FEDERALIZATION

As employer contribution rates and benefits plummeted, Roosevelt administration officials grew increasingly disillusioned with the federal-state UI system. According to Social Security Board Chair Arthur Altmeyer, who had served on the Committee on Economic Security, the program's early years confirmed that it "suffered from a fundamental defect ... there were no minimum benefit standards." Moreover, he lamented, by allowing states to offer firms tax credits for maintaining a good employment record, "federal law actually created a powerful incentive for individual states to keep benefit rates low." Thus, instead of achieving its "fundamental purpose" of preventing a competitive race to the bottom, the law "actually increased that danger" (Altmeyer 1966, 85).

Would-be reformers, emboldened by the removal of the principal obstacle to a purely national program – Supreme Court opposition – following a series of personnel changes and "about-face" decisions in the high court in the late 1930s and early 1940s, began to push for federalization (Witte 1942, 42). In its 1940–1941 annual report, for instance, the Social Security Board argued that "a federal system would obviate the marked disparities in the proportion of workers protected under state laws and the degree of protection afforded" (Altmeyer 1966, 134). The Board made similar recommendations in its 1942, 1943, and 1944 annual reports. Labor organizations and liberals in Congress supported the idea.

However, by this time a new obstacle to the enactment of a federal system had emerged: the vested interests of state officials in preserving the status quo.

As early as March 1939, a knowledgeable expert and participant in the development of the unemployment insurance provisions of the Social Security Act, in commenting on the likelihood of a federal unemployment insurance law, observed that "on the contrary, the fifty-one unemployment compensation systems now have a vested interest in maintaining their present status." (Hight 1982, 617)

State unemployment agency directors formed a lobbying organization known as the Interstate Conference of Employment Security Agencies (ICESA) in 1937. They "successfully organized themselves to help defeat attempts to eliminate or to reduce their role in the employment service," and became "a strong force in resisting attempts to centralize and federalize unemployment insurance" (Blaustein, O'Leary, and Wandner 1997, 37; Lieberman 1998, 185). State elected officials, including individual governors and lobbying groups such as the Council of State Governments, regularly joined the ICESA in fighting federal UI reform efforts (Haber and Murray 1966).

State officials' resistance to reform reflected both their desire to defend their administrative turf and political pressure from powerful state-level economic interests seeking to "prevent a nationalization of benefits that would hinder economic strategies based on low wages and stingy social provision" (Pierson 1995b, 325). Decentralization of policymaking authority, combined with capital mobility, enables business interests to "play off one political jurisdiction against another," often resulting in less generous social policies (Pierson 1995b, 306). Employers recognized that the decentralized UI system worked in their favor, as states competed with one another to provide an attractive business climate. Equating nationalization with liberalization – particularly in the context of the Roosevelt administration's expansive social policies – employer groups urged sympathetic state officials to defend the status quo. Thus, UI became a "common carrier" bringing together a new coalition of state officials and business groups with a shared stake in resisting reform. As a byproduct of protecting their turf, state officials pulled the unemployment insurance system in a "generally conservative, pro-employer direction" (Lieberman 1998, 185).

Northern and southern officials alike fiercely guarded their authority over the program. Regardless of political persuasion, "states generally resented and resisted federal efforts to control or dominate the program" during its early years (Blaustein 1993, 187). Southern conservatives mobilized in part to protect racist labor practices (Ikenberry and Skocpol 1987). Yet northern states with relatively liberal UI provisions also fought federalization. For instance, in 1941 the governors of the six New England states sent a telegram urging President Roosevelt not to approve proposals to nationalize UI ("Oppose Job Federalization" 1941). And in 1945, Governor Edward Martin of Pennsylvania, chairman of the National Governors' Conference, testified that he spoke for all 48 governors when he said "the states are opposed to any bill or plan designed to federalize the administration of unemployment compensation" ("All States Oppose Job Insurance Federalization" 1945). State officials were not responding to constituent demands in resisting nationalization. In a 1942 poll, 53 percent of respondents agreed that UI should be "mostly controlled by the federal government" while only 20 percent felt that it should be "mostly controlled by each state government."[5] Rather, state officials were motivated by a combination of pressure from business interests and a desire to retain their own jurisdiction and power.

These motives only intensified with the onset of World War II and the accompanying threat of wide-scale nationalization. After the Japanese attack on Pearl Harbor in December 1941, the president transferred all state-affiliated offices of the US Employment Service from state to federal control. In a telegram to the governors, Roosevelt requested their "full cooperation so that the conversion of the present employment service into a truly national service may be accomplished without delay." State leaders cooperated but "bitterly denounced" the move and alleged that it was part of the administration's broader "desire to 'federalize' the entire existing federal-state unemployment

---

[5] The Post-War Problems Survey was conducted by the National Opinion Research Center in March 1942 and was based on 2,505 interviews. Other responses included "Don't know" (14 percent), "Neither" (2 percent), and "Both" (1 percent).

insurance system" (Altmeyer 1966, 130–132). The administration denied this claim. Although the employment service was returned to the states in 1946, its temporary federal takeover turned out to be a "development of great importance," shaping political battles over the UI program for years to come (Altmeyer 1966, 130).

In this context of war and expanding national power, state officials' fears of federalization led them to resist even the slightest expansion of the national government's role. In 1942, for example, the Roosevelt administration proposed to temporarily supplement UI with a national war displacement benefits program. State administrators, suspecting an attempt to nationalize the UI system, lobbied heavily against the proposal. The administration, backed by powerful labor organizations, was unable to overcome the opposition, and the measure died in committee. As one observer noted, "the Ways and Means Committee was strongly influenced in its decision against the bill by a wave of protests from state officials who saw in the plan an insidious plot to federalize the state unemployment insurance systems" ("Wrong Approach" 1942).

State officials also blocked more overt attempts at federalization. For instance, in 1944 the prospect of massive postwar unemployment led Congress to consider overhauling the UI system. After seven months of consideration by five committees, lawmakers ultimately decided that control of unemployment compensation during the reconversion period would remain primarily with the states; "in making its decision the Congress was impressed by the testimony of many state administrators and governors" (Social Security Administration 1944, 3). For instance, ICESA President Claude Williams had appeared before the Senate Special Committee on Post-War Economic Policy and Planning and declared that "no greater evil has grown during the past few years than ... the tendency on the part of the federal government during this period of emergency, under the guise of aiding the war effort, to usurp many functions which unquestionably belong to the states." He had concluded his statement with a forceful argument against "any attempt at federalization of our state unemployment compensation system either directly or indirectly through subsidy or otherwise."[6]

Although Congress did not federalize the program in 1944, it did press the states to adopt more generous benefits. The report of the Senate Special Committee on Post-War Economic Policy and Planning urged state authorities to "give immediate consideration to improving the state laws, particularly with respect to increasing the duration and level of benefits"; it observed that "more adequate state benefits would do much to weaken the argument for federalization" (Social Security Administration 1944, 3). In 1945, a majority of states complied by enacting legislation to substantially modify their UI programs. The changes included increasing the maximum weekly

---

[6] Senate Special Committee on Post-War Economic Policy and Planning, *The Problem of Unemployment and Reemployment after the War*, 78th Cong., 7th sess., June 1, 1944, 921.

benefit to $20 or more, increasing the maximum duration of benefits to twenty weeks or more, and reducing the waiting period to one week. These laws "provided better protection against unemployment to larger numbers of workers than before," although the states' policies were also "more varied than ever before" (Reticker 1945, 9).

Despite these measures, wage growth outstripped benefit increases and UI benefits continued to shrink as a proportion of workers' weekly wages. The reconversion period brought a spike in joblessness. However, the mass unemployment many had feared did not materialize, emboldening business groups to continue their lobbying efforts and leading state lawmakers to keep employer contributions low (Wagenet 1960). As a result of the "constant worry over interstate competition for business in state legislatures," many state unemployment insurance systems lacked adequate resources and faced "chronic fiscal crises" throughout the late 1940s and 1950s (Harpham 1986, 160–161).

FEDERAL STANDARDS

As it became evident that the opposition of state officials and business groups posed a formidable obstacle to the adoption of a federal system of unemployment insurance, reformers changed tactics and began to support federal standards instead. Starting in 1945, the Social Security Board began recommending, in its annual reports, federal standards for weekly benefit amounts, duration of benefits, qualifying requirements, and disqualifications from benefits. Over the course of several decades, Congress considered a series of bills that would have imposed such standards. For instance, in 1945 the Roosevelt administration championed a bill that would have established a federal standard of $25 per week for 26 weeks; in states with benefits below $25, the federal government would have provided supplementary benefits to make up the difference.

State political leaders and program administrators fiercely and unanimously opposed the federal standards, fearing such reforms were a "camel's nose under the tent" to federalize the system. Earlier reform efforts had created a "lasting suspicion" among the states that any proposal to enlarge federal authority was a move toward full national government control (Haber and Murray 1966, 140, 455). When Edward Martin, Chairman of the National Governors' Conference, appeared before the Senate Finance Committee in 1945 to warn that the states remained "opposed to any bill or plan designed to federalize the administration of unemployment compensation," a senator replied, "This bill does not touch the federalization of unemployment compensation at all."[7] For its part, the ICESA was, according to Social Security Board Chairman Altmeyer, "paranoiac

[7] Senate Finance Committee, *Emergency Unemployment Compensation*, 79th Cong., 1st sess., August 31, 1945, 287.

in feeling that the federal government was trying to take over the administration of the state unemployment compensation act" (Coming 1966). The "ghost of federalization" hovered over this and subsequent attempts to impose federal benefit standards (Haber and Murray 1966, 140).

Although state elected officials have largely opposed federal benefit standards throughout the program's history, there have been occasional exceptions in which some liberal governors expressed support, particularly in the context of economic downturns. For instance, during the 1958 recession, several Democratic governors from northern states sent a telegram to President Eisenhower urging him to adopt a number of recession-fighting policies including federal benefit standards for UI. The telegram read, "Realistic federal minimum standards in unemployment insurance should be established. Unemployment compensation is one of the greatest weapons we have to maintain purchasing power when there is mass unemployment."[8] Some of the governors were turning to Congress for help because they had tried to expand unemployment benefits in their respective states but had been stymied by resistance from conservative state legislatures. Nonetheless, such cases of support were the exception rather than the rule.

Federal reformers repeatedly took aim at not only the program's benefits but also its tax provisions. In 1949, for example, the Senate Finance Committee's Advisory Council on Social Security observed that "the present arrangements permit States to compete in establishing low contribution rates for employers and therefore discourage the adoption of more adequate benefit provisions." Rather than recommending federal benefit standards, which it deemed "inappropriate in a state-federal system," the council concluded that "the best way to encourage the liberalization of unemployment compensation is to remove, or at least greatly diminish, the incentive which states now have to reduce their unemployment insurance contribution rates." To remedy the situation, the council recommended "the imposition of a federal minimum for the state contribution rate, so that the rate will not be allowed to fall below a point which will be sufficient to pay adequate benefits in the great majority of states" (Social Security Administration 1949, 13–17).

State unemployment administrators and business leaders unleashed a "heavy barrage of criticism" against the proposed federal tax standards. At a National Institute for Unemployment Compensation, held under the auspices of the US Chamber of Commerce, the director of Colorado's Department of Employment Security argued that retaining the present system of experience rating was "a must," calling it "the primary means by which employers' interest in the program is maintained" (Stark 1949, 22). In arguing for the preservation of state autonomy over employer contributions, state officials were joined by

---

[8] House Ways and Means Committee, *Emergency Extension of Federal Unemployment Compensation Benefits*, 82nd Cong., 2nd sess., March 31, 1958, 151.

several large employers including the General Motors Corporation. The proposal was dead on arrival.

The closest the national government came to imposing federal standards was in 1966, when a strong Democratic president, large Democratic majorities in Congress, and a brief softening in the states' position opened a window for reform (Pierson 1995b). In a message to Congress, President Johnson observed that the UI system had "not kept pace with the times," as "no major improvements [had] been made since its original enactment 30 years ago."[9] With the strong support of organized labor, the administration proposed a bill requiring that the maximum weekly benefit equal two-thirds of a state's average wage. The bill also called for the elimination of experience rating and the extension of benefits during recessions. The prospect of fiscal relief during hard times led a handful of Democratic governors to support the proposal. With reform appearing all but inevitable, a "sharply divided" ICESA made a major concession, narrowly agreeing by a vote of 24 to 21 to accept a federal benefit standard of one-half of a state's average wage – below the two-thirds sought by the administration. However, when the House Ways and Means Committee solicited the ICESA's input on the bill, the group complained that "the imposition of a federal standard would mean, in effect, virtually wiping off the books the kind of program that that state had. It was not just a matter of increasing the amount they paid but it was a matter of actually changing their whole philosophy of paying benefits."[10] State officials' protests were echoed by business leaders, one of whom contended that the "proposed standards and requirements are so high as to effect federalization" (Greenough 1966, B52). Accordingly, the House dropped federal standards from its bill, instead proposing "a set of modest modifications that confirmed state-level control over the program" (Pierson 1995b, 311). State administrators were "overwhelmingly in favor" of this "watered-down" version of the administration's proposal.[11] However, the two chambers of Congress were unable to work out their differences, and the reform died in conference.

Subsequent attempts to impose federal standards also floundered. In 1973, for instance, when the Nixon administration drafted a bill calling for states to provide minimum benefits equal to two-thirds of the average state weekly wage of covered workers, the legislation could not even attract a Senate sponsor. As usual, a coalition of state administrators and business leaders blocked the measure. One frustrated labor official called state officials "one of the toughest but quietest lobbies you are going to see anywhere" (Hyatt 1974, 15).

[9] Lyndon B. Johnson, *Special Message to the Congress on Labor*, May 18, 1965, www.presidency.ucsb.edu/ws/index.php?pid=26972.
[10] Senate Finance Committee, *Unemployment Insurance Amendments of 1966*, 89th Cong., 2nd sess., July 15, 1966, 113–114.
[11] Senate Finance Committee, *Unemployment Insurance Amendments of 1966*, 89th Cong., 2nd sess., July 15, 1966, 113–114.

In short, fear of federalization was historically an "important element in opposition to expansion of UI" (Lieberman 1998, 212.).[12] The united opposition of state administrators and employer groups succeeded in blocking any major changes to the program's overarching structure. Despite widely acknowledged inadequacies in the amount and duration of benefits, attempts to broaden the program repeatedly failed, and "preference for retention of state control of these matters was a major factor in the outcome" (Blaustein, O'Leary, and Wandner 1997, 38).

"PIECEMEAL REMEDIES"

Although efforts at wholesale reform have repeatedly failed, Congress has succeeded in enacting a series of adjustments to the UI system, including gradual expansions of eligibility, increases in the federal payroll tax rate and taxable wage base, and temporary expansions in the duration of benefits during recessions. One observer likened these modifications to "reaching for a first aid kit instead of calling for the ambulance" (Hyatt 1974, 15). As a result, unemployment insurance has seen "a subtle shift in the federal-state balance in favor of the federal partner" over time (Hight 1982, 617). However, these "piecemeal remedies" reflect a "reluctance to consider structural changes," despite widespread acknowledgment of the program's inadequacies, owing to the "federal-state structure of unemployment insurance, which granted the states substantial control over the program, [and] was thus a continuing obstacle" to reform (Weir 1992, 141–142).

First, national lawmakers have on several occasions expanded eligibility for unemployment insurance. Originally, coverage had been limited to primarily industrial and commercial workers in the private sector. In 1954, Congress passed, and President Eisenhower signed, legislation extending coverage to federal civilian employees as well as employers with 4 or more workers (instead of 8, as provided by the previous law), bringing an additional 3.7 million workers and 270,000 employers into the system. In 1970, Congress extended coverage to firms with one worker or more and mandated coverage for certain nonprofit organizations, among other changes, bringing in an additional 4.8 million workers. In 1976, Congress expanded protection to 8.6 million additional workers in industries such as farm employment and domestic employment in private households, among others (Price 1985). In 2000, Congress extended coverage to workers performing services for federally recognized Indian tribes.

Second, lawmakers have made several adjustments to the unemployment insurance system's financing over the years. Congress raised the permanent

---

[12] The racial implications of policy change were also important, as southerners worried that it would promote the expansion of coverage to occupations in which African-American workers were concentrated.

payroll tax rate several times, most recently to 6 percent (with a maximum offset of 5.4 percent). It also increased the federal tax base from the first $3,000 of covered wages (where it had stood since 1939) to $4,200 in 1970, $6,000 in 1976, and $7,000 in 1982; these increases are rather modest once inflation is taken into account (Price 1985). And in 1954, the Reed Act established a federal fund to provide interest-free loans to states whose unemployment insurance trust funds were insufficient to support benefit payouts.

Finally, Congress has extended unemployment benefits during recessions on many occasions. The first of these extensions occurred in 1958 when, in response to an economic downturn, Congress passed and President Eisenhower signed the Temporary Unemployment Compensation Act (TUCA). TUCA offered interest-free loans to states wishing to extend the duration of regular state benefits by the lesser of 50 percent of the regular entitlement or an additional 13 weeks. However, "not only did the federal government's role in the system as a whole continue to remain minimal, but full financial responsibility for benefits and coverage continued to lie with the individual state governments." During the congressional debate over this legislation, there had been "strong support in Congress for giving the federal government a much larger role to play in the unemployment insurance system as a whole" but such attempts had been "soundly defeated" in favor of this decentralized approach (Harpham 1986, 164–165).

The subsequent extension of unemployment benefits in 1961 created a temporarily larger role for the federal government, establishing an important precedent. In response to the 1960–1961 recession, President Kennedy proposed and Congress passed the Temporary Extended Unemployment Compensation (TEUC) Act. Like TUCA before it, this act offered advances to states that wished to extend their regular benefits by the lesser of 50 percent of the regular entitlement or an additional 13 weeks, but this time the extended benefits were financed by a temporary 0.4 percentage point increase in the federal unemployment tax. TEUC was effectively "a federal program grafted upon the existing decentralized unemployment insurance system." Although TEUC "gave the federal government a new, albeit temporary, role to play," it "did not permanently alter the relationship that existed between the federal government and the individual state governments" (Harpham 1986, 166–167).

The single most significant change to the unemployment insurance system since its creation in 1935 arguably occurred in 1970, with passage of the Federal-State Extended Unemployment Compensation Act of 1970. Unlike its temporary predecessors, this act created a permanent federal-state program to extend benefits for workers who exhausted their regular UI benefits during periods of high unemployment, with the cost shared equally by the federal and state governments. As before, the duration of extended benefits was the lesser of 50 percent of the regular entitlement or an additional 13 weeks.

Despite the existence of this permanent program, Congress subsequently saw the need to enact numerous temporary extensions during recessions. These included the Emergency Unemployment Compensation Acts of 1971, 1974, and 1977; the Federal Supplemental Compensation Act of 1982; the Emergency Unemployment Compensation Act of 1991; Unemployment Compensation Amendments of 1992 and 1993; the Temporary Extended Unemployment Compensation Act of 2002; the Unemployment Compensation Extension Act of 2008; and the American Recovery and Reinvestment Act of 2009, among others.[13] These extensions were federally financed and governed by federal rules, and thus temporarily increased the federal role in unemployment insurance.

Elected state leaders, enticed by the offer of additional federal financial assistance during economic downturns, typically welcomed these temporary extensions. For instance, Michigan's Democratic Governor, Mennen Williams, testified in 1958: "I do strongly urge that the Congress enact a program which would provide an extension of benefits to those who have exhausted their eligibility under state law. I believe that the duration of such benefits should be uniform, and not tied to the individual's eligibility under state law."[14] The following year, as the extended benefits were about to expire, President Eisenhower invited the governors to the White House and asked them to increase the amount and duration of state benefits to limit the need for further federal intervention (Brooks 1961). The governors demurred, instead issuing a statement that endorsed the status quo. They asserted the states' right to run UI programs "without imposition of federal standards governing eligibility, duration or the amount of benefits" and advocated the continuation of "federal advances to meet emergencies where the problems of unemployment are beyond the ability of the affected state governments" (Trussell 1959).

For their part, state administrators initially objected to these piecemeal remedies as setting a dangerous precedent of federal intrusion on their turf. Since the adjustments left the federal-state balance of power largely intact, however, they tended to elicit relatively mild responses. For instance, in 1958, several state administrators testified against the temporary federal extension of benefits in response to the recession. The chairman of North Carolina's employment security commission testified that "supplementation of the state programs whether in terms of amount of weekly benefit payments or duration of benefits is a matter that can best be done by each individual state through state legislation."[15] Similarly, in 1962, a representative of Virginia's employment commission argued against the federal extension of benefits,

---

[13] See Whittaker and Isaacs (2013) for a full list and description of each program.

[14] House Ways and Means Committee, *Emergency Extension of Federal Unemployment Compensation Benefits*, 82nd Cong., 2nd sess., March 31, 1958, 150.

[15] House Ways and Means Committee, *Emergency Extension of Federal Unemployment Compensation Benefits*, 82nd Cong., 2nd sess., April 1, 1958, 322.

noting that "the vast majority of the states have at their disposal the necessary reserves or the taxing authority to provide additional temporary benefit extensions if the need for such extensions actually exists."[16]

Yet starting in the mid 1960s, state administrators began to grudgingly accept temporary benefit expansions as the lesser of two evils. During the Johnson era, when federal benefit standards suddenly seemed imminent, the ICESA overwhelmingly endorsed the temporary expansion of benefits as a tolerable compromise, as discussed in the previous section. Similarly, in 1970, the ICESA "strongly advocate[d]" the creation of a permanent federal-state program to extend benefits during periods of high unemployment, calling the proposal a substantial improvement over the Nixon administration's bill, which had included several unattractive provisions including a larger increase in the taxable wage base.[17] Indeed, ICESA President John Crosier observed in 1976 that state employment security administrators "generally have welcomed" temporary benefit extensions, finding them less objectionable than other, more intrusive reforms.[18]

State business leaders remained hostile to these incremental expansions, many of which entailed increasing employer contributions. In rejecting changes to the status quo, they often invoked states' rights arguments. In response to the proposed temporary extension of benefits in 1958, for instance, Leslie Dikovics, a member of the Council of State Chambers of Commerce, complained that the payment of benefits for up to 16 additional weeks "sets the precedent, in our minds, for federal domination of the state unemployment compensation programs through federal standards," and "would be a major step in the attrition of the prerogative of the states to exercise their own judgments as to how their programs should be shaped to meet their own needs."[19] Joseph Shaw, President of the Associated Industries of New York State, was even more blunt, warning that "federal intervention into the state administered unemployment insurance law is intrinsically bad and entirely unwarranted," not to mention "a violation of New York State's constitutional right to determine what are the needs of the working men and women within its boundaries and to legislate in accordance with these needs."[20] Lacking the support of their typical allies – state politicians and administrators –

---

[16] House Ways and Means Committee, *Extended Temporary Unemployment Compensation Benefits*, 87th Cong., 2nd sess., August 23, 1962, 97.

[17] Senate Finance Committee, *Unemployment Compensation*, 91st Cong., 2nd sess., February 5, 1970, 243.

[18] Subcommittee on Unemployment Compensation, House Ways and Means Committee, *Extend and Modify the Federal Supplemental Benefits and Special Unemployment Assistance Programs*, 94th Cong., 2nd sess., April 28, 1976, 52–53.

[19] House Ways and Means Committee, *Emergency Extension of Federal Unemployment Compensation Benefits*, 82nd Cong., 2nd sess., April 1, 1958, 272–273.

[20] House Ways and Means Committee, *Emergency Extension of Federal Unemployment Compensation Benefits*, 82nd Cong., 2nd sess., April 1, 1958, 366.

and in the face of powerful political counter-pressures on federal lawmakers to respond to pressing economic needs, business groups typically lost these battles.

CONCLUSION

Despite decades of controversy and repeated attempts at reform, the UI system "has been quite stagnant, and it has undergone less significant reform than any other American welfare policy" (Lieberman 1998, 177). Just as Roosevelt's Committee on Economic Security predicted, vested interests – namely, a powerful coalition of state officials and business groups – quickly mobilized to protect state control over benefits, eligibility, and financing. As a result, "the inertial force of its beginnings has kept unemployment insurance primarily a state program" (Graetz and Mashaw 1999, 79). In contrast to other examples of self-reinforcing feedback effects that led to the expansion of programs like Social Security (Derthick 1979; Hacker 2002), the mobilization of state officials and the business community preserved a status quo that limited the generosity and scope of UI.

Key features of UI's policy design, in combination with the timing of its enactment, help explain why state officials joined forces with other stakeholders to fiercely defend the program against national reform initiatives. Its broad state administrative discretion, powerful financial incentives, permanent authorization, and strong coalition potential proved especially influential in an era of national government liberalism and wartime mobilization. This political environment fostered fears that even modest changes were the precursor to the nationalization of the program. The self-reinforcing feedback that characterized UI's developmental trajectory stands in stark contrast to the subject of Chapter 3, the Sheppard–Towner Act, where a policy featuring limited state autonomy, meager funding, temporary authorization, and limited coalition potential struggled to take root amidst the conservative political environment that characterized its early years. This interaction of policy design and timing led state officials to stand by indifferently as Congress dismantled the Sheppard–Towner Act shortly after its enactment.

3

The Brief Life of the Sheppard–Towner Act

The centerpiece of the Sheppard–Towner Act, which was signed into law in 1921, was a matching grant program that funded infant and maternity programs. Sparked both by substantive concerns about high rates of infant and maternal mortality in the United States and uncertainty about the political implications of the ratification of the Nineteenth Amendment, the Sheppard–Towner Act originally received strong bipartisan support in both houses of Congress. By the time the law came up for reauthorization a few years later, however, its political prospects were considerably more tenuous. It lacked a strong coalition of supporters, and a more powerful and mobilized group of opponents insisted that national government financial support for the services that it provided was no longer necessary. After a lengthy congressional debate, a "compromise" was reached that extended the Sheppard–Towner Act for two years but automatically repealed it on June 30, 1929, less than eight years after its adoption.

This chapter examines the developmental trajectory of the Sheppard–Towner Act, focusing on the reception that it received from state governments. Key state officials, such as governors, generally supported the broad objectives of the program but nevertheless had misgivings and reservations about its specific provisions. Their reservations did not dissipate over time, and even though the grant program was capped at a relatively low level, the states consistently spent less than their full allotment of Sheppard–Towner funds. The tepid support of state leaders was one of many factors that undermined proponents of an extension when the effort to extend the law's authorizations began in the mid 1920s. In sum, the Sheppard–Towner Act generated negligible feedback effects. State leaders neither rose to the program's defense nor lobbied for major structural changes. Instead, they greeted the program's demise with a collective shrug.

The Sheppard–Towner Act illustrates the importance of policy design, timing, and their interaction. In this particular case, those factors combined to limit state officials' enthusiasm about the policy and their political engagement when members of Congress debated its future. Specific features of the law help explain its inability to generate self-reinforcing feedback. State government support was broad but not especially deep due to the small size of the available grants, the peripheral institutional position of the state agencies charged with their administration, and the law's various constraints on state autonomy. One especially consequential constraint was the fact that Sheppard–Towner programs could not provide direct payments to physicians, health care providers, or program beneficiaries, limiting their coalition potential. Instead, the law inadvertently generated strong opposition from medical professionals, creating a crucial political obstacle to its reauthorization. Moreover, the temporary authorization of the Sheppard–Towner Act left it vulnerable to changes in the partisan composition of Congress. This feature of the law was especially important because Sheppard–Towner was a progressive policy innovation adopted at the outset of a conservative era. This combination of factors helps explain why the Sheppard–Towner Act failed to take root and flourish.

THE ORIGINS AND ENACTMENT OF THE SHEPPARD–TOWNER ACT

The Sheppard–Towner Act can be traced to intellectual and cultural shifts that began in the latter half of the nineteenth century. Rapid advances in medicine and the creation of state and local health departments drew heightened attention to issues of maternal and child health (Schmidt 1973, 419). Social settlement reformers, female professionals, and others developed a "feminine vision of public preventive health care" that legitimated government activity in this policy arena by drawing upon the cultural resources of the "separate sphere" of nineteenth-century American women (Skocpol 1992, 511; see also Rothman 1978). Their wide-ranging efforts had many important consequences, but the creation of a federal Children's Bureau in 1912 was especially significant. One of its earliest activities was the collection of systematic data on infant and maternal mortality, and the bureau found that rates in the United States were worse than those in many other countries.[1]

In 1917 Children's Bureau Director Julia Lathrop recommended that Congress establish a federal-state matching grant program with the goal of improving child and maternal health. This recommendation launched the

---

[1] For more on the creation and early activities of the federal Children's Bureau see Lemons (1990), Lindenmeyer (1997), Meckel (1990), Rothman (1978), and Skocpol (1992). In 2012, the agency produced an e-book called *The Story of the Children's Bureau: 100 Years of Serving Our Nation's Children and Families* that also discusses the origins and early years of the bureau. http://cb100 .acf.hhs.gov/CB_ebrochure. Date of access: August 29, 2016.

congressional struggle that eventually led to the passage of the Sheppard–Towner Act. Representative Jeannette Rankin (R-MT) introduced legislation based on the bureau's recommendation a year later. Her bill focused on "promoting the care of maternity and infancy in rural districts"[2] where the Children's Bureau identified "practically no organized effort to meet the need for instruction in prenatal and infant hygiene and for trained care during pregnancy and confinement."[3] The proposal's focus on rural areas helped insulate it against the charge that the measure was usurping state governments' traditional management of public health policy. Supporters argued that the national initiative was necessary because states often struggled to meet the needs of nonurban residents; they also emphasized that the matching grant framework would limit the national government to a supporting role.

Even so, there was lingering uncertainty about the constitutionality of the grant-in-aid mechanism at the heart of the program. In the early twentieth century, Congress started to rely more heavily on intergovernmental grants and other policy instruments that facilitated or even required the establishment of new state-level agencies and associations (Clemens 2006; Johnson 2007). However, relatively few of these intergovernmental policy instruments addressed issues of social welfare policy.[4] With the notable exception of Civil War pensions (Skocpol 1992), the national government's involvement in social policy had been limited. Proponents of maternity and infant hygiene legislation therefore buttressed their case by drawing on the "abundant precedent for Federal aid to State work in rural areas." They pointed to the Smith–Lever Act of 1914, through which the national government provided matching funds for county extension agents to teach farmers new agricultural methods: "Like the Smith–Lever Act, the present bill is primarily for the purpose of educational extension ... In the same way, the proposed measure would bring to the woman on the farm modern knowledge about the care of her children and her own care during pregnancy and

---

[2] H.R. 12634, 65th Cong., 2nd sess., introduced June 29, 1918.

[3] House Committee on Labor, *Maternity Aid and Infant Hygiene*, 65th Cong., 3rd sess., 1919, Report No. 1062, 4.

[4] Kimberley S. Johnson (2007, 165–167) provides a comprehensive catalog of intergovernmental policy instruments (IPIs) enacted by Congress between 1877 and 1931, categorizing these efforts based on the type of instrument on which they relied and their substantive content. The Sheppard–Towner Act is categorized as a social welfare policy that established an intergovernmental grant. Only ten of the 102 IPIs enacted prior to the Sheppard–Towner Act fall into the "social welfare" category, and only two of those ten relied on a grant-in-aid program rather than intergovernmental regulations. Thus the proposal that Rankin put forward embodied a rare, but not wholly unprecedented, expansion of national government activity. Even so, the matching grant was "considerably more conservative" than other policy solutions that were being considered at the time, including free or subsidized medical services and the payment of pensions to new mothers (Meckel 1990, 205).

confinement."[5] In sum, supporters argued that the proposal was a constitutionally appropriate way to provide rural residents with essential public health services that they often lacked.

Once Rankin left Congress,[6] the legislative baton passed to Senator Morris Sheppard (D-TX) and Representative Horace Mann Towner (R-IA). Their efforts during the 66th and 67th Congresses faced considerable opposition, especially in the House of Representatives.[7] In 1920, however, the matching-grant idea got a jolt of momentum from the ratification of the Nineteenth Amendment giving women the right to vote. Women's groups, including the General Federation of Women's Clubs, the National League of Voters, and a coalition of fourteen national interest groups known as the Women's Joint Congressional Committee, pushed hard for the legislation. Their efforts were especially influential because the "women's vote was an unknown quantity at the time," with suffragists claiming that women would vote as an issue-oriented bloc that would reject the major political parties (Lemons 1990, 157–158). The uncertain partisan implications of the Nineteenth Amendment led many legislators "to register publicly their approval when the bill finally came up for a vote. Indeed, fear of being punished at the polls by American women ... seems to have motivated Congress to vote for [the Sheppard–Towner Act]" (Meckel 1990, 211). The measure received strong bipartisan support in both chambers; it was approved 63–7 in the Senate and 279–39 in the House. President Warren G. Harding signed it into law on November 23, 1921.[8]

State government officials generally endorsed the objectives of the Sheppard–Towner Act, but they did not play a significant role in the campaign that led to its enactment. When the editor of *Good Housekeeping* testified before the Senate Committee on Public Health and National Quarantine in May 1920, he provided "letters and telegrams that show that 33 of the Chief Executives of the States are in favor of maternal and infant welfare work at the public expense."[9] Even some of the supportive governors, however, expressed

---

[5] House Committee on Labor, *Maternity Aid and Infant Hygiene*, 65th Cong., 3rd sess., 1919, Report No. 1062, 5. It is also revealing that physician Dorothy Reed Mendenhall, who had conducted "extension work in Wisconsin under the Smith–Lever fund," appeared at two committee hearings in January 1919. House Committee on Labor, *Hygiene of Maternity and Infancy: Hearings on H.R. 12634*, 65th Cong., 3rd sess., January 15 and 28, 1919.

[6] Rankin's first congressional term lasted from 1917 to 1919. After a hiatus of over two decades, she won reelection to the House of Representatives and served another term from 1941 to 1943.

[7] The multi-session trajectory of the Sheppard–Towner Act illustrates the "softening up" process identified by John Kingdon (1995) in his classic study of congressional policymaking. See Chepaitis (1972) for a more comprehensive congressional history of the Sheppard–Towner Act.

[8] During the 1920 campaign, Harding had spoken in favor of a precursor to the Sheppard–Towner Act in a "well-publicized speech delivered one month before the election" (Lindenmeyer 1997, 81). The matching-grant idea had been endorsed by the Democratic, Socialist, Prohibition, and Farm Labor Parties.

[9] Senate Committee on Public Health and National Quarantine, *Protection of Maternity and Infancy: Hearing on S. 3259*, 66th Cong., 2nd sess., May 12, 1920, 27.

reservations about the details of the bill. West Virginia Governor John J. Cornwell enthusiastically pledged that his state would "cooperate to the limit" if the legislation was enacted,[10] but many of his counterparts mentioned existing efforts to protect maternal and infant health in their states and questioned whether it was necessary for new state agencies to be created. South Carolina Governor R. A. Cooper emphasized that it was "important for [the] bill to retain [the] feature providing that this fund should be handled by State health machinery already existing, otherwise there might arise annoying duplication."[11] In addition, governors and other state officials did not lobby energetically on behalf of the proposal. The governors did not appear at this congressional hearing, which featured witnesses affiliated with the Children's Bureau, the medical profession, and women's organizations.

Between 1919 and 1921, congressional committees held several hearings on proposals to establish a matching grant program to promote the health of infants and mothers.[12] The witnesses at these hearings represented a wide range of interests, yet subnational officials played only a minor role in these discussions. Four distinct individuals represented the interests of states and localities: a member of the State Child Welfare Board of New Mexico; the director of the Bureau of Child Hygiene of New York City; the director of the Division of Child Hygiene in the State Department of Health in Pennsylvania; and the State Health Commissioner of Virginia.[13] While each of these individuals possessed significant expertise in the subject being discussed, none of them would be classified as a central figure in state politics. In addition, the number of witnesses representing state governments paled in comparison to twenty-two witnesses who testified on behalf of women's organizations, which included supportive organizations like the National Congress of Mothers and the Woman's Christian Temperance Union and several antisuffrage groups that opposed the bills. The health care field was also strongly represented, with thirty-one witnesses appearing on behalf of groups like the American Child Hygiene Association and the National Organization for Public Health Nursing.[14] The result was a spirited debate about the desirability and structure of the intergovernmental program.

[10] Senate Committee on Public Health and National Quarantine, *Protection of Maternity and Infancy: Hearing on S. 3259*, 66th Cong., 2nd sess., May 12, 1920, 29.

[11] Senate Committee on Public Health and National Quarantine, *Protection of Maternity and Infancy: Hearing on S. 3259*, 66th Cong., 2nd sess., May 12, 1920, 29.

[12] The figures cited in this paragraph consider five congressional proposals: H.R. 12634 (1919), S. 3259 (1920), H.R. 10925 (1920), S. 1039 (1921), and H.R. 2366 (1921).

[13] In 1921, the officials from New York City and Pennsylvania appeared at hearings for both S. 1039 and H.R. 2366.

[14] A total of 114 witnesses appeared at the hearings. There were also thirteen witnesses who represented the Children's Bureau and seven who represented the Public Health Service. Finally, thirty-five witnesses fall into a catch-all category that includes current and former members of Congress, individuals affiliated with a national government agency other than the Children's Bureau or the Public Health Service, party officials, labor groups, media outlets,

Indeed, the overwhelmingly supportive final congressional vote on the law should not be interpreted as a sign of minimal opposition. During congressional hearings and floor debates, the Sheppard–Towner Act was "roundly denounced by … antisuffrage groups, by defenders of states' rights, by some medical groups, and by forces trying to protect the bureaucratic prerogatives of the Public Health Service" (Skocpol 1992, 500). In part, the opposition of these groups reflected broader trends in American politics. Historian Richard Hofstadter (1955) famously described the era from 1890 to 1940 as the "age of reform," but the political context in the 1920s departed in critical ways from the Progressive Era that preceded it and the New Deal period that followed it. The decade was not a propitious political moment for progressive reforms of the sort represented by the Sheppard–Towner Act. Indeed, it has been described as "a period made almost unique by an extraordinary reaction against idealism and reform" (Link 1959, 833). This reaction included a growing ideological conservatism and the prioritization of the "associative state" and welfare capitalism (Ikenberry and Skocpol 1987).[15] Although the uncertain political implications of the Nineteenth Amendment and the energetic lobbying of women's groups helped Sheppard–Towner supporters achieve their progressive goals in 1921, their victory ultimately proved fleeting as key features of the law interacted with a relatively unfavorable political context.

Opponents of the Sheppard–Towner Act leveled several specific critiques at the proposal. Fiscal conservatives lamented its high cost. States' rights advocates alleged that it threatened the integrity of the states by inserting the national government into a policy area that had traditionally been under state control. Although the medical profession was divided over the measure,[16] the American Medical Association (AMA) relentlessly attacked it as "a step toward state or socialized medicine" that would usurp the authority of the medical profession (Chepaitis 1972, 219). The Sheppard–Towner Act was "one of the

religious organizations, other interest groups across the political spectrum, and individuals representing themselves. Only once (individuals testifying on S. 1039 on their own behalf) did the number of witnesses in any of these subcategories exceed two.

[15] Although the preceding characterization of the 1920s is widely shared, not every historian endorses it. For more on the distinctive features of the era and fluctuations in the nature of the conservative reaction, see May (1956) and Keller (1987). This scholarly disagreement reflects the broader analytical challenges inherent to periodization in the study of American history (Sklar 1992).

[16] The opposition of the American Medical Association (AMA) was significant because the political power of the professional association was increasing dramatically at the time (Burrow 1963; Starr 1982). However, the AMA did not represent the entirety of the medical profession. The Sheppard–Towner Act received support from the Pediatrics Section of the AMA, Medical Women's National Association, American Child Health Association, Association of Women in Public Health, National Organization of Public Health Nursing, American Association of Hospital Social Workers, Women's Health Foundation, and the Life Insurance Institute of New York (Lindenmeyer 1997, 87–88). In addition, some "doctors organized the Sheppard–Towner Emergency Committee to support the bill" (Chepaitis 1972, 219).

first pieces of federal legislation to catch the brunt of the AMA's new fear of state medicine" (Lemons 1990, 159–160), and the *Journal of the American Medical Association* published numerous editorials denouncing the bill. Witnesses representing organizations like the American Medical Liberty League raised similar concerns. Even though foes were unable to derail the Sheppard–Towner Act, their critiques are important for two major reasons. First, they reappeared when the law came up for reauthorization in the mid 1920s. Second, during the legislative process critics extracted several crucial amendments that hindered the Sheppard–Towner Act's ability to generate self-reinforcing feedback effects.

POLICY DESIGN AND FEEDBACK POTENTIAL

The central feature of the Sheppard–Towner Act was its matching grant program. State governments had to enact enabling legislation, develop a detailed plan for carrying out Sheppard–Towner programs, and allocate funds to infant and maternity programs. In addition, they could only receive federal funds once they established state agencies that would coordinate their health programs with the Children's Bureau; the agencies had to be separate units whose "concern with children could not be diluted with any other responsibility" (Rothman 1978, 141). State plans had to be approved by a Federal Board of Maternity and Infant Hygiene that included the chief of the Children's Bureau, the surgeon general, and the commissioner of education.[17] Participant states received a lump-sum $5,000 grant, and they were eligible for an additional $5,000 if they provided matching funds. Matching funds exceeding $5,000 were distributed on the basis of state population.

The general contours of the matching grant program resembled the original proposal that Julia Lathrop made in 1917. Successfully navigating the legislative process, however, required several critical amendments. Even though opponents were unable to defeat the bill, they altered key dimensions of Sheppard–Towner's design in ways that influenced the program's short- and medium-term political prospects. For instance, urban members of Congress insisted on altering the original language of the bill "so that the program would encompass rural as well as urban areas" (Johnson 2007, 144). As a result, the maternal and infancy services funded by the grant would be available statewide. Two especially consequential changes were made at the behest of fiscal conservatives. The original bills provided for a maximum appropriation of $4,000,000, but a Senate amendment reduced that amount to $1,480,000. When the Sheppard–Towner Act gained enactment and the

---

[17] The inclusion of the surgeon general and the commissioner of education resulted from a legislative amendment that reflected opponents' desire to limit the authority of the Children's Bureau.

program was operational, the law made only $1,201,725 available to the states each year.[18] Thus limited generosity was one of the defining attributes of the Sheppard–Towner Act. In the words of historian J. Stanley Lemons (1990, 158), "In retrospect, this pioneering bill seems pitifully small."[19] For comparison, consider that $8,020,000 was available for cooperative vocational education and $76,197,294 was available for the national highway construction system during the 1929 fiscal year.[20] During its campaign to defeat the Sheppard–Towner Act, in fact, the AMA "claimed that the limited funds available for the program could not produce any significant results" (Lindenmeyer 1997, 86). With so little money at stake, the law was unlikely to generate self-reinforcing feedback effects.

Fiscal conservatives' second significant victory concerned the duration for which the law was authorized. The final legislation included a temporary authorization, and it was scheduled to expire on June 30, 1927. This feature of the law placated many of its opponents but rendered it unstable. By definition, temporary authorizations require that programs be reevaluated and reapproved, which can hinder implementing agencies' ability to plan, develop policy changes, and accommodate new demands and constituencies (Lieberman 1998, 18–19). In addition, they also make extant programs especially vulnerable to changes in the ideological, political, or economic environment. The congressional debate over the reauthorization of the Sheppard–Towner Act highlights these vulnerabilities and illustrates the profound potential significance of a temporary authorization. The critical impact of this design feature in the Sheppard–Towner case derived in part from its interaction with other variables, particularly those linked to timing. The interaction of a temporary authorization and a changing political environment helped undermine the program's medium-term prospects.

The opposition of states' rights advocates led to important administrative changes as the program navigated the congressional process. Many members of Congress "feared an imbalance in the federal-state relationship" and hoped to establish a program that deferred to state authority (Chepaitis 1972, 217).[21]

---

[18] House Committee on Interstate and Foreign Commerce, *Protection of Maternity and Infancy*, 66th Cong., 3rd sess., 1921, Report No. 1255, 1. The law appropriated $1,480,000 for the 1921–1922 fiscal year and $1,240,000 for each of the next five years. The $1,201,725 figure excludes various administrative and other expenses.

[19] Johnson (2007, 144) attributes the phrase "pitifully small" to Julia Lathrop, the Children's Bureau's first director.

[20] These figures come from the House Committee on Interstate and Foreign Commerce, *Extension of Maternity and Infancy Act: Report to Accompany H.R. 17183*, 70th Cong., 2nd sess., 1929, 18 (Exhibit H).

[21] One congressional committee claimed that its efforts were "actuated by the desire to encroach as little as possible on the rights of States, but on the other hand to encourage them to take on the work of guarding its maternity and infancy interests as completely as possible within the borders of each." House Committee on Interstate and Foreign Commerce, *Protection of Maternity and Infancy*, 67th Cong., 1st sess., 1921, Report No. 467, 7.

Even so, the Sheppard–Towner Act placed significant constraints on state autonomy as part of a general effort to limit government intervention in family life. For example, in 1921 the House Committee on Education and Labor adopted a "substantial" amendment that forbade "any official, or agent, or representative [from] entering any home over the objection of the parents."[22] Other strictures, especially the provision disallowing the payment of any maternity or infancy pensions, stipends, or gratuities, were more politically consequential.[23] State Sheppard–Towner programs also could not reimburse physicians for the provision of medical services.[24] These restrictions on how states could spend the available funds are important not only because they hamstrung state officials. In addition, they made it quite unlikely that either individual beneficiaries or the medical profession would come to the program's defense, reducing the law's coalition potential and eliminating two potential paths through which the program might generate self-reinforcing feedback effects.

The administrative provisions of the Sheppard–Towner Act were also the subject of much debate as members of Congress discussed where state programs should be housed. Occurring at a time when state governments' institutional capacities were relatively limited, these discussions reflected the particularities of the 1920s. The law required that state governments establish new agencies devoted exclusively to the emerging field of child welfare. While the impulse behind this provision was understandable, it also brought the legislation into conflict with individuals heading existing state agencies. At a January 1919 congressional committee hearing, for example, the president of the American Public Health Association submitted a letter from the Secretary of the North Carolina State Board of Health. The state official wrote, "Infant hygiene work is strictly public health work and it seems to me that the public health work of the United States Government should be carried on under the United States Public Health Service and not through the Department of Labor."[25] Four officials from the US Public Health Service also raised this administrative issue at a hearing of the House Committee on Interstate and Foreign Commerce in December 1920.[26] This debate pitted the female reformers within the

---

[22] Senate Committee on Education and Labor, *Protection of Maternity and Infancy*, 67th Cong., 1st sess., 1921, Report No. 61, 1.

[23] A House committee described these provisions as an effort to preserve parental autonomy. House Committee on Interstate and Foreign Commerce, *Protection of Maternity and Infancy*, 67th Cong., 1st sess., 1921, Report No. 467, 7.

[24] Sheppard–Towner funds also could not be "applied, directly or indirectly, to the purchase, erection, preservation, or repair of any building or buildings or equipment, or for the purchase or rental of any buildings or land." S. 1039, 67th Cong., 1st sess., reported in the House November 14, 1921, 15.

[25] House Committee on Labor, *Hygiene of Maternity and Infancy: A Hearing on H.R. 12634*, 65th Cong., 3rd sess., 1919, 47.

[26] Three of the four officials from the Public Health Service also appeared at a congressional committee hearing the following July.

Children's Bureau against the mostly male public health community (Rothman 1978; Skocpol 1992). Even though the final legislation ultimately reflected the priorities of the former, the prominence of the issue suggests that the administrators of state Sheppard–Towner programs would struggle to build strong working relationships and political coalitions with their peers in state government.

In sum, several features of the Sheppard–Towner Act seemed more likely to dampen state officials' excitement about the program than to generate the self-reinforcing feedback effects that would facilitate its entrenchment. The limited generosity of the matching grant program, which was capped at a low level, made it unlikely that state lawmakers would feel invested in the policy initiative. The law's temporary authorization was an inherently destabilizing feature that left it vulnerable to changes in the economic and political environment. In addition, the states' inability to provide direct payments to individuals or physicians was a politically consequential constraint that reduced the likelihood that either the beneficiaries of the program or the medical profession would mobilize in its defense. Finally, the new child welfare agencies that states established to gain access to national government funds had the potential to come into conflict with extant state agencies as well as the US Public Health Service.

Moreover, Sheppard–Towner was a progressive policy adopted at a time of limited state administrative capacity and the outset of a conservative political era. Despite the existence of a relatively favorable economic environment, overall the timing of its enactment seemed to limit its feedback potential. Nevertheless, members of Congress were confident that the initiative would be well received at the state level. In 1920, the Senate Committee on Public Health and National Quarantine said that "the States are ready and eager to avail themselves of the provisions of this bill";[27] referring to state activities that were already underway, it claimed that "only the stimulus of Federal action is needed to make the work flourish."[28] A few months later, a House committee used similar language, asserting that the Sheppard–Towner Act would reduce infant and maternal mortality "by merely enlarging the activities of the States."[29] National legislators expected state officials to be enthusiastic about the new matching grant program. How did the states actually respond once Sheppard–Towner funds became available on March 20, 1922, and what were the political implications of their reaction for the initiative's short- and medium-term trajectory? The next section addresses these questions.

---

[27] Senate Committee on Public Health and National Quarantine, *Protection of Maternity and Infancy*, 66th Cong., 2nd sess., 1920, Report No. 650, 2.

[28] Senate Committee on Public Health and National Quarantine, *Protection of Maternity and Infancy*, 66th Cong., 2nd sess., 1920, Report No. 650, 3.

[29] House Committee on Interstate and Foreign Commerce, *Protection of Maternity and Infancy*, 66th Cong., 3rd sess., 1921, Report No. 1255, 5.

STATE GOVERNMENTS' RESPONSE TO THE SHEPPARD–TOWNER ACT

The Sheppard–Towner Act was authorized for only five years, so its ability to take root necessitated a rapid positive response from state officials. This section focuses primarily on one of the forms of mobilization described in Chapter 1, namely, the decisions that state officials made about the creation and operation of Sheppard–Towner programs. Scholars offer competing descriptions of state governments' reactions. On the one hand, historian J. Stanley Lemons (1990, 169) claims that the law was "well received by the state authorities." On the other hand, political scientist Kimberley S. Johnson (2007, 140) argues that "national bureaucrats had uneven support from the states." There is an element of truth in each of these claims. Most state governments took the necessary steps to establish programs serving mothers and infants, but many of them did not take full advantage of the matching grant's meager financial incentives. Other states fought the law, none more so than Massachusetts, which challenged the constitutionality of the Sheppard–Towner Act in a case that went to the Supreme Court. A close examination of state government reactions to the law suggest that its state-level support was broad but not deep, indicating that it did not generate self-reinforcing feedback.

Few state legislatures met annually in the early 1920s, posing an immediate challenge to the law because the receipt of national matching funds required state legislative approval. Since "very few of the legislatures were in session in 1922," only twelve had accepted the act by June 30, 1922.[30] States where the legislature did not meet could receive funds on an interim basis with gubernatorial approval, however, and thirty additional states used that option to accept the law "pending the next regular session of the legislature."[31] Technically the additional states were "in the process of compliance" (Lindenmeyer 1997, 93), but seven states that took advantage of this alternative later failed to uphold the governor's acceptance.[32]

After the national law received legislative or gubernatorial approval, two other important steps needed to be taken. First, state governments had to establish Sheppard–Towner programs. Many states were "quick" to set up programs, a "particularly noteworthy" development in many southern and western states where "maternal, infant, and early childhood health programs ... had been all but nonexistent" prior to the adoption of the Sheppard–Towner Act (Meckel 1990, 212). Second, state governments had to allocate funds for their programs in order to take advantage of the matching

[30] *Eleventh Annual Report of the Chief, Children's Bureau, to the Secretary of Labor: Fiscal Year Ended June 30, 1923*. Washington, DC: Government Printing Office, 1923, 1.

[31] *Tenth Annual Report of the Chief, Children's Bureau, to the Secretary of Labor: Fiscal Year Ended June 30, 1922*. Washington, DC: Government Printing Office, 1922, 6.

[32] The seven states included Connecticut, Illinois, Kansas, Louisiana, Vermont, Maine, and Massachusetts (Johnson 2007, 147).

TABLE 2 *State Government Responses to the Sheppard–Towner Act*

Fiscal Year	Maximum Amount Available to States in Matching Funds	Amount Accepted by States (Percentage)	Number of States Accepting Maximum Amount
1922	$477,500.00	$316,554.02 (66.3%)	16
1923	$1,201,725.96	$716,333.40 (59.6%)	13
1924	$1,201,725.96	$877,122.04 (73.0%)	26
1925	$1,201,725.96	$932,754.69 (77.6%)	28
1926	$1,201,725.96	$947,959.59 (78.9%)	23
1927	$1,201,725.96	$977,866.97 (81.4%)	28
1928	$1,201,725.96	$966,509.51 (80.4%)	28

Source: House Committee on Interstate and Foreign Commerce, *Extension of Maternity and Infancy Act: Report to Accompany H.R. 17183*, Report No. 2751, 70th Cong., 2nd sess., February 26, 1929, Exhibit A, 8–9.

grant. Once the Federal Board of Maternity and Infant Hygiene approved a state plan, that state became eligible for its share of the $477,500 that Congress had allocated for the 1922 fiscal year. Each participating state received a lump-sum grant of $5,000 from the national government and an additional appropriation that required a state match based on state population. Table 2 reveals that only sixteen states took full advantage of Sheppard–Towner Act funds during the 1922 fiscal year by accepting their entire allocation; all the rest left money on the table. In some cases, states rejected federal funds despite gubernatorial acceptance of the law; California, Illinois, and Vermont all "returned their 1922 funds to the U.S. Treasury unspent" (Lindenmeyer 1997, 93). Thus the first year of the Sheppard–Towner Act was a mixed bag, a troubling development for a program with a temporary authorization.

The program's second year also produced a combination of successes and setbacks. Most state legislatures were in session in 1923, and the number of legislative approvals increased from twelve to forty. This growth represented the most promising sign of increased momentum at the state level. The law even made some progress in the eight remaining states, winning majorities in at least one legislative chamber in four of them.[33] State spending patterns, in contrast, provided mixed signals. During the 1923 fiscal year, the total amount of matching funds accepted by states more than doubled to $716,333.40. Part of the increase stemmed from the fact that the previous year's allocation had been prorated to reflect the Sheppard–Towner Act's November passage. In fact, fewer states accepted the maximum allocation from the national government, and the states claimed only 59.6 percent of the available funds, down from 66.3 percent during the 1922 fiscal year. In sum, during its first two years the Sheppard–Towner Act received a warm but not overly enthusiastic reception at the state level.

Indeed, resistance to the national initiative appeared in every region of the country. The eight states that did not accept the program by June 30, 1923 were Connecticut, Illinois, Kansas, Louisiana, Maine, Massachusetts, Rhode Island, and Vermont. The Sheppard–Towner debate in Connecticut was particularly contentious. A 1919 law authorized the state health department to accept federal funds for the promotion of public health, but four years later the state legislature "instructed the health department not to accept the funds available under the [Sheppard–Towner Act]."[34] Legislators rejected Sheppard–Towner funds on the grounds that the national initiative infringed on the rights of the state even though Connecticut had accepted matching funds for many other purposes. They also "declared that such legislation expanded the federal government beyond its means and therefore it was time to stop the federal aid process," another claim that struck the law's proponents as hollow (Lindenmeyer 1997, 93). Eventually the state legislature established a state program for maternity and infancy protection, but it appropriated fewer funds than were available under the Sheppard–Towner Act. Moreover, funds for the new program came at the expense of a "major cut in funds for the Bureau of Child Welfare" that had been created in 1921 (Lemons 1990, 171).

Resistance to the Sheppard–Towner Act was also very strong in Massachusetts, one of only two states that chose not to participate in the program throughout its brief history.[35] Even before the national law was passed, the state had rejected proposals for maternity and infancy protection in 1919, 1920, and 1921. The opposition of the medical profession was "particularly vigorous" during those debates (Lemons 1990, 171). Catholic and antisuffrage groups expressed their opposition as well. In 1922, as the state began to consider enabling legislation, its attorney general "issued an opinion

---

[33] Acceptance acts were endorsed by the state senates in Illinois, Kansas, and Louisiana, and legislation cleared both houses of the legislature in Maine but was vetoed by the governor. *Eleventh Annual Report of the Chief, Children's Bureau, to the Secretary of Labor: Fiscal Year Ended June 30, 1923.* Washington, DC: Government Printing Office, 1923, 1.

[34] *Eleventh Annual Report of the Chief, Children's Bureau, to the Secretary of Labor: Fiscal Year Ended June 30, 1923.* Washington, DC: Government Printing Office, 1923, 1.

[35] Illinois was the other state that did not participate in the Sheppard–Towner Act before its termination in 1929.

that the Sheppard–Towner Act ... was unconstitutional because it violated the reserved rights of the states" (Lemons 1990, 171).[36] The state filed suit with the US Supreme Court to enjoin the law, arguing that its funds "are for purposes not national, but local to the states, and together with numerous similar appropriations constitute an effective means of inducing the states to yield a portion of their sovereign rights."[37] In response, ten states and the Association of Land Grant Colleges filed briefs in defense of the act.[38] Massachusetts resident Harriet Frothingham, a member of the antisuffragist group Woman Patriots, brought a separate suit against the law in the Supreme Court of the District of Columbia. The US Supreme Court combined the cases, concluding that they "must be disposed for want of jurisdiction, without considering the merits of the constitutional questions."[39] However, its unanimous opinion included language that seemed to reject the claims of the Act's opponents. The Court argued "that the powers of the state are not invaded, since the statute imposes no obligation but simply extends an option which the state is free to reject," and it concluded that the central question raised by the suits "is political, and not judicial in character, and therefore is not a matter which admits of the exercise of the judicial power."[40]

The Supreme Court decision did not dramatically alter state government responses to the Sheppard–Towner Act. State spending patterns changed somewhat from fiscal year 1923 to fiscal year 1924; the number of states that accepted their maximum allocation increased from 13 to 26, and states accepted 73 percent of the funds that the national government made available. As the decade continued, however, these numbers plateaued. Table 2 shows that no more than 28 states accepted their maximum allocation during the life of the law, and the proportion accepted by the states as a whole never exceeded 81.4 percent. Considering the relatively limited funds at stake, these patterns are striking. Although opposition continued across the country, states with large Catholic populations, like Massachusetts, represented especially hostile terrain due to concerns about government intervention in family life. As anti-Catholic sentiment increased in the 1920s, "some members of the Catholic hierarchy feared that [the law] might lead to further religious discrimination and the dissemination of birth control information" (Lindenmeyer 1997, 92–93). Concerns about government intervention were not limited to Catholic families, especially in the aftermath of the Red Scare, yet the issue of

---

[36] The state attorney general was "an anti-suffragist who had ruled women off the ballot and out of the jury box in Massachusetts" (Lemons 1990, 171).

[37] *Massachusetts v. Mellon*, 262 US 447 (1923).

[38] *Eleventh Annual Report of the Chief, Children's Bureau, to the Secretary of Labor: Fiscal Year Ended June 30, 1923*. Washington, DC: Government Printing Office, 1923, 6. The ten states included Arkansas, Arizona, Colorado, Delaware, Indiana, Kentucky, Minnesota, Oregon, Pennsylvania, and Virginia.

[39] *Massachusetts v. Mellon*, 262 US 447 (1923).

[40] *Massachusetts v. Mellon*, 262 US 447 (1923).

family autonomy appeared to resonate particularly strongly among that constituency.

In sum, state governments generally reacted positively but not overly enthusiastically to the Sheppard–Towner Act and its matching grant. To be sure, the program accomplished a great deal despite this tepid reaction; by the mid 1920s, supporters could offer several facts and figures to buttress their claims that the law had spurred the creation of "more widespread medical and nursing facilities" and the provision of services designed to improve maternal and infant health.[41] During the 1925 fiscal year, Sheppard–Towner nurses conducted 370,591 home visits and home demonstrations and 31,529 American women attended mothers' classes. In the 43 states that were administering federal funds that year, there were 18,154 child health conferences where 290,846 infants and preschool-age children were examined and another 3,781 prenatal conferences with a total of 36,690 women in attendance. Nineteen states held midwife classes that were attended by 10,693 women. Up to that point, the states had established 607 children's health centers and 65 permanent prenatal centers.[42] Supporters took great pride in the maternity and infancy activities that the grants had funded and hoped the program's wide reach would lead to its reauthorization. Ironically, however, these activities arguably undercut the Sheppard–Towner Act's medium-term political prospects rather than enhancing them.

The provision that prohibited state Sheppard–Towner programs from reimbursing physicians for medical services limited the law's coalition-building potential. Had the medical profession benefited financially from the activities documented in the previous paragraph, its initial ambivalence toward the Sheppard–Towner Act might have evaporated and it might have become one of the law's most ardent defenders. Indeed, doctors' and hospitals' reaction to the creation of Medicaid, which will be discussed in more detail in Chapter 4, illustrates the plausibility of this claim. Lacking a similar financial incentive in the context of state Sheppard–Towner programs, the medical profession was unlikely to feel a stake in their continuation. Not only did the Sheppard–Towner Act fail to generate support from the medical community; broader changes in American medicine meant that physicians were increasingly inclined to view the law as a competitor.

During the 1920s, the AMA and local medical societies encouraged private physicians to transform their practices by offering preventive health services and advice on personal hygiene for the first time. They offered in-person courses that taught doctors how to examine expectant mothers, healthy children, and

---

[41] House Committee on Interstate and Foreign Commerce, *Extension of Public Protection of Maternity and Infancy Act: A Hearing on H.R. 7555,* 69th Cong., 1st sess., January 14, 1926, 8.

[42] House Committee on Interstate and Foreign Commerce, *Extension of Public Protection of Maternity and Infancy Act: A Hearing on H.R. 7555,* 69th Cong., 1st sess., January 14, 1926, 8–9.

healthy adults, and they circulated lengthy instructions about how to conduct the checkups. These outreach activities promoted an alternative model of health care delivery that, among other things, transferred responsibility for infant and maternal health from public health nurses to the medical profession (Rothman 1978). By drawing attention to and providing the services that the AMA now encouraged its members to embrace, the Sheppard–Towner Act "was in some respects the victim of its own success" (Meckel 1990, 218). It demonstrated the value of prenatal, infant, and maternal care to both the public and medical professionals, encouraging the public to seek out these health services. The increased demand for the services gave physicians a financial incentive to provide them. The Children's Bureau and state Sheppard–Towner program directors made every effort to assure the medical profession that their programs did not intrude on doctors' domains; ironically, their efforts "helped to educate their own medical competition" (Skocpol 1992, 516). As doctors took an increased interest in the services provided by the law, their opposition to its continuation grew stronger. The hostility of this powerful constituency, in combination with the Sheppard–Towner Act's failure to spur the mobilization of state officials, was apparent during congressional debates over the law's reauthorization.

POLITICAL CHANGE, ELITE FEEDBACK, AND THE DEMISE OF SHEPPARD–TOWNER

In 1926, Sheppard–Towner supporters began to lobby Congress for an extension of the law's appropriations, which were scheduled to expire the following year. Proud of the maternity and infancy activities the grants had funded, they anticipated minimal opposition. Extension bills "were introduced into both houses, but were met with surprising resistance" (Chepaitis 1972, 222). Opponents made the same arguments that they had advanced when the initial legislation was being considered, but three key political changes put Sheppard–Towner supporters on the defensive.

First, the renewal debate took place in a more conservative political environment. After World War I, the United States entered into "an era characterized by growing ideological conservatism ... and renewed Republican Party dominance" (Johnson 2007, 148). The Sheppard–Towner Act, a progressive policy innovation, had nevertheless gained enactment in 1921 due to profound uncertainty over the partisan implications of the Nineteenth Amendment and a fairly favorable partisan alignment in Congress.[43] By the mid 1920s, however, the law faced a more hostile environment. President Calvin Coolidge had been elected in a landslide in 1924. A strong believer in fiscal responsibility and limited national

---

[43] Joseph B. Chepaitis (1972, 222) contends that "Congress was controlled by progressive elements, particularly the Farm Bloc," in 1921.

government activity, the president "endorsed more funds for Sheppard–Towner, but only for an interim period during which he expected the states to prepare themselves for a full takeover of its programs" (Skocpol 1992, 513). Coolidge's landslide victory also "signaled the emergence of conservative southern Democrats as decisive powers within the weakened party" as "Democrats lost whatever cohesion they had achieved" during the presidency of Woodrow Wilson (Johnson 2007, 148). Republican empowerment and Democratic fragmentation were apparent in Congress, which experienced massive turnover in the 1920s. The original Sheppard–Towner Act had been supported by seventy-four senators in 1921, but by 1927 only thirty-two of those supporters were still in office (Chepaitis 1972, 222).[44]

Second, by the time the renewal debate occurred, elected officials had a better sense of whether and how the enfranchisement of American women would affect national politics. The results of the 1922 and 1924 elections suggested that women, like men, voted along partisan lines. Women did not vote in blocs according to the issues, contrary to suffragists' claims, and the potential clout of female voters weakened since "the politicians' fear of wrathful women voting as a bloc against them had been quelled" (Chepaitis 1972, 223). The reauthorization debate highlights the combined impact of the conservative shift and decreased uncertainty surrounding the female vote, although these changes did not cause support for the Sheppard–Towner act to collapse completely.

The third key political change concerned the organized interests working against renewal, as the law faced a more powerful and mobilized set of adversaries. By 1926, "opponents had a number of powerful allies they did not have before" (Meckel 1990, 214). The Daughters of the American Revolution supported the original measure but opposed its renewal.[45] Developments at the state level had showcased the objections of Catholic groups, who had not played a major role during the adoption debate but were more outspoken against renewal, and especially the medical profession, which was more unified and more strongly mobilized in opposition.[46] Thus renewal

---

[44] Moreover, three of the holdovers were Democrats who changed their support to opposition (Johnson 2007, 148).

[45] The Daughters of the American Revolution had been a member of the Women's Joint Congressional Committee (WJCC), but it withdrew from the coalition and "ceased espousing progressive causes after 1923–24" (Lemons 1990, 172; see also Lindenmeyer 1997, 100). By the middle of the decade, the Daughters of the American Revolution "had become a reactionary organization dedicated to principles of militarism, nationalism, and, above all, antiradicalism"; in the late 1920s it engaged in a heated battle with its former WJCC allies (Wilson 2007, 166–168).

[46] Even though the medical profession as a whole was largely unified in its opposition to the renewal of Sheppard–Towner, the Pediatric Section of the AMA supported the program's continuation. However, the AMA's House of Delegates ruled that the section could not publish its views independently, a rebuke which contributed to the 1930 founding of the American Academy of Pediatrics (Schmidt 1973, 422).

advocates were operating in a less hospitable political environment without one of the resources that contributed to their initial success, and they had to contend with a more cohesive and active set of adversaries. Moreover, state governments' mixed response to the law foreshadowed their surprisingly limited role during the reauthorization debate. Powerful state-level actors failed to come to the law's defense, yet another factor that contributed to its demise.

The Reauthorization Debate

State Sheppard–Towner programs provided a striking range of maternal and infant health services, yet supporters knew that the programs were not well entrenched and required additional federal funds in order to be placed on sounder footing. At a congressional committee hearing in January 1926, Children's Bureau director Grace Abbott explained, "If we were to withdraw the Federal assistance at this moment, a great deal of the work would be undone, and the money that has already been expended would, to a very considerable extent, be lost, because much of the work has not been developed into permanent activity."[47] Abbott's concerns about the long-term prospects of the Sheppard–Towner Act highlight the impact of its temporary authorization, which rendered the program inherently unstable and placed it at the mercy of Congress. On December 21, 1925, Secretary of Labor James J. Davis sent a letter to Congress supporting an extension of the law's appropriations: "For the purpose of Budget estimates next autumn, and in order that the State legislatures meeting in January, 1927, may know what funds will be available, action with reference to this appropriation should be taken by the present Congress. I therefore submit for your consideration a proposal which would authorize continuing this appropriation for the fiscal years 1928 and 1929."[48] The questions of whether and for how long to extend appropriations for the Sheppard–Towner Act took center stage in January when a House committee discussed the law's future.

When Abbott was asked about a possible two-year extension of the law's appropriations, she responded, "Well, I do not consider it sufficient if it is to end at the two-year period."[49] Her rejoinder to this line of questioning sparked a lively exchange that was joined by Representatives John Fredericks (R-CA), Clarence Lea (D-CA), Sam Rayburn (D-TX), and Robert Crosser (D-OH). Fredericks pressed Abbott to estimate how long it would be before the

---

[47] House Committee on Interstate and Foreign Commerce, *Extension of Public Protection of Maternity and Infancy Act: Hearing on H.R. 7555*, 69th Cong., 1st sess., January 14, 1926, 10–11.

[48] House Committee on Interstate and Foreign Commerce, *Extension of Public Protection of Maternity and Infancy Act: Hearing on H.R. 7555*, 69th Cong., 1st sess., January 14, 1926, 28.

[49] House Committee on Interstate and Foreign Commerce, *Extension of Public Protection of Maternity and Infancy Act: Hearing on H.R. 7555*, 69th Cong., 1st sess., January 14, 1926, 12.

national government could "step out of this endeavor" and make the maintenance of maternity and infancy programs a state government responsibility. He asked, "The primary purpose of the law was to induce the States to take this matter on their own shoulders, eventually, was it not?"[50] Abbott expressed her preference for a five-year extension, but her congressional interlocutors continued to emphasize that the program should be ceded to the states in short order. The Director of Administration of the Sheppard–Towner Act for the State of Pennsylvania was pressed on this point by Fredericks and Representative Schuyler Merritt (R-CT). Asked whether and when her state would be able to carry out the work without national government assistance, she responded, "I do, temporarily. I absolutely agree … that there is no reason why in time we should not gradually shift over to the place where the State bears its own responsibility for help, but I think we are gradually doing that."[51] Had the Sheppard–Towner Act received a permanent authorization, this issue most probably would not have been raised.

While the proper duration of the program was the subject of considerable attention, the congressional hearings also led its supporters and opponents to revisit their general arguments for and against its very existence.[52] The claims on both sides were familiar, so much so that during a reauthorization hearing the chair of the House Committee on Interstate and Foreign Commerce limited each side to forty minutes because his "committee heard this subject for months and months during the Sixty-Seventh Congress."[53] Opponents continued to characterize Sheppard–Towner as an encroachment on states' rights that violated parental autonomy, with one witness describing it as endorsing a "very dangerous paganistic principle [that] the child belongs to the State."[54] One witness supplemented these familiar claims by alluding to the public's increasing conservatism: "Since this maternity bill was first passed, I believe that you will agree with me that there has been a very great change in public opinion on such legislation as this."[55] This assertion cannot be validated due to a lack of systematic polling data on the law, but it resonates with most scholars'

[50] House Committee on Interstate and Foreign Commerce, *Extension of Public Protection of Maternity and Infancy Act: Hearing on H.R. 7555*, 69th Cong., 1st sess., January 14, 1926, 13.

[51] House Committee on Interstate and Foreign Commerce, *Extension of Public Protection of Maternity and Infancy Act: Hearing on H.R. 7555*, 69th Cong., 1st sess., January 14, 1926, 18. She also explained that before the Sheppard–Towner Act was adopted, "[state] plans were simply laid aside because there was no money to carry them on."

[52] Reflecting continued objections to the law in his home state, Representative A. Piatt Andrew (R-MA) introduced legislation to repeal the Sheppard–Towner Act. The House took no action on his proposal. H.R. 10986, 69th Cong., 1st sess., introduced April 5, 1926.

[53] House Committee on Interstate and Foreign Commerce, *Extension of Public Protection of Maternity and Infancy Act: Hearing on H.R. 7555*, 69th Cong., 1st sess., January 14, 1926, 1.

[54] House Committee on Interstate and Foreign Commerce, *Extension of Public Protection of Maternity and Infancy Act: Hearing on H.R. 7555*, 69th Cong., 1st sess., January 14, 1926, 22.

[55] House Committee on Interstate and Foreign Commerce, *Extension of Public Protection of Maternity and Infancy Act: Hearing on H.R. 7555*, 69th Cong., 1st sess., January 14, 1926, 26.

descriptions of the 1920s. Sheppard–Towner supporters responded by emphasizing the necessity of maternal and infancy protection and the constitutionality of the matching grant approach. In addition to making these familiar claims, they also highlighted the services that state programs had already provided. Eventually the House of Representatives endorsed a two-year extension of the program's appropriations in a 218–44 vote.

While the Sheppard–Towner Act received a skeptical but ultimately positive reception in the House, its reception in the Senate was more hostile. The reauthorization debate "renewed the 1921 battle with an extra measure of bitterness in opponents," who were also energized by their recent defeat of the federal child labor amendment (Lemons 1990, 172).[56] The general contours of the Senate debate were similar to those of the House, and the program's adversaries continued to question the need for an extension of its appropriations. The Senate Committee on Education and Labor, headed by Lawrence Phipps (R-CO), proposed to authorize aid for one additional year, instead of the two-year extension endorsed by the House. The committee report asserted that the "original purpose and intent of Congress to encourage the States to take up this important work is rapidly approaching fulfillment, if indeed that time has not already come"; it portrayed the one-year extension as providing state legislatures with the extra time they needed, since they did not meet every year, to prepare for the cessation of the grant-in-aid program.[57]

The temporary extension of the Sheppard–Towner Act was not the preferred outcome for Phipps, one of "a small but powerful group of archconservative senators" who wanted to block any extension legislation from coming to the Senate floor but settled for a campaign to force the law's supporters to accept a single additional year of funding (Meckel 1990, 218). Senator James Reed (D-MO) led the fight against renewal on the Senate floor, making the case that there should be no continuation in any form. Morris Sheppard (D-TX) was his most prominent adversary; the Senate sponsor of the 1921 law argued "that neither he nor Congress intended for the bill to be limited to a five-year test and that a two-year extension was too short" (Lindenmeyer 1997, 102). Neither side was willing to acquiesce to the other's demands. No vote was taken, and Phipps and his conservative allies launched a filibuster that delayed action on the extension for eight months. Sheppard–Towner supporters lacked the votes

---

[56] The federal child labor amendment would have granted Congress "the power to limit, regulate, and prohibit" the labor of individuals under the age of 18. After the Supreme Court invalidated two congressional attempts to regulate child labor, the amendment cleared Congress in 1924. Six state legislatures ratified the amendment between 1924 and 1932, while it was rejected by one or both houses of the legislature in thirty-two states during that time. See The Child Labor Amendment, 1924–1934 (1934). *Editorial Research Reports 1934* (Vol. 1). Washington, DC: CQ Press. The interest group politics of the amendment are covered in more detail in Lemons (1990) and Wilson (2007).

[57] Senate Committee on Education and Labor, *Amend the Maternity Act: Report to Accompany H. R. 7555*, 69th Cong., 1st sess., 1926, Report No. 745, 2.

they needed to break the filibuster, and they knew that the law's original appropriations were on the verge of expiring. With this deadline looming, they reluctantly agreed to a "compromise" that extended appropriations for two more years but automatically repealed the Sheppard–Towner Act on June 30, 1929. The extraordinarily high cost of the additional funding was the termination of the program.[58]

What role, if any, did state officials play during the reauthorization debate? Were they a highly mobilized constituency that came to the defense of Sheppard–Towner, working with other groups affected by the law? The historical record suggests that, as the fate of the matching grant program hung in the balance, most state government leaders were uninvolved in national politics. In 1926, two directors or administrators of state Sheppard–Towner programs testified at a congressional hearing on reauthorization; several others submitted material for the record.[59] This constituency had a vital stake in the continuation of the state programs, yet they were neither independently powerful nor allied with other influential groups. The recent origins of the state agencies they headed were a crucial disadvantage, and state directors' influence was limited by "the far weaker and fragmented position child welfare departments held in state governments" (Johnson 2007, 140). When state Sheppard–Towner directors testified before Congress, they represented only themselves – not other powerful officeholders like governors.

In addition, the limited coalition potential of the Sheppard–Towner Act meant that state administrators lacked the support of additional allies. The strong opposition of the AMA made clear that the "disproportionately female professional employees of Sheppard–Towner programs [were] already marginal in their public health professions" (Skocpol 1992, 520). They could not claim to have the support of the medical profession. Moreover, no other state-level constituency joined the program's defenders at congressional hearings. The matching grant program lacked a "strong, easily identifiable, and mobilized constituency at the state level [or] the ability to supply discrete or tangible benefits to draw the support of other powerful, organized groups" (Johnson 2007, 149). In contrast to the unemployment insurance case, where business

---

[58] Scholars disagree about why Sheppard–Towner supporters agreed to the legislative compromise. Some argue that advocates hoped a more progressive political climate would exist by 1929 and lead to the Act's restoration (Lemons 1990, 173); others say that advocates "misjudged the compromise appropriation act as only a temporary difficulty" (Lindenmeyer 1997, 103). Theda Skocpol (1992, 521) contends that Sheppard–Towner's supporters underestimated the political prowess of American women and "may have given in too quickly, agreeing to a 'compromise' whose terms were worse than necessary for their cause."

[59] House Committee on Interstate and Foreign Commerce, *Extension of Public Protection of Maternity and Infancy Act: Hearing on H.R. 7555*, 69th Cong., 1st sess., January 14, 1926. Five other witnesses testified at the hearing; they represented the Children's Bureau, the Women's Committee for the Extension of the Sheppard–Towner Act, Sentinels of the Republic, the Massachusetts Public Interest League, and the League of Catholic Women of Boston, Massachusetts.

organizations joined state officials in lobbying for the preservation of the status quo, state Sheppard–Towner program administrators lacked strong allies.

Policy design helps explain why the Sheppard–Towner Act proved unable to galvanize a strong supporting coalition. The new state agencies established in response to its requirements lacked solid relationships with other powerful state government actors, such as the public health officials who would have been logical allies. Perhaps these relationships would have emerged if the financial stakes of the program had been higher, but the funds authorized for state Sheppard–Towner programs represented less than 1 percent of the funds available to state governments for cooperative undertakings during the 1929 fiscal year.[60] Similarly, individual beneficiaries and the medical community might have come to the law's defense had state programs been permitted to deliver stipends or other cash benefits. The challenges faced by Sheppard–Towner proponents were exacerbated, moreover, by the interaction of timing and program design, contributing to its ultimate demise. The law was especially vulnerable to short-term political shifts, such as changes in the distribution of power in Congress, because it did not provide a permanent entitlement to its services and it lacked automatically renewed appropriations (Skocpol 1992). As its five years of appropriations reached their conclusion, the effort to extend the life of the grant-in-aid program took place in a politically hostile environment. The Sheppard–Towner Act failed either to provide resources or to alter incentives in ways that generated feedback effects among state officials. Its provisions did, however, manage to provoke the strong opposition of the increasingly powerful medical profession. These political dynamics help explain its termination.

AFTERMATH

After the demise of the Sheppard–Towner Act, many state governments continued to fund maternity and infancy aid programs. The law had succeeded in raising awareness of the problems confronting mothers and young children, and most states possessed the necessary administrative apparatus to try to address them. The absence of federal appropriations, however, restricted their efforts. Nineteen state legislatures "appropriated funds equal to or exceeding the combined state and national funds provided under the act" (Johnson 2007, 151), but maternity and infancy programs took a financial hit in a majority of the states.[61] The onset and deepening of the Great

---

[60] House Committee on Interstate and Foreign Commerce, *Extension of Maternity and Infancy Act*, 70th Cong., 2nd sess., 1929, Report No. 2751, 6.

[61] The nineteen states were Delaware, Kentucky, Maine, Maryland, Michigan, Missouri, New Hampshire, New Jersey, New Mexico, New York, North Carolina, North Dakota, Pennsylvania, Rhode Island, South Dakota, Tennessee, Vermont, Virginia, and Wisconsin (Abbott 1930, 95). This estimate may be high. Lemons (1990, 175) contends that "only sixteen states appropriated enough money to exceed or equal the previous total."

Depression made program maintenance even more challenging, forcing many states to reduce their spending or drop their programs altogether in the early 1930s (Lemons 1990, 175).

Working with allies like the Women's Joint Congressional Committee, the leaders of the Children's Bureau tried to buttress the state programs by reviving the Sheppard–Towner Act or enacting equivalent legislation. Fourteen bills, none of which gained enactment, were introduced between 1928 and 1933 (Chepaitis 1972, 223). One liberal alternative apportioned funds based on need, not population, and "specified that the money would be spent in cooperation with the states, but did not require either acceptance by the state legislature or matching funds" (Lemons 1990, 174). Other bills adhered more closely to the precedent set by the Sheppard–Towner Act, either by extending or reviving the law or by creating programs focused on maternal and infant hygiene in rural areas. The political obstacles that had confronted the renewal campaign of the mid 1920s remained in place; in some ways they were even more formidable. Conservatives maintained congressional control, elected officials no longer worried about being punished by a women's voting bloc, and President Herbert Hoover retained his predecessor's strong commitment to fiscal responsibility and limited national government activity.[62] In addition, the interest groups that had opposed renewal, such as the AMA, continued their energetic lobbying against national legislation.

Indeed, the alignment of interest groups supporting and opposing the Sheppard–Towner Act and similar proposals changed little over time. When Congress considered maternity and infancy legislation in 1929 and 1931, state health officials from Kentucky, Virginia, and New York offered supportive testimony,[63] just as a similarly situated group had in the years leading up to the law's enactment. However, experience with Sheppard–Towner programs had not led other state leaders, such as governors, to join them, indicating the absence of self-reinforcing elite feedback. Meanwhile, witnesses representing the medical profession, health organizations, or women's organizations continued to outnumber state and local officials.[64]

The rhetorical contours of the debate over national government funding of maternity and infancy programs also changed little after the legislative compromise that extended funds for two years but terminated the Sheppard–Towner Act. One congressional committee report, published as the expiration date loomed, is illustrative. Supporters pointed to the state-level activity that the law had spurred, emphasizing that 45 states were cooperating with the

---

[62] While Hoover was not enthusiastic about legislation to revive the Sheppard–Towner Act, he "issued perfunctory formal statements which urged its enactment; and refusing to press the matter, he allowed the first federal social welfare law to lapse" (Lemons 1990, 174).

[63] The 1929 hearing focused on H.R. 14070, while there was a joint hearing on S. 255 and H.R. 12995 in 1931. The official from Kentucky appeared at both hearings.

[64] Of the 42 witnesses who appeared at the two hearings, 8 represented women's organizations while 12 represented health organizations or medical professionals.

Children's Bureau and 11 of them had "appropriated additional funds for child health over and above the amount set up for matching Federal funds under the maternity and infancy act" during the fiscal year that ended on June 30, 1928.[65] They sought to illustrate the law's beneficial impact through statistics on state appropriations and infant and maternal mortality rates. The minority report, which was signed by Representatives Schuyler Merritt (R-CT) and James M. Beck (R-PA), responded that the effort to revive the law was "a good illustration of the difficulty of stopping any Federal activity when it is once started, and especially when it provides funds for State activities which in turn provide employment for a great number of people."[66] Recapitulating earlier debates, it did not dispute the value of the services that the matching grant program provided. However, it sharply questioned whether the national government should allocate additional funds to those services, describing the initial activities as "demonstration work" that state governments should continue without any national government assistance.[67] It quoted a January 7, 1927 Budget Message from President Coolidge, saying, "The States should now be in a position to walk alone along the highway of helpful endeavor, and I believe it in the interest of the States and the Federal Government to give them this opportunity."[68] By parrying every effort to revive the Sheppard–Towner Act, opponents effectively brought this "opportunity" to fruition.

Advocates' inability to secure additional national government funding for state maternity and infancy programs, combined with the fiscal pressures sparked by the Great Depression, led to a sharp decline in state spending between 1928 and 1934 (Johnson 2007, 153).[69] The Great Depression also led to the passage of the Social Security Act of 1935, however. Title V of that comprehensive social welfare legislation authorized grants to the states for maternal and child welfare, which historian J. Stanley Lemons (1990, 175–176) has described as a "restoration" of the Sheppard–Towner Act that "authorized appropriations of $5,820,000 for maternity and infancy protection."[70] Supporters and opponents spoke of Title V as reviving the

---

[65] House Committee on Interstate and Foreign Commerce, *Extension of Maternity and Infancy Act*, 70th Cong., 2nd sess., 1929, Report No. 2751, 4.

[66] House Committee on Interstate and Foreign Commerce, *Extension of Maternity and Infancy Act*, 70th Cong., 2nd sess., 1929, Report No. 2751, 19.

[67] House Committee on Interstate and Foreign Commerce, *Extension of Maternity and Infancy Act*, 70th Cong., 2nd sess., 1929, Report No. 2751, 21.

[68] House Committee on Interstate and Foreign Commerce, *Extension of Maternity and Infancy Act*, 70th Cong., 2nd sess., 1929, Report No. 2751, 22.

[69] Cumulatively, states were spending "about $1.2 million" in 1934 as opposed to "approximately $2.8 million" in 1928, of which $1.02 million came from the national government. In 1934, "twenty-two states reported spending half the amount spent in 1928, while nine states spent no money at all on maternal and child health" (Johnson 2007, 153).

[70] Johnson (2007, 153) provides a smaller estimate of available funds, saying that "approximately $3.8 million was appropriated for maternal and child health."

Sheppard–Towner Act; the repealed measure served as "a model for apportioning funds, cooperating with state health agencies, reviewing state plans, and inspecting state activities" (Chepaitis 1972, 226).

In several important ways, however, Title V of the Social Security Act differed from its legislative predecessor. It was simultaneously more generous and more targeted. It allotted more funds to the states, and potential beneficiaries included both preschool and school-age children. Indeed, the enhanced generosity of Title V helps explain "the alacrity with which states matched funds"; by 1936, every state was cooperating with the Children's Bureau and operated a maternal and child health division that was headed by a full-time director (Johnson 2007, 153–154). Title V was more targeted by virtue of its incorporation in the Social Security Act, which "mandated that special attention be given women and infants in economically depressed areas – thus moving its programs in the direction of temporary medical relief" (Meckel 1990, 222).

In addition, several provisions of Title V reflected its sponsors' desire to avoid provoking opposition from the medical community. Physicians were unlikely to claim that the new program created unfair competition because it did not provide services to all families but instead targeted families in economic distress, and Title V supporters took several additional steps to mollify this increasingly powerful constituency. It "granted to the medical profession authority to determine that which was best for promoting the health of mothers and infants," and the Children's Bureau "courted medical specialists to design and approve programs and ... also granted local and state medical societies the right to approve or disapprove plans" (Meckel 1990, 222–223). Physicians were not entirely satisfied with the program, but these steps helped prevent the strong opposition that undermined the Sheppard–Towner Act. In this sense, Title V of the Social Security Act of 1935 addressed some of the crucial program design features that had diminished the political prospects of its legislative predecessor.

CONCLUSION

Based on both the policy decisions state leaders made in their own jurisdictions and the tepid lobbying efforts they undertook during congressional debates, the Sheppard–Towner Act clearly failed to generate self-reinforcing or self-undermining policy feedback. Key features of the program – its limited generosity, its temporary authorization, its constraints on how state governments could allocate funds, and its weak coalition potential – help explain why powerful state officials generally did not come to its defense during the renewal debates of the mid 1920s. Moreover, the timing of the law's adoption interacted with these provisions in ways that left it politically vulnerable. A progressive policy innovation adopted at the outset of a conservative era, the Sheppard–Towner Act faced a highly mobilized set of adversaries when it came up for renewal in an inhospitable political environment. It also failed to mobilize a supportive coalition among the individuals who benefited from its services or the state government officials charged with its implementation, and the end result was a legislative compromise that cemented its termination.

In sum, the trajectory of the Sheppard–Towner Act illustrates how certain provisions of a program shape its ability, or inability, to spark future political mobilization. Most state officials failed to view themselves as having a strong stake in the continuation of the law, and the ones who were especially likely to come to its defense were marginalized professionally. Its failure to generate self-reinforcing feedback effects among government elites was one of many factors that facilitated the demise of Sheppard–Towner. Intergovernmental relations alone cannot account for the trajectory of the matching grant program, yet the evidence presented in this chapter clearly demonstrates that they did make its elimination more likely.

4

The Remarkable Expansion of Medicaid[*]

When Congress created Medicaid under Title XIX of the Social Security Amendments of 1965, national lawmakers envisioned it as a safety net for only the poorest and most vulnerable citizens. They predicted that state officials would be measured and circumspect about participating in the new program, as they had been with previous health care programs for the poor, thereby limiting federal outlays. Upon the program's inception, however, state officials "rudely jostled their way toward the Title XIX trough, to the increasing consternation of legislators and administrators in Washington" (Stevens and Stevens 2003, 81). The program's chief architect, fiscally conservative House Ways and Means Chairman Wilbur Mills (D-AR), later called Medicaid the most expensive mistake of his career (Zelizer 1998, 262). He and other lawmakers began drafting legislation to scale back the program almost immediately, but state officials successfully fought off these and subsequent efforts at retrenchment. On several occasions the governors also lobbied for federal policy changes to greatly expand eligibility for the program. Medicaid today covers more people than any other US health insurance program (75 million people or about 1 in 5 Americans), comprises more than half of all federal grants to state and local governments, and represents the single largest item in the typical state's budget.

Medicaid's expansion exemplifies self-reinforcing feedback, illustrating the lasting impact of program design and timing. Financed with an unprecedentedly generous open-ended matching grant, the program created strong incentives for states to adopt liberal Medicaid plans and to protect the program against federal funding cuts. Several other expansive provisions, including loosely drawn eligibility standards and mandated coverage of a broad array of services, further contributed to this dynamic. Another feature of Medicaid's

[*] This chapter draws heavily on Rose (2013).

policy design – permanent authorization – helped it survive an early period of vulnerability. And since Medicaid – unlike the Sheppard–Towner program discussed in Chapter 3 – reimburses health care providers on behalf of those who would probably otherwise be uninsured, organized medicine has often (though not always) worked in tandem with state officials to advocate for the program's maintenance and expansion. Moreover, Medicaid was introduced at a time of relative prosperity and liberal state leadership, and its rollout coincided with the mobilization of the state government lobby in Washington. Indeed, a combination of policy design and timing helps explain why Medicaid experienced self-reinforcing feedback whereas similar health care programs that came before it did not.

ORIGINS AND ENACTMENT

In 1965, Congress enacted two new health care programs: Medicare, a universal program for the elderly, and the Medical Assistance Program – commonly known as Medicaid – a means-tested program for poor elderly persons, people with disabilities, and families. In reality, Medicaid was not a new program at all, but rather an incremental expansion of an existing program – the Kerr-Mills Program of Medical Assistance to the Aged – which itself was an expansion of an earlier program of medical vendor payments. Medicaid thus has certain elements in common with these antecedents, yet critical differences in program design set it apart.

In 1950, the federal government began allowing states to use federal public-assistance funds for direct payments to doctors and hospitals on behalf of welfare recipients. These so-called "medical vendor payments" were governed by the funding limits on public-assistance programs – Old Age Assistance (OAA), Aid to the Blind (ATB), and Aid to Dependent Children (ADC) – which had been created under the Social Security Act of 1935. Initially, OAA and ATB matched state spending at a rate of 50 percent up to a maximum payment of $30 per person per month, and ADC provided a 33 percent match up to $18 per month for the first child and $12 for additional children. This matching structure was designed to incentivize states to spend their own resources. However, due to meager federal funding as well as constraints on state political commitment, taxing authority, and administrative capacity, states adopted skimpy cash assistance programs and only a handful of states authorized medical vendor payments at all. To increase state participation, Congress incrementally raised the matching rates and caps for public assistance programs several times between 1935 and 1960. It also introduced a progressive matching formula with a maximum rate of 65 percent in order to spur low-income states in particular to expand coverage. Forty states were using federal funding for medical vendor payments by 1960, but the total level of spending remained quite modest at $514 million.

Meanwhile, political pressure for greater access to health insurance, particularly for the elderly, continued to build. The elderly population was growing rapidly, and one-third of the elderly lived in poverty in 1960 (US Census Bureau 1961). Medical costs were skyrocketing, and senior citizens had few affordable health insurance options. John F. Kennedy announced his support for Medicare – a universal, payroll-tax-financed health care program for all elderly persons, regardless of income – during his 1960 presidential campaign. But conservatives, including Ways and Means Chairman Wilbur Mills, feared it would be too costly and would threaten the financial integrity of the Social Security system.

These developments paved the way for the 1960 passage of a means-tested alternative to Medicare: the Kerr-Mills Program of Medical Assistance to the Aged. Named for its sponsors, Senator Robert Kerr (D-OK) and Chairman Mills, the program provided federal matching funds to the states for medical care for the poor elderly. Kerr-Mills shared much in common with medical vendor payments. It left most of the initiative, including the decision of whether or not to participate, up to the states. However, it featured several provisions designed to increase state participation. First, it increased the top matching rate from 65 to 80 percent and, unlike medical vendor payments, did not place a cap on the amount of federal aid states could receive. Although it went largely unnoticed at the time, the adoption of open-ended matching grants was unprecedented. Second, it extended eligibility by creating a new optional category of beneficiaries known as the "medically needy" – elderly persons whose incomes were not low enough to qualify them for public assistance but whose resources were insufficient to meet the costs of necessary medical services.[1] Third, it required participating states to cover some institutional and some noninstitutional care, and gave states the option of covering a broad range of physician, hospital, nursing home, and other services.

During the congressional debate over the Kerr-Mills bill, progressive members worried that a voluntary state-based program would be insufficient to meet the needs of the poor elderly due to the states' proven lack of capacity and commitment. Senator Patrick McNamara (D-MI) remarked that "it would be the miracle of the century if all of the states – or even a sizeable number – would be in a position to provide the matching funds to make the program more than just a plan on paper" (Marmor 1970, 36).

These fears turned out to be well founded. Senator Kerr had predicted that 10 million recipients would benefit from the Kerr-Mills program, but by 1965 – five years after passage – fewer than 300,000 recipients (less than 2 percent of the elderly) were covered.[2] Nor did many states choose to provide more

---

[1] Medically needy blind people and people with disabilities were made eligible in 1962.

[2] "Public Assistance: Number of Recipients and Average Payments, by Program and State," Table XIV, *Social Security Bulletin*, Vol. 28, December 1965, 46–47.

generous benefits than they had under medical vendor payments (Stevens and Stevens 2003). Although the majority of states established Kerr-Mills plans, the most active participation came from the handful of high-income states that had adopted the most substantial medical vendor payment programs prior to 1960. Indeed, by 1965, five such states – New York, California, Massachusetts, Minnesota, and Pennsylvania – were receiving nearly two-thirds of the Kerr-Mills funds (Stevens and Stevens 2003). A congressional report concluded that the program "has proved to be at best an ineffective and piecemeal approach" to the health problems of the poor elderly.[3] Mills argued that the program simply needed more time to take effect, but acknowledged that "as time develops" some "modifications" might be necessary (Zelizer 1998, 220).

Disappointment with Kerr-Mills contributed to the mounting clamor for Medicare. After President Kennedy's assassination and the subsequent Democratic landslide in the 1964 election, the proposal suddenly gained momentum. As Congress began to seriously consider Medicare legislation, the American Medical Association grew alarmed at the prospect of large-scale national government intrusion in health care markets. Hoping that a "stepped-up campaign to popularize the Kerr-Mills Act as a solution to the needs of the elderly would be enough to block Medicare in Congress" (Wehrwein 1964, 72), the organization drafted a plan for a program called Eldercare, which was essentially a "spruce-up" of Kerr-Mills (Large 1965). The AMA ran television and newspaper ads emphasizing the fact that, unlike Medicare, Eldercare would cover physician and surgical services, drugs, nursing home fees, diagnostic and laboratory fees, and other outpatient services. The proposal was widely unpopular on the left and right, however. Labor unions called it "Eldersnare" and accused the AMA of making empty promises since the proposal would make only cosmetic changes to the Kerr-Mills program (Kooijman 1999). Republican lawmakers distanced themselves from the proposal, largely out of concern that their partnership with the AMA in opposing Medicare had contributed to their party's losses in the 1964 election.

The proposal to "spruce up" Kerr-Mills was also unpopular with state leaders. During legislative hearings in 1964 and 1965, no governor or state legislator testified before Congress on behalf of liberalizing the program. In fact, a series of governors – primarily Democrats who supported the expansion of access to health insurance and had developed some of the most ambitious Kerr-Mills plans in the nation – bemoaned its shortcomings while endorsing the federal Medicare program as superior. Endicott Peabody (D-MA) observed that if Congress passed the Medicare legislation, his state would save over $10 million in Kerr-Mills spending, adding: "I do not need to emphasize the

[3] Subcommittee on Health of the Elderly, *Medical Assistance for the Aged: The Kerr-Mills Program, 1960–1963*, 88th Cong., 1st sess., 1963. A Report to the Special Committee on Aging, United States Senate.

importance of this relief" to his "hard-pressed" state.[4] John Reynolds (D-WI) argued that "the Kerr-Mills program cannot do the basic job of providing medical security, with dignity, to our older citizens" and that Medicare would "ease the financial impact of Kerr-Mills on our State budget."[5] Similarly, Karl Rolvaag (D-MN) testified that Medicare would be an improvement over the "degrading" system whereby an elderly person had to "surrender the rights to his worldly possessions in return for state assistance."[6] The leaders of several other states, including New Jersey, New York, Washington, and West Virginia, echoed this preference for Medicare over an expansion of Kerr-Mills.

Nonetheless, the Lyndon Johnson administration saw merit in the AMA's proposal, viewing it as a complement, not an alternative, to Medicare. As Johnson's Under Secretary of Health, Education, and Welfare (HEW), Wilbur Cohen, later explained, "At that time most people felt the Kerr-Mills was the substitute for Medicare. It was my position that you ought to have both of them."[7] Cohen worried that even if Medicare passed, there was still "the entire issue of what to do about people who were not covered by Medicare or, if they were covered by Medicare and their coverage was not sufficient to take care of everything."[8] Thus, the Johnson administration convinced Mills to attach a "major revision and liberalization" of the Kerr-Mills program to the Medicare legislation. The idea appealed to Mills as a "face-saving operation" because the eponymous program's failure to catch on had become a source of personal embarrassment.[9] Creating a small safety net for the poor also had the advantage, in Mills's eyes, of heading off subsequent pressure for costly expansions of Medicare (Marmor 1970). Strategically, the move also allowed Mills to "turn [the AMA's] propaganda against them and say that he was doing what they were asking."[10]

Thus, Title XIX: the Medical Assistance Program was added to the Medicare bill. It was modeled on the AMA's Eldercare proposal and soon renamed Medicaid. Congress passed the measure by a wide margin, reflecting the popularity of Medicare among the large Democratic majority. Since Medicaid

---

[4] House Committee on Ways and Means, *Medical Care for the Aged*, 88th Cong., 2nd sess., January 23, 1964, 1753.

[5] House Committee on Ways and Means, *Medical Care for the Aged*, 88th Cong., 2nd sess., January 22, 1964, 1587.

[6] House Committee on Ways and Means, *Medical Care for the Aged*, 88th Cong., 2nd sess., January 23, 1964, 1761.

[7] Transcript, Wilbur J. Cohen, December 8, 1968, Interview with David G. McComb, Tape #1, Oral History Collection, Lyndon Baines Johnson Library.

[8] Lewis E. Weeks, *Wilbur J. Cohen, In First Person: An Oral History*. Hospital Administration Oral History Collection, 1984, www.aha.org/research/rc/chhah/oral-histories.shtml.

[9] Memo, Lawrence F. O'Brien to the President, January 27, 1964, EX LE/IS1, Box 75, White House Central File, LBJ Library.

[10] Lewis E. Weeks, *Nelson H. Cruikshank, In First Person: An Oral History*, Hospital Administration Oral History Collection, 1984, www.aha.org/research/rc/chhah/oral-histories.shtml.

had been tacked on at the last minute, the provision largely flew under the radar. A legislative draftsman said that only half a day was devoted to consideration of its provisions (Smith and Moore 2008, 21), while the *New York Times* reported that there had been "little floor debate" on the program ("Medicare" 1966, 87). This inattention largely reflected the belief that Medicaid was not a new program at all, but rather a minor extension of the tiny Kerr-Mills program. Mills actively promoted this belief. Eager both to fix the program that bore his name and to brand the new legislation as his own, he repeatedly referred to Title XIX as a "continuation of the Kerr-Mills program" or "the revised Kerr-Mills program."[11] When President Johnson signed the Social Security Amendments of 1965, he spoke at great length about the historical significance of Medicare but did not mention Title XIX once in his remarks.[12]

Despite Medicaid's humble origins, by the program's first year observers were already predicting that "Medicaid would eventually be a far greater and more significant program than Medicare" (Jaffe 1966, 83). The initial estimates of Medicaid's cost proved to be "absurdly low" ("Medical Economics Revolution" 1970, 36). A federal study reported that within Medicaid's first three years the program was already contributing to "vast increases in government health expenditures" and "crippling inflation in medical costs" (Finch and Egeberg 1969). One White House official explained: "Our original estimate of the cost of the program was conservative because we really had no way of determining which states would adopt Title XIX or what programs they would develop" (Kotulak 1966, 12). State officials' surprisingly enthusiastic response was a product of the interaction between policy design and timing, as outlined in the next two sections.

POLICY DESIGN

Since Medicaid was billed as a "spruce up" of Kerr-Mills, it is not surprising that the two programs shared many design features in common. Like Kerr-Mills, Medicaid is financed with a generous (by historical standards), progressive, open-ended matching grant. Medicaid also carried over from Kerr-Mills two other critical provisions (Grogan and Patashnik 2003). First, both programs authorized states to set eligibility based on medical indigence; like Kerr-Mills, Medicaid let the states define "medically needy" however they liked, establishing no income ceiling. Second, both programs authorized the states to offer comprehensive coverage of a broad array of services. For these reasons,

---

[11] Memo, Theodore C. Sorenson to Wilbur Mills, June 14, 1966, Folder 580, Box 51, Series 10.3, Record Group 15, Nelson A. Rockefeller Papers, Gubernatorial, Rockefeller Family Archives, Rockefeller Archive Center, Sleepy Hollow, New York.

[12] President Lyndon B. Johnson, "Remarks With President Truman at the Signing in Independence of the Medicare Bill," July 30, 1965, www.lbjlib.utexas.edu/johnson/archives .hom/speeches.hom/650730.asp.

Kerr-Mills had substantial latent potential for expansion. "In theory the new program could have provided extensive services to a substantial proportion of the elderly population ... It could have thus met a considerable share of the needs of those who fell into the gap between adequate coverage of their medical bills through private health insurance schemes and those receiving cash payments under public assistance" (Stevens and Stevens 1970, 355).

Why, then, did Medicaid elicit an enthusiastic response among many state officials, whereas Kerr-Mills did not? Part of the answer is policy design. Despite their similarities, Medicaid was intentionally designed to stimulate greater state participation than Kerr-Mills. Wilbur Cohen later explained that he had been "acutely aware of the inadequacies of the State medical assistance plans in the 1960's" as he helped draft the legislation (Cohen 1983, 10). Based on the Kerr-Mills experience, Cohen knew that any federal-state health care program "would be operative only to the extent States undertake the financial responsibility to carry out the program."[13] Thus, he convinced Wilbur Mills that in order to correct the failures of the Kerr-Mills program – and to create an effective fence around Medicare – it would be necessary to incorporate a number of carrots and sticks to encourage greater state participation.

First, whereas Kerr-Mills had limited eligibility to the low-income elderly, Medicaid required participating states to cover all persons receiving public assistance. Coverage extended beyond the aged to the blind, people with disabilities, and families with dependent children – a particularly sympathetic and "deserving" group. It also gave states the option of covering medically needy persons in these same categories.

Second, Medicaid required participating states to provide all beneficiaries with five mandatory services: inpatient hospital care, outpatient hospital care, laboratory and X-ray tests, physician services, and nursing home services. Although many of these services had been authorized under Kerr-Mills, the only requirement under that program had been for the states to provide some institutional and some non-institutional care, and few states had chosen to adopt comprehensive coverage. Mandatory coverage of nursing home services was particularly consequential, especially since Medicare (and most private insurance) did not cover long-term care. Medicaid also allowed states to cover, and receive matching federal grants for, a long list of "optional" services including prescription drugs, dental care, eyeglasses, prosthetic devices, hearing aids, and physical therapy.

Third, the law included a "maintenance of effort" provision specifying that states must expand eligibility and the scope of covered services as a condition of receiving federal funding. Section 1903 of the statute stated that:

---

[13] Memo, Wilbur J. Cohen to the President, February 25, 1965, EX LE/IS1, Box 75, White House Central File, LBJ Library.

The Secretary shall not make payments under the preceding provisions of this section to a State unless the State makes a satisfactory showing that it is making efforts in the direction of broadening the scope of the care and services made available under the plan and in the direction of liberalizing the eligibility requirements for medical assistance, with a view toward furnishing by July 1, 1975, comprehensive care and services to substantially all individuals who meet the plan's eligibility standards with respect to income and resources, including services to enable such individuals to attain or retain independence or self care.

This provision was designed in part to prevent state officials from using federal dollars to supplant, rather than supplement, current state spending.

Finally, and most importantly, Medicaid offered the states stronger financial incentives to participate than had existed under Kerr-Mills. Title XIX increased the average state's matching rate by five percentage points relative to Kerr-Mills (Cohen and Ball 1965). States with national average income received a federal match of 55 percent instead of 50 percent, while those with the lowest incomes received 83 percent in contrast to 80 percent under Kerr-Mills. Moreover, the law permitted states that established Medicaid plans to apply this more liberal matching formula to AFDC and other cash assistance programs, which were still funded with capped matching grants at that time (Smith and Moore 2008). As an additional inducement, states that did not establish Medicaid programs by 1970 would lose their Kerr-Mills funding.

By providing unprecedentedly generous financial incentives and giving the states broad discretion over eligibility and benefits, Title XIX paid scant attention to cost containment. This might seem surprising in light of the fiscal conservatism of its sponsor, Wilbur Mills. However, as Moore and Smith (2005, 49) note:

The legislation seems to have been acceptable to those who worried about costs because it was based on a presumption – not unreasonable given the history of Kerr-Mills – that States would be slow and careful about taking up this option, would set eligibility standards and income and assets tests close to those for public assistance recipients, and would, therefore, limit both State and Federal financial outlays.

This assumption turned out to be incorrect, however, due in part to the unique timing of Medicaid's enactment.

TIMING

Medicaid's timing was conducive to self-reinforcing feedback for several reasons. First, the national economy was in the midst of a long expansionary period when the program was established in 1965. The resulting growth of state revenues increased the feasibility of adopting a Medicaid plan with generous eligibility and coverage provisions for states that were so inclined. By contrast, Kerr-Mills's self-reinforcing feedback potential had been limited by back-to-back recessions in 1957–1958 and 1960–1961.

Second, the public mood and political climate became increasingly receptive to government intervention and redistribution during the 1960s. After a period of relative conservatism during the 1950s and early 1960s, the mid to late 1960s were characterized by growing concern about poverty, inequality, and social justice (Stimson 1999). Following President Kennedy's assassination and the 1964 electoral landslide, Democrats controlled the presidency and enjoyed enormous margins in both chambers of Congress – although some, particularly southern Democrats like Wilbur Mills, were fiscally conservative and at times obstructionist. State capitals were also dominated by liberals; two-thirds of the nation's governors were Democrats throughout most of the 1960s. Even Republican leaders of the day, such as Governor Nelson Rockefeller of New York, were remarkably progressive by historical standards.

Third, Medicaid's arrival coincided with a dramatic transformation in the American governorship. Traditionally, governors had few formal powers, tiny staffs, and small budgets. Many served two-year terms, while others were limited to a single four-year term in office. Since the governorship offered few advantages, it tended to attract "good-time Charlies" who were primarily interested in the social and ceremonial aspects of office rather than substantive policy matters (Sabato 1983). However, following a flurry of new federal-state programs introduced under the banners of the Great Society and War on Poverty, state leaders in the 1960s suddenly encountered a rapidly expanding set of duties and resources. As state officials struggled to meet the new demands of office, they began to modernize state administrative structures. Pressure for change also came from the federal government, with an eye toward seeing its programs executed competently. Citizens, too, expected more of their state leaders, as postwar prosperity increased the demand for government services. These pressures unleashed a series of state reforms giving the governors additional administrative powers, expanding staffing, creating state budget offices, extending term lengths, and loosening term limits (Bowman and Kearney 1986). A growing number of states adopted income and sales taxes or raised existing tax rates, greatly increasing state resources, and many states switched from biennial to annual legislative sessions to allocate those resources more effectively. Together, these reforms attracted a "new breed" of politician to state capitals around the country. Almost overnight, the "political pipsqueaks" who had run state governments earlier in the century were replaced with state leaders who were "capable, creative, forward-looking, and experienced" and therefore willing and able to take full advantage of a complex new federal-state program like Medicaid (Sabato 1983, 1–2).

Finally, Medicaid's arrival also coincided with the establishment of the intergovernmental lobby in Washington. Prior to the 1960s, the governors had expressed little concern with what was going on in the nation's capital. When they did try to lobby federal lawmakers, they "scored few if any victories and nearly all defeats," were at most "mildly obstructive on federal-state matters," and "generally proved ineffectual as a national political interest group" (Haider 1974, 22). All that changed in the mid 1960s, when the national government began to intervene in state affairs to an unprecedented degree. Federal policy was suddenly high-stakes for the governors, and they became increasingly concerned about their lack of organization and influence in Washington. As one governor explained, "We simply weren't going anywhere under the then existing structure" (Haider 1974, 23). The governors' desire to organize themselves more effectively also reflected the increased competence and motivation of the new breed of governors entering office: "as the governors grew more capable and directed, this development was reflected in their organization" (Sabato 1983, 172). In 1967, the governors established a permanent office in Washington, DC. The pace of the governors' activities in the nation's capital subsequently accelerated. They began to regularly issue policy statements, informing national officials of their collective opinions on national policy matters, and testified with much greater frequency before Congress. In short, the 1960s saw the governors evolve from a disorganized group of "political homebodies with few responsibilities or interests beyond the boundaries of their home states" to "a tightly organized, hard-working group committed to a program of action" (Brooks 1961, vii, 6).

In summary, the expansionary features embedded in the Kerr-Mills Program and extended in Title XIX reflected the mistaken assumption that states would continue to lack the political commitment and fiscal and administrative capacity to adopt liberal Medicaid plans. But at the time of Medicaid's introduction, state leaders were suddenly exceptionally receptive to the new program's incentive structure.

NEW YORK UNLOCKS MEDICAID'S POTENTIAL

When federal Medicaid funding became available for the first time in January 1966, the large, liberal, high-income states that had developed relatively generous Kerr-Mills plans were first in line. Governor Nelson Rockefeller of New York took a particularly keen interest in the new program. "Indisputably liberal on one issue, health care," Rockefeller eagerly "seized upon the federal plan" to expand access to health insurance in his state (Persico 1982, 224). In early 1966, he announced his intention to implement a Medicaid plan so generous that 45 percent of the state's population, or eight million people, would be eligible for coverage. Title XIX allowed the states to define "medically needy" however they liked, and Rockefeller defined it as a family of four with an income of $6,000 or less, which was close to the median household income at that time. Several other large, high-income states such as California and Pennsylvania proposed standards around $4,000 for a family of four – lower than New York's but still well above the federal poverty level of $3,100.

The new program's financial incentives for state participation elicited a strong response in New York and elsewhere. Indeed, Rockefeller observed that his plan was designed to "enable New York State to receive the maximum federal aid under Title XIX."[14] The estimated federal cost of New York's program – $217 million – was more than Johnson administration estimates had initially suggested Medicaid would cost for all 50 states combined.[15] The scope of the New York program prompted Senator Jacob Javits (R-NY) to exclaim: "My God, Nelson, at the rate you're going, New York State will use up all the Medicaid money that Congress appropriated for the whole country" (Persico 1982, 224).

Medicaid's generous financial incentives also prompted swift legislative approval of Rockefeller's ambitious plan. The governor urged the State Assembly to vote quickly, noting that if New York enacted a plan before April 1, the federal government would provide retroactive aid for the first quarter of 1966.[16] By creating a sense of urgency over the potential loss of federal funds, Rockefeller was able to move the bill through the legislature after the briefest of hearings and with virtually no floor debate. The bill passed both chambers by wide margins: 64 to 1 in the Senate and 132 to 21 in the Assembly.[17] This "rush-hour lawmaking" happened so quickly that few legislators seemed to comprehend what they had voted for ("Rush-Hour Lawmaking" 1966, 23; Sibley 1966, 14).

Suddenly, the news media was full of stories about how New York had unlocked Medicaid's potential. The *Wall Street Journal* reported that New York had "turned a spotlight on Medicaid by showing just how generous a state can make its Title XIX programs" (Prial 1966, 1). The *New York Times* noted that "it was not until New York State established the plans for its program . . . that most persons realized Medicaid would eventually be a far greater and more significant program than Medicare" (Jaffe 1966, 83).

The political backlash from New York voters and interest groups was swift. Following the vote, lawmakers from conservative parts of the state returned home to face a "storm of protest" and "mass hysteria" over the alleged "socialization of medicine" (Edstrom 1966, A16; Reeves 1966, 1). One Republican legislator from Erie County who had voted for the bill subsequently led an unsuccessful campaign to repeal the entire act. In response to the mounting furor, the governor delivered a series of speeches and statewide television addresses to allay widespread "fear and misunderstanding" of the program (Sibley 1966, 14). The uproar suggests

---

[14] "Statement to the Legislature, March 9, 1966," Folder 577, Box 50, Series 10.3, Record Group 15, Nelson A. Rockefeller Papers, Gubernatorial, Rockefeller Family Archives, Rockefeller Archive Center, Sleepy Hollow, New York.

[15] House Committee on Ways and Means, *Social Security Amendments of 1965: Report of the Committee on Ways and Means on H.R. 6675*, 89th Cong., 1st sess., Report No. 213, 1965, 75.

[16] T. N. Hurd to Earl W. Brydges, Folder 585, Box 51, Series 10.3, Record Group 15, Nelson A. Rockefeller Papers, Gubernatorial, Rockefeller Family Archives, Rockefeller Archive Center, Sleepy Hollow, New York.

[17] *Journal of the Assembly of the State of New York* (1966, Vol. 2), 2883.

that Medicaid's explosive early growth can be traced to elite-level feedback rather than the program's popularity. That is, the governor developed an expansive Medicaid plan in response to the financial incentives and flexibility built into the new program – not because doing so was politically expedient.

The reaction of organized medicine was decidedly mixed. In keeping with the AMA's longstanding support of welfare medicine as an alternative to Medicare, the New York State Medical Society grudgingly endorsed Rockefeller's plan (Stevens and Stevens 1970). However, several of the society's upstate chapters "bitterly attacked it" (Sibley 1966, 14). And although the Association of New York State Physicians and Dentists had supported the federal Medicaid law, the organization sent a letter to dozens of members of key congressional committees calling New York's plan a "careless, almost wanton, distortion of the worthwhile purpose intended by Congress" and recommending that Congress establish stricter limits on eligibility.[18]

The uproar over Rockefeller's proposal extended to the nation's capital. When New York officials presented their plan in Washington, the House Ways and Means Committee and Senate Finance Committee summoned Wilbur Cohen to Capitol Hill and demanded to know how a state could do such a thing. The answer was simple: the law Congress had written encouraged states to adopt expansive plans, and unless Congress rewrote the law, the administration had no grounds for withholding approval (Miller 1966). Thus, only six months after Medicaid went into effect, congressional leaders hurriedly set out to rewrite the law so as to restrict the scope of New York's plan and prevent other states from following suit.

GOVERNORS FIGHT OFF FEDERAL RETRENCHMENT

Not surprisingly, Wilbur Mills – the bill's fiscally conservative sponsor – was among the first members of Congress to attempt to rewrite the Medicaid law. Realizing that he had miscalculated in creating Medicaid as a check on the growth of public health care spending, and embarrassed by media coverage of the "great goof" Congress had made in designing the law, Mills began to see the program as an "intolerable blot" on the Ways and Means Committee's proud record (Miller 1966, 18).

Chairman Mills led the Ways and Means Committee in considering several alternative approaches to curbing Medicaid spending in the summer of 1966. Recognizing that Medicaid's open-ended matching grants were enticing states to adopt generous plans, Mills first proposed to place a ceiling on federal Medicaid contributions to each state. One such formula would have limited

---

[18] Association of New York State Physicians and Dentists to Appropriations Committee members, July 21, 1966, Folder 580, Box 51, Series 10.3, Record Group 15, Nelson A. Rockefeller Papers, Gubernatorial, Rockefeller Family Archives, Rockefeller Archive Center, Sleepy Hollow, New York.

federal Medicaid spending to $12 per capita per year. This revision would have capped New York's annual allocation at its estimated first-year cost of $217 million, a major change since its allocation was expected to soar to $700 million within a few years under the original law. The committee also considered imposing tighter income limits on eligibility to prevent states from adopting expansive definitions of the medically needy. The proposed income standard for New York was rumored to be $4,150 for a family of four, which was considerably less than Governor Rockefeller's $6,000 limit (Stevens and Stevens 2003).

Mills's plan to obstruct New York's Medicaid plan was a potentially embarrassing development for Rockefeller, particularly as the governor campaigned for reelection and touted the program as one of his most important achievements. Thus, as Mills began to draft a Medicaid bill, Rockefeller called on Representative Eugene Keogh (D-NY), a senior member of Ways and Means, to block the bill from making it out of committee. Despite belonging to different political parties, Rockefeller and Keogh shared the desire to expand access to health care and to promote their state's financial interests. They therefore formed a "firm, if unaccustomed" alliance (Miller 1966, 18).

Like their chairman, most members of the Ways and Means Committee worried that Medicaid's unintended growth reflected poorly on their legislative craftsmanship and initially seemed predisposed to rewrite the law. However, when Keogh notified the representatives of California and Massachusetts, which also had ambitious Medicaid plans, of the committee's plans to curtail their states' funding, they joined him in warning the committee against any legislative changes. Suddenly, the committee's near-unanimous support for Medicaid reform disintegrated as members realized that there was no way to curb federal spending without squashing the plans of several powerful states. One committee member admitted, "We got cold feet." As another put it, "We're like the man who casually invited his country cousin to come have dinner someday and then has the guy arrive on his doorstep with his whole damn family. You'd like to slam the door in his face but how the hell can you do it?" After the proposal died in committee, media reports marveled that despite much "huffing and puffing," the powerful Ways and Means Committee was "helpless to prevent states from grabbing all the goodies in the surprise package" (Miller 1966, 18).

Mills was unwilling to concede defeat, however. Realizing that any large, visible cut in federal aid would spark resistance from powerful state leaders, he took a different approach. Instead of capping federal matching grants, he sought to clarify the definition of medically needy, specifying that the federal government would not provide any matching funds for able-bodied adults under 65 who were not on welfare. This measure was significantly less severe than the first, as it would have cost New York an estimated $50 million instead of $500 million in lost federal funding per year (Schanberg 1966, 25). Over

Keogh's protests, the Ways and Means Committee reported this relatively mild bill to the House floor in October 1966.

As the Senate began to consider parallel action, Rockefeller again lobbied the New York delegation to kill the measure. The governor convinced Javits, a member of the Senate Finance Committee, to demand that the committee delay consideration of the bill until Rockefeller had had a chance to testify. Javits's effort to stall the legislation came as a surprise, as the senator had irked Rockefeller only a few months earlier by speaking of the urgent need to set "reasonable limits" on federal Medicaid commitments (Tolchin 1966, 19). Some speculated that Javits's reversal was related to the fact that he had since become the governor's campaign manager (Miller 1966, 18). As a result of the delay, the Democratic leadership announced that no action would be taken on Medicaid until the following year. Many observers registered shock that legislative action that had seemed like a virtual certainty earlier in the year somehow failed to materialize (Robinson 1966, 1).

Determined to revise the Medicaid law, Mills resumed his efforts in 1967. As a growing number of states submitted ambitious Medicaid plans, pressure to rewrite the law mounted. In an effort to find a middle ground, the Johnson administration put forward a proposal of its own. Wilbur Cohen, eager to avoid imposing federal limits on the definition of medical indigence, proposed instead to tie the means-test level for Medicaid to the cash assistance standard in each state, thereby retaining state control over eligibility (Stevens and Stevens 2003). Under the administration's proposal, the national government would only help pay for Medicaid coverage for recipients with incomes under 150 percent of the state's standard to qualify for welfare payments. Mills drafted a bill that made this limit slightly more restrictive, calling for the standard to decline in stages from 150 percent in 1968 to 133 percent by 1970. This tightening of eligibility rules would affect 14 of the 35 states that had enacted Medicaid programs by this time.[19]

The compromise measure enjoyed widespread support in Congress. During Senate Finance Committee hearings, Senator Albert Gore, Sr. (D-TN) argued forcefully for limiting the definition of medically needy, questioning "the justice of taxing a person in Nebraska who has earnings of $4,000 a year to pay the medical expenses of a citizen in New York who earns $6,000 a year."[20] The Senate Finance Committee report on the bill noted that:

The tendency of some States to identify as eligible for medical assistance under title XIX large numbers of persons who could reasonably be expected to pay some, or all, of their

---

[19] Senate Committee on Finance, *Social Security Amendments of 1967: Part 1*, 90th Cong., 1st sess., August 22–24, 1967, 280. The states were California, Connecticut, Delaware, Illinois, Iowa, Kentucky, Maryland, Michigan, Nebraska, New York, Oklahoma, Pennsylvania, Rhode Island, and Wisconsin.

[20] Senate Committee on Finance, *Social Security Amendments of 1967: Part 3*, 90th Cong., 1st sess., September 20–22 and 26, 1967, 1551.

medical expenses has not only significantly increased the amount of Federal funds flowing into this program currently but has developed future cost projections of a level totally inconsistent with the expectations of the Congress when it enacted title XIX in 1965.[21]

Governor Rockefeller fought the measure both personally and through his state's congressional delegation. In congressional testimony, he protested that his Medicaid plan was merely an attempt to comply with Title XIX's "maintenance of effort" provision, which specified that states could only qualify for increased aid if they expanded eligibility, so as not to merely replace existing state funding with federal funding. "We already had high standards and we went higher in order to fulfill the intent of the Federal law as written by the Congress – then there was a tremendous reaction in the Congress ... This was not our fault. We complied with the law in order to get the maximum funds."[22] At Rockefeller's urging, Representative Jacob Gilbert (D-NY) told his colleagues that his and other states had acted in "good faith" in establishing Medicaid programs in accordance with federal law, that the program's rising costs were a sign of success rather than failure, and that his home state would suffer greatly if the law was amended.[23]

Nonetheless, in a rare defeat for Rockefeller, Congress passed the bill and President Johnson signed it into law as part of the Social Security Amendments of 1967. The prospect of diminished federal aid prompted New York lawmakers to reduce the income eligibility cap for a family of four from $6,000 to $5,000 by 1969, resulting in the elimination of one million individuals from the Medicaid rolls (Sparer 1996, 81). Still, New York's program and, to a lesser extent, those of several other states continued to be significantly more generous than Congress had intended. Although the Social Security Amendments of 1967 imposed limits on the concept of medical indigence, which was one of the "expansionary seeds embedded in Medicaid's beginnings," two other expansionary seeds – open-ended matching grants and comprehensive benefits – remained available (Grogan and Smith 2008, 228).

Thus, in 1968 fiscally conservative Senate Finance Committee Chairman Russell Long (D-LA) proposed to reduce matching rates from 50–83 percent to 25–69 percent for the medically needy. This amendment was directed at states such as New York, where, in Long's words, "middle-income people were being made eligible as medical indigents ... if the states want to be more liberal

---

[21] Senate Committee on Finance, *Social Security Amendments of 1967*, 90th Cong., 1st sess., 1967, Report No. 744, 176.

[22] Subcommittee on Intergovernmental Relations of the Senate Committee on Government Operations, *Creative Federalism*, 90th Cong., 1st sess., February 1, 1967, 549.

[23] Senate Committee on Finance, *Social Security Amendments of 1967*, 90th Cong., 1st sess., 1967, Report No. 744, 197–198.

than we intended to be, let them put up a higher percentage of money to be liberal with" (Madden 1968a, 41).[24]

Governor Rockefeller again urged New York's congressional delegation to block the bill, which he called "very disturbing" in a letter to Senators Javits and Robert F. Kennedy (D-NY) ("Assails Medicaid Cut" 1967, 23). A few days later, Javits carried Rockefeller's message to the Senate, arguing that it was "discriminatory to cut the federal share of costs of benefits for the medically indigent who were not eligible for or did not choose to accept public assistance" (Morris 1967, 35). Rockefeller also sent President Johnson a telegram, cosigned by New York City Mayor John Lindsay, imploring him "to do everything possible" to kill the measure, which he alleged would have a "serious impact on many destitute children, their families, and the medically needy of this state" ("Appeal on Medicaid" 1967, 39). The governor also testified before Congress, noting that "it is very difficult . . . to have Federal legislation passed and then have the legislation changed. The States must then backtrack and that is not easy."[25]

This time, Rockefeller's was not the only state leader's voice heard in Washington. He was joined by Massachusetts's Republican Governor, John Volpe, who sent a telegram to key members of Congress complaining that his state stood to lose $30 million per year if the measure passed. Volpe argued that cutting the federal matching rate would deal a "telling blow" to state finances, not only in his state but also around the country ("Volpe Protests" 1967, 48).

Despite the governors' efforts, the Senate Finance Committee passed the measure in September 1968, and its action sent "shock waves" throughout the Johnson administration and state capitals alike. Wilbur Cohen called the reduction "absolutely unrealistic," noting that many states would be forced to cut eligibility and services, and predicted that the governors would join him in "vigorously opposing" the amendment (Edstrom 1968, A2). Indeed, Rockefeller blasted national lawmakers for failing to honor their commitments to "the needy sick who cannot pay for the health care they require and to states who accepted, in good faith, Federal approval of their Medicaid programs." He denounced the bill, which would cost New York an estimated $130 million per year, as a "planned act of reneging" that would be even more damaging than the Social Security Amendments of 1967 (Illson 1968, 36).

Once again, Rockefeller's most potent weapon was his influence with his state's congressional delegation. In October 1968, Senators Javits and Charles Goodell (R-NY) used a filibuster to kill the measure, speaking at length against the Medicaid cutbacks and lining up other senators to speak and offer

---

[24] Long had introduced this measure before, as part of the Social Security Amendments of 1967, but it had been rejected in the House.

[25] Subcommittee on Executive Reorganization of the Senate Committee on Government Operations, *Health Care in America*, 90th Cong., 2nd sess., April 24, 1968, 411.

amendments. Long was forced to withdraw the provision, announcing: "I have been defeated by a successful filibuster" (Madden 1968b, 1). When Long vowed to resume his efforts to curtail federal Medicaid contributions the following year, Javits warned that he and Rockefeller would continue to work together to block the legislation.

Shortly thereafter, President Richard Nixon, having won the 1968 election on a campaign platform of reining in federal spending, put forward a new proposal to curb Medicaid's growth. Since a broad reduction in matching rates had proven politically difficult, and since institutional care was the largest and fastest-growing component of Medicaid spending, Nixon proposed to reduce federal matching funds for nursing homes and mental institutions. He defended his proposal on the grounds that the program's original purpose was to provide medical treatment rather than "custodial care" (Kilpatrick 1970, 22).

The president's proposal elicited strong objections from a chorus of governors. As the Senate Finance Committee began considering the measure, Nebraska's Republican Governor, Norbert Tiemann, wired committee member Carl Curtis (R-NE) to complain that the bill would cost their state nearly $3 million per year.[26] Governor William Cahill (R-NJ) submitted testimony that his state's losses would be nearly $17 million per year.[27] And Governor Marvin Mandel (D-MD) warned that cutting federal funding for nursing homes and other long-term care facilities would be "an act of bad faith by the federal government." Mandel argued that the states did not have the money to pay a larger share of health costs, and faulted the federal government for "grossly" underestimating the cost of Medicaid prior to enactment.[28] Under pressure from their states' leaders, congressional support dwindled and the measure died.

Tellingly, Rockefeller was no longer acting alone to protect the states' financial stake in Medicaid. The flurry of telegrams and testimony reflects the dramatic transformation of the governorship and its impact on both state and national politics. In 1962, the Pulitzer Prize–winning journalist James Reston had observed that "the governors of the states, taken as a whole, are a poor lot," singling out Nelson Rockefeller as a notable exception (Reston 1962). By the late 1960s, however, Rockefeller had been joined by a "new breed" of governor – ambitious, organized, and highly influential in the nation's capital.

Rockefeller's efforts were also supported by organized medicine, albeit tentatively and with misgivings, in a striking illustration of Medicaid's

---

[26] Senate Committee on Finance, *Social Security Amendments of 1970: Part 2*, 91st Cong., 2nd sess., September 21, 1970, 813.

[27] Senate Committee on Finance, *Social Security Amendments of 1970: Part 2*, 91st Cong., 2nd sess., September 16, 1970, 564.

[28] Senate Committee on Finance, *Social Security Amendments of 1970: Part 2*, 91st Cong., 2nd sess., September 17, 1970, 705.

coalition potential. Notwithstanding the AMA's initial concern about government intrusion in health care markets, providers soon realized that they had a financial stake in the new program because it reimbursed them for services previously rendered for free (or not at all). Indeed, "when physicians began to be paid for their services ... under title XIX in 1965, they received a sudden and significant increase in their incomes" (Stevens and Stevens 1970, 409). In some states, such as Virginia, the initial pressure to establish a Medicaid plan came from physicians; elsewhere, physicians lobbied vigorously for increases in provider reimbursement rates (Stevens and Stevens 1970). The AMA's leadership even fought federal eligibility cuts on occasion, when doing so served their purposes. For instance, in 1967 Dr. Milford O. Rouse, president of the AMA, testified before Congress that "any income limit placed on eligibility for title XIX benefits should not be so rigid as to exclude those who are clearly unable to pay for needed health care, especially those whose need is such that they are already receiving cash assistance."[29]

AFTERMATH

State leaders' efforts to preserve Medicaid's basic structure in the face of repeated federal attempts at retrenchment helped the program survive its vulnerable early period and establish a firm toehold in the American polity. It also established a persistent pattern that has played out repeatedly over the past five decades. Moreover, in seeking to secure additional federal Medicaid funds for their states, governors have caused Medicaid eligibility to expand over time. The rest of this chapter discusses state leaders' repeated rejection of proposals to convert Medicaid to a block grant and their efforts to expand eligibility.

Block Grants

Periodically throughout Medicaid's history, Republican leaders in Washington have proposed to convert the program's financing arrangement from open-ended matching grants to block grants. Such proposals were seriously considered in 1981, 1991, 1995, and 2003.[30] By offering the states additional flexibility over eligibility and benefit policies and delivery systems, they hope to entice state leaders into accepting a fixed amount of federal funding regardless of enrollment. And by breaking the link between state effort and federal funding – an inherent feature of open-ended matching grants – they hope to

---

[29] Senate Committee on Finance, *Social Security Amendments of 1967*, 90th Cong., 1st sess., August 28, 1967, 755.

[30] In 2017, Congress considered a per capita cap on federal Medicaid payments – similar to a block grant in many respects – as part of an effort to repeal and replace the Affordable Care Act, as discussed in chapter 8.

rein in the states' expansionary incentives and bring federal Medicaid outlays under control.

Despite the attractiveness of additional flexibility, concerns about the financial implications of a Medicaid block grant have typically led state leaders to vehemently reject such proposals. Perhaps most obviously, block grants are designed to cut federal spending and thus shift costs to the states. A block grant would also replace the federal entitlement – whereby individuals who meet eligibility criteria have a right to benefits specified under federal law – with an annual lump sum and thereby expose the states to increased economic risk as Medicaid costs spike during recessions and epidemics. Finally, removing the Medicaid entitlement would leave the program vulnerable to additional funding cuts in the future. According to NGA Executive Director Raymond Scheppach, "once they break the entitlement, there's nothing to preclude Congress from saying I'll give you $150 billion one year and $100 billion the next."[31]

The governors' resistance to block-granting Medicaid has been a critical obstacle because their buy-in is seen as essential in Washington. Without the endorsement of the state leaders who ultimately would have to implement the reforms, swing voters in Congress typically refuse to go along. Since governors are closer to the electorate than their counterparts on Capitol Hill, their support is seen as "hugely helpful" in communicating to the public that Medicaid reform is the right thing to do (Drew 1997, 84). Moreover, only a handful of members of Congress know much about Medicaid, making state leaders an indispensable source of expertise on the technical details of structuring a block grant due to their practical experience running the program.[32]

More often than not, state leaders' resistance has been bipartisan and virtually unanimous. When President Reagan floated the idea in 1981,[33] a spokesman for the NGA announced that an "overwhelming majority" of governors of both parties "violently opposed" the idea (Ayers 1981). Underscoring the governors' influence within Congress, one of Reagan's advisors warned the president: "If they are united in their opposition to the Administration's program when it is presented on the Hill, we will, in all probability, lose."[34] Reluctant to proceed without state leaders' support, the Reagan administration dropped the idea. When President George H. W. Bush floated a similar plan in 1991, the governors fervently shot it down and the administration "quickly abandoned that suggestion as politically unrealistic" (Olson 2010). The two abandoned

---

[31] Interview with Raymond Scheppach, July 14, 2011.

[32] David G. Smith and Judith D. Moore, "Interview with Alan Weil," CMS Oral History Project, 2003–2006, August 13, 2003, 774, www.cms.gov/History/Downloads/cmsoralhistory.pdf.

[33] Earlier that year, the White House proposed to permanently cap Medicaid matching grants, but state leaders successfully lobbied Congress to instead adopt a much smaller, temporary cut in federal matching rates (Rose 2013).

[34] Memo, Richard S. Williamson to Kenneth Cribb, October 23, 1981, Folder "Entitlements (2 of 3)," Box OA 5665, Richard Williamson Files, Ronald Reagan Library.

reform attempts illustrate the impact of self-reinforcing elite feedback effects, as strong gubernatorial opposition effectively prevented the serious consideration of an alternative that would have fundamentally altered Medicaid's trajectory.

In 2003, the George W. Bush administration proposed a block grant that was financially advantageous to the states in the short run. The proposal strategically traded short-term financial assistance for elimination of the federal government's open-ended financial commitment in the long term. The administration aggressively courted the governors' endorsement, seeing it as essential for passage. As one White House official noted: "It will be hard for Congress to pass any legislation unless it has strong bipartisan support from governors ... If they don't want to do it, it's not going to happen" (Pear 2003; Connolly 2003). However, governors of both parties – even the president's brother, Republican Governor Jeb Bush of Florida – flatly rebuffed the proposal. Although they wanted the temporary infusion of federal funds as well as the increased flexibility to cut state spending, they feared a block grant would not provide sufficient protection against economic downturns like the one they were recovering from at the time.

The closest the GOP has come to block-granting Medicaid was in the mid 1990s. An examination of this episode illustrates how, even when conditions are ripe for reform, state leaders have successfully preserved the status quo. In 1995, a highly visible and influential group of conservative governors embraced the idea of a Medicaid block grant for the first time. This shift can be traced to a unique set of political and economic conditions, including rising party polarization, a large number of Republican governors, and a strong national economy that increased openness to federal funding cuts among some state leaders. However, gubernatorial support was by no means universal or unqualified. Democratic governors uniformly resisted the idea, fearing that it would leave the states with insufficient resources to maintain their current eligibility and benefit policies. Many moderate Republicans privately expressed similar reservations; according to Scheppach, they were "weak-kneed" at the thought of losing billions of dollars in federal funds, and "although they might not say so publicly, it was clear most of them weren't going to push the proposal forward."[35]

Even the handful of conservative state leaders who wholeheartedly embraced the principle of a block grant found themselves engaged in a bitter formula fight over the distribution of funds. Replacing the open-ended federal commitment with a lump-sum payment designed to meet a federal deficit-reduction target created a zero-sum game that pitted the states against one another as they struggled over a fixed pot of money. According to Scheppach, moderate Republican governors grew increasingly "edgy" and "wishy-washy" about the reform as they started negotiating the details.[36]

---

[35] Interview with Raymond Scheppach, July 14, 2011.
[36] Interview with Raymond Scheppach, July 14, 2011.

Whereas disagreements over the general principle of a block grant were primarily partisan in nature, the formula fight largely broke down along geographical lines. The governors of northeastern and midwestern states, which tend to have generous Medicaid programs, wanted to base the block grant formula on a state's current level of spending. However, southern governors argued that block grants should not reward states that had been granting "excessive benefits," and northern governors replied that Congress should not privilege states that had been "miserly" and "unwilling to commit resources."[37] Since the poor elderly population and the number of people with disabilities in the "Sun Belt" were growing much more rapidly than in the northeast or midwest, southern governors hoped to base the formula on a state's demographic characteristics rather than current spending. As the negotiations dragged on, congressional leaders repeatedly urged the governors to overcome their differences and agree on a formula (Shillinger 1995). Senate Majority Leader Robert Dole (R-KS) told state leaders, "We can't do it without you ... if there's a big split with the Governors, it makes it more and more difficult."[38]

To help break the logjam, the National Governors Association created a task force of six governors – three Republicans and three Democrats – with the goal of developing a bipartisan proposal that would serve as a "middle ground" between the Republican-controlled Congress and the Democratic White House.[39] Eager for political cover, the Clinton administration urged the Democratic governors to "very publicly walk away" from the negotiating table.[40] The governors did so, and the task force fell apart. Without a bipartisan compromise among the governors, the Republican-controlled Congress passed its block grant bill and President Clinton vetoed it. A Clinton administration official explained: "There is no question that we would not have succeeded in the block grant fight in '96 if ... the Democratic governors hadn't stepped up."[41] Internal divisions among the governors had doomed the proposal's prospects in Washington. Once again, state leaders' efforts to protect their states' financial interests served to protect the program against retrenchment.

Eligibility Expansions

In addition to blocking federal retrenchment, the nation's governors have also sought expansionary changes to federal Medicaid policy on a number of

---

[37] David G. Smith and Judith D. Moore, "Interview with Sheila Burke," CMS Oral History Project, 2003–2006, June 20, 2003, 115, www.cms.gov/History/Downloads/cmsoralhistory.pdf.

[38] National Governors Association, "National Governors Association 87th Annual Meeting, Closing Plenary Session," August 1, 1995, 24.

[39] National Governors Association, "Transcript of Proceedings, National Governors Association Winter Meeting, Plenary Session and Executive Committee," February 4, 1996, 14.

[40] Democratic Governors Association conference call with Tom Daschle and Leon Panetta, May 1, 1996, Bruce Reed Files, Box 25, Folder "NGA [1]," William J. Clinton Presidential Library.

[41] David G. Smith and Judith D. Moore, "Interview with Jack Ebeler," CMS Oral History Project, 2003–2006, January 22, 2003, 142, www.cms.gov/History/Downloads/cmsoralhistory.pdf.

occasions. For instance, in the 1990s the governors of Oregon and Tennessee secured waivers from the Clinton administration, giving them the additional administrative flexibility needed to expand coverage to hundreds of thousands of low-income residents (Rose 2013). But perhaps the most striking example occurred in the 1980s, when state leaders lobbied Congress to loosen federal eligibility rules to allow them to enroll more pregnant women and infants in Medicaid.

In the mid 1980s, state leaders were struggling to cope with a confluence of economic, budgetary, and public health pressures. Following Reagan's 1981 budget cuts, the 1981–1982 recession, and the resulting state cuts to Medicaid, the share of the nation's poor covered by the program dropped from approximately two-thirds to half (Engel 2006, 184). The infant mortality rate rose precipitously, particularly in the south, with its large numbers of poor, uninsured single mothers and its traditionally limited Medicaid programs. As the ranks of the uninsured ballooned, uncompensated care costs more than doubled from $3.5 billion to almost $9 billion nationwide between 1980 and 1987, with public hospitals bearing most of the burden (Fraser 1991, 304). In many states, interest groups representing hospitals, nursing homes, physicians, and insurers lobbied lawmakers for help with these mounting problems and costs. Their lobbying underscored the tremendous coalition potential of a federal program that reimburses medical providers on behalf of groups that would otherwise be uninsured. As the economy began to improve in 1984, a number of state leaders were eager to expand Medicaid coverage, particularly for pregnant women and infants, and to shift the states' mounting health care costs to the national government.

Governors encountered two types of obstacles to Medicaid expansion, however. The first was the longstanding link between Medicaid eligibility and a state's standard for Aid to Families with Dependent Children (AFDC). Under federal law, Medicaid was only available to single mothers and their children who either qualified for AFDC or were "medically needy," with incomes under 133 percent of the state's AFDC standard. Due to budgetary stress and AFDC's unpopularity, many states had allowed their standards to be heavily eroded by inflation; by the early 1980s, two-thirds of poor women and children did not qualify for cash assistance (Omenn 1985). States that wanted to extend Medicaid eligibility further could not do so without also extending AFDC eligibility – something most state leaders could not or would not do. Moreover, women who were pregnant for the first time and therefore did not have the children necessary to qualify for AFDC as well as poor children in two-parent families were ineligible for Medicaid.

Governors encountered a second set of obstacles within their own states. Progressive southern Democrats faced "bruising, uphill battles" with conservative state lawmakers reluctant to appropriate funds for Medicaid expansion (Applebome 1989). State leaders also encountered collective action problems stemming from intergovernmental competition (Posner 1998). If one state voluntarily made its Medicaid program more generous than its neighbors', it risked scaring away businesses and wealthy taxpayers. Thus, some governors hoped that federal action to raise Medicaid standards across the board would provide "political cover" if state lawmakers objected or taxpayers threatened to "vote with their feet" (Conlan 1991, 57).

Thus, in 1984, the governors began to ask Congress for help. Democratic Governor Richard Riley of South Carolina created the Southern Regional Task Force on Infant Mortality with the goals of publicizing the infant mortality problem and compelling Congress to allocate more resources to address it. The task force was a joint undertaking of the Southern Governors Association (of which Riley was chairman) and the Southern Legislative Conference. The decision to focus on maternal and infant health was largely a response to rising infant mortality rates, but it was also a politically astute calculation. State leaders realized that a broad increase in eligibility would be a hard sell due to complicated racial politics and antiwelfare sentiments, so they decided to focus on a widely attractive and less divisive subset of the poor (Smith and Moore 2008). Moreover, they hoped it would appeal to fiscal conservatives, given the growing awareness that investing in preventive prenatal and neonatal care was cost-effective because it reduced the astronomical costs of neonatal intensive care as well as disability, mental retardation, and other health, learning, and behavioral problems later in life.[42]

Congress was receptive. Democrats had solidified their control of the House in 1982, and while the Senate remained in Republican hands, Reagan's declining popularity, the recession, and a growing sense of sympathy for the poor led many Republican senators to take a more moderate stance. One member of Congress, Representative Henry Waxman (D-CA), was particularly sympathetic. Waxman chaired the Commerce Committee's Subcommittee on Health and the Environment, which had jurisdiction over the Medicaid program. The entrepreneurial lawmaker soon figured out how to use a relatively new tool known as budget reconciliation to tuck Medicaid provisions into fast-tracked omnibus budget bills, thereby increasing the odds of passage relative to proposing a standalone measure (Howard 2007).

Southern Democratic governors, with Waxman's help, were the driving force behind a series of Medicaid eligibility expansions beginning in 1984. The Deficit Reduction Act of 1984 (DEFRA 1984) authorized nearly $300 million in new federal matching grants per year. It also required states to provide Medicaid coverage to several groups meeting AFDC income and resource requirements: first-time pregnant women; pregnant women in two-parent families with an unemployed parent; and children up to age five in

---

[42] See for example US Office of Technology Assessment, "The Implications of Cost Effectiveness: Analysis of Medical Technology: Background Paper 2: Case Studies of Medical Technologies: Case Study 10: The Costs and Effectiveness of Neonatal Intensive Care," August 1981.

two-parent families.[43] The Consolidated Omnibus Budget Reconciliation Act of 1985 (COBRA 1985) required states to cover all pregnant women meeting state AFDC income and resource standards, regardless of family structure or employment status. The Omnibus Reconciliation Act of 1986 (OBRA 1986) gave states the option of extending coverage to pregnant women and children up to age five in families below the federal poverty level, even if they did not qualify for AFDC. This decoupling of Medicaid eligibility from cash assistance was a major juncture in the program's history, reducing the stigma associated with Medicaid and setting it on a distinct political trajectory. The Omnibus Reconciliation Act of 1987 gave states the option to cover pregnant women and infants in families with incomes up to 185 percent of the poverty level. The legislation also extended coverage of children under DEFRA 1984 up to age eight. The Family Support Act of 1988 required states to extend a year of transitional Medicaid coverage to families leaving the AFDC rolls due to earnings from work, and to cover all two-parent families with incomes below the AFDC standard in which the primary earner was unemployed. All told, these laws extended coverage to over half a million pregnant women and more than 4 million children (Rosenbaum 1993).

In interviews and during congressional proceedings, numerous federal lawmakers gave southern governors credit for these expansions. During the congressional debate over OBRA 1986, Senator Lloyd Bentsen (D-TX) commended Governor Riley's Task Force for "developing a set of policy goals and for the educational campaign which they undertook in an effort to improve public understanding of the need for these changes."[44] When Senator Edward Kennedy (D-MA) introduced the legislation, he noted that "The Southern Governors Association has recommended the change in the law I am introducing today. The National Governors Association unanimously endorsed it. It is time for Congress to do its part."[45] In an interview, Henry Waxman recalled that:

The Southern governors were tremendously helpful in pushing for this. A big part of their economy in some of these states was health care under the Medicaid program. And this was a large amount of federal dollars that they could use to cover people ... Southern governors were coming to us and urging that we start mandating some of these Medicaid proposals so that they could ... get their states to go along with drawing down the federal dollars.[46]

---

[43] "Deficit Reduction Act of 1984: Provisions Related to the Medicare and Medicaid Programs," *Social Security Bulletin*, November 1984 (Vol. 47, No. 11).

[44] *Medicaid Maternal and Infant Amendments of 1986*, S. 2333, 99th Cong., 2nd sess., *Congressional Record* 132 (April 17, 1986): S7991.

[45] Senate Committee on Labor and Human Resources, *Barriers to Health Care/Children's Health*, 99th Cong., 2nd sess., July 16, 1986, 7.

[46] David G. Smith and Judith D. Moore, "Interview with Henry Waxman," CMS Oral History Project, 2003–2006, January 25, 2005, 752, 745, www.cms.gov/History/Downloads/cmsoral-history.pdf. However, after Congress shifted its focus from pregnant women and children to the

As Waxman observed, Medicaid's policy design, and particularly its generous open-ended matching grants, had created powerful incentives for state leaders to advocate for the program's expansion.

In addition to the governors, organized medicine also advocated for Medicaid's expansion during the 1980s. Lobbying by the medical profession was a crucial factor in several states' decisions to expand Medicaid during this period (Nathan, Doolittle, and Associates 1987). Indeed, during the political tug-of-war over scarce state resources in the Reagan era, the "well-organized and politically strong" associations representing medical providers gave Medicaid a major advantage over other welfare programs (Nathan, Doolittle, and Associates 1983, 201).

Several empirical studies have corroborated this linkage, finding a positive association between the strength of a state's health care interest groups and the generosity of its Medicaid eligibility, covered services, and/or provider reimbursement policies (Barrilleaux and Miller 1988; Grogan 1994; Camobreco 1996; Kousser 2002; Pracht and Moore 2003; Lukens 2014). Michael Sparer (1996, 66) observes that state variation in Medicaid spending per beneficiary can partly be explained by the amount of pressure exerted by interest groups. In low-spending states, officials are "relatively insulated from interest-group politics" whereas high-spending states tend to have "powerful interest groups" including "institutional medical providers ... most of whom have an interest in generous spending."

CONCLUSION

Medicaid emerged in 1965 as a last-minute, largely overlooked addition to the Medicare bill. State leaders had not lobbied for it, most members of Congress who voted for it knew little about it, and the president did not even mention it at the signing ceremony. Despite its modest origins, however, the program quickly expanded beyond anyone's wildest expectations and grew to become the nation's largest health insurance program in terms of enrollment. Medicaid's policy design (open-ended matching grants, loose eligibility standards, comprehensive benefits, permanent authorization, and strong coalition potential) and timing (during a period of economic prosperity, liberal state leadership, and mobilization of the intergovernmental lobby) contributed to a dynamic of self-reinforcing feedback whereby state leaders adopted much more generous plans than Congress had anticipated and successfully fought federal efforts to cut the program's funding.

Medicaid established such a secure toehold that in 2010 it became a prominent feature of the Patient Protection and Affordable Care Act (ACA), the most sweeping health care legislation since 1965 (and the subject of Chapter 8). This

elderly and people with disabilities in 1988, the governors became increasingly vocal in opposing Medicaid expansion mandates.

surprising development underscores the power of self-reinforcing policy feedback. When Medicaid and Medicare were created in 1965, progressives saw the universal Medicare program as a potential stepping stone to national health insurance. Meanwhile, the programs' fiscally conservative architect, Wilbur Mills, hoped that Medicaid – designed as a safety net for only the poorest, most vulnerable Americans – would serve as a firewall around Medicare to prevent such an eventuality. Yet, as Chapter 8 discusses in greater detail, ultimately it was Medicaid, and not Medicare, which became the springboard for health care reform.

5

The Rise and Demise of General Revenue Sharing

In 1972, President Richard Nixon signed into law the State and Local Fiscal Assistance Act, creating a program of general revenue sharing with state and local governments. At the signing ceremony, Nixon proclaimed that the new program would "give these hard-pressed governments the dollars they need so badly" and "the freedom they need to use those dollars as effectively as possible."[1] With virtually no strings attached, general revenue sharing offered state and local governments unprecedented spending discretion. And at the time of passage, its $30 billion price tag over the first five years made it the largest federal grant-in-aid ever enacted (Stephens and Wikstrom 2007, 39). Not surprisingly, state and local officials had lobbied vigorously for its passage; indeed, Nixon observed that its enactment would have been impossible without their support. Puzzlingly, however, state leaders hardly resisted when Congress discontinued the state portion of general revenue sharing eight years later.[2]

This chapter examines the rise and surprising demise of general revenue sharing. It argues that the program failed to generate self-reinforcing feedback among state government elites as a result of both specific features of its design and the particular timing of its enactment. Although the program's size and flexibility were conducive to feedback effects, its diffuse benefits – and the resulting absence of pressure from state-level special interest groups – along with its temporary authorization contributed to the program's downfall. Moreover, the timing of its enactment also helps explain state leaders' failure to mobilize to protect the program. General revenue sharing was established just before a period of party turnover, federal deficits, state surpluses, intergovernmental tension over budget policy, and the emergence of a fiscal regime of austerity.

[1] Richard Nixon, "Statement About the General Revenue Sharing Bill," Philadelphia, PA, October 20, 1972, The American Presidency Project, www.presidency.ucsb.edu/ws/?pid=3636.
[2] The local portion ended in 1986, as discussed later in the chapter.

ORIGINS AND ENACTMENT

General revenue sharing first appeared on the national agenda in 1964, when a special task force appointed by President Lyndon Johnson and headed by economist Joseph Pechman proposed the idea. The task force's proposal drew on the ideas of Walter Heller, Chairman of the Council of Economic Advisors, and thus became known as the Heller-Pechman Report. Advocates of the proposal saw general revenue sharing as a solution to two related budgetary problems. The first was "fiscal drag," as an overflowing Treasury combined with high national unemployment threatened to depress aggregate demand. The second was "fiscal mismatch," as state and local governments' revenues lagged behind rapidly mounting service demands. Many localities had bumped up against strict limits on municipal taxes and borrowing. Although states faced fewer institutional barriers to raising revenue, many faced stiff voter opposition to tax increases. State officials feared taxpayer flight, particularly at a time when the national government was lowering taxes. In sum, "Where the high-priority public service needs were, the money was lacking; and where the money was ample, the high-priority needs were lacking" (Break 1980, 144).

President Johnson ultimately rejected the proposal, however. In part, this was due to competing priorities, including the Vietnam War, as well as opposition from a federal bureaucracy eager to retain control of domestic programs (Thompson 1973, 57). General revenue sharing was also apparently a victim of a strange twist of fate. As Walter Heller sat in the White House lobby for several hours, waiting to brief the president on his proposal, Johnson was managing a breaking sex scandal involving his top aide, Walter Jenkins. Before Heller had an opportunity to brief the president, the proposal was leaked to the media, provoking outrage from the AFL-CIO and other groups that both distrusted state legislatures and feared that revenue sharing might reduce support for other federal grant programs. The timing of the leak, right before the 1964 election, was awkward for the White House. In an effort at damage control, Johnson ordered all copies of the Heller-Pechman Report burned, and the subject was reportedly off limits for the remainder of his term (Wallin 1998, 35). Instead, Johnson focused on the creation of categorical grant programs – in areas such as health care, education, and transportation – to address the problems of fiscal drag and fiscal mismatch while also achieving his administration's policy goals under the banners of the Great Society and War on Poverty.

Nixon's First Proposal (1969–1970)

General revenue sharing got a second look when Richard Nixon took office in 1969. Nixon believed that the complex maze of categorical grant programs, which dated back to the early twentieth century and had proliferated under Johnson, had created a bloated federal bureaucracy and cumbersome red tape that hampered the autonomy and efficiency of subnational governments. In his August 1969 national address on domestic programs, the new president bemoaned the "trend toward ever more centralization of government in Washington, DC" and unveiled his vision of a "New Federalism" in which "power, funds, and responsibility will flow from Washington to the States and to the people." General revenue sharing was to be the centerpiece of the New Federalism, as Nixon vowed to send state and local governments "a share of Federal revenues ... with a minimum of Federal restrictions on how those dollars are to be used."[3]

By this time, the nation's fiscal outlook had changed considerably since Pechman and Heller had first proposed revenue sharing. Fiscal drag was no longer an issue. Government spending had risen sharply due to the Great Society, War on Poverty, and Vietnam War, wiping out the federal surplus. Fiscal mismatch remained, however, and the financial challenges faced by states and localities were only compounded by rising inflation and the 1969–1970 recession. As state and local debt mounted, many officials were forced to cut basic services, raise taxes, or both. Against this backdrop, the primary objective of revenue sharing had shifted: "No longer was the program intended to distribute surplus revenues, but instead, provide assistance to floundering states and localities, while avoiding the problems which had come to plague the growing array of categorical programs" (Thompson 1973, viii).

State leaders, eager for an infusion of federal grant money with no strings attached, enthusiastically supported the plan. Indeed, the National Governors Association (then known as the National Governors' Conference, or NGC) had supported general revenue sharing since the idea had first appeared on the national agenda several years earlier. An NGC committee had called for a new study of the Heller-Pechman plan in 1965, and in 1966 the governors had voted overwhelmingly in favor of a program of general revenue sharing (Thompson 1973, 57). Interest groups representing local government officials, such as the US Conference of Mayors (USCM) and National Association of County Officials (NACO) followed suit with similar resolutions.

Revenue sharing was particularly appealing to Republican leaders, who tended to place a premium on increased flexibility to spend federal funds in accordance with local preferences. As Figure 1 illustrates, gubernatorial support for the proposal was especially strong in 1969–1970 because a majority of governors were Republicans. Democrats traditionally had been more supportive of categorical programs that targeted the poor and other vulnerable groups, but they were enticed by the prospect of additional federal funds and joined their Republican counterparts in supporting the proposal.

At the forefront of the state and local push for general revenue sharing throughout the late 1960s and early 1970s was Republican Governor Nelson

---

[3] Richard Nixon, "Address to the Nation on Domestic Programs," Washington, DC, August 8, 1969, The American Presidency Project, www.presidency.ucsb.edu/ws/?pid=2191.

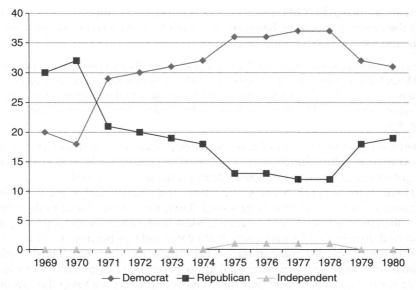

FIGURE 1 Governors' Party Affiliations, 1969–1980
Source: National Governors Association, "Governors' Party Affiliations, 1900–2017"
(https://classic.nga.org/files/live/sites/NGA/files/pdf/directories/PartyAffiliation.pdf).

Rockefeller of New York. The unofficial "senior statesman for the governors," Rockefeller wielded considerable power in Washington due to his famous name, connections, and political acumen (Haider 1974, 229). For Rockefeller, the appeal of revenue sharing was as much practical as philosophical; the governor faced an enormous budget deficit and feared that raising the state's income tax – already among the highest in the nation – to meet growing demand for public services would drive more high-income residents to relocate to Connecticut and New Jersey (Thompson 1973, 102). In a series of speeches in the winter of 1969, Rockefeller explained the state's fiscal problems and presented revenue sharing as the solution, imploring: "We don't need Band-Aids on the problems, with little bitty Federal help. We need a blood transfusion" (Clarity 1969, 1). The governor made the case before President Nixon and his Urban Affairs Council in February 1969, urging him to place the proposal at the center of his domestic agenda (Haider 1974, 230).

The Congress, under Democratic control, did not enact Nixon's proposal, however. The idea of revenue sharing was popular, with 71 percent of Americans in favor (ACIR 1970). Yet this broad public support was not deep because revenue sharing "was not an issue that could sell itself ... it was, in fact, an issue without emotional appeal or deeply held conviction as far as the mass of the public was concerned" (Dommel 1974, 121–122). Meanwhile, several powerful organizations mobilized against the proposal, including the aforementioned AFL-CIO and the US Chamber of Commerce, which feared that the program would be financed with a tax hike. As a result, the position of state and local officials would be critical:

The real constituency for revenue sharing was the nation's governors, state legislators, and local leaders. Therefore, if Congress was to be pressured into action, it would not be by any national Presidential appeals on television or popular barnstorming, but by selling the idea to the key state and local leaders and to their lobbying organizations. (Dommel 1974, 122)

Despite supporting the idea of revenue sharing, state and local leaders failed to throw their weight behind Nixon's proposal, however. Without pressure from the governors and mayors, revenue sharing was dead on arrival.

There were several reasons for state and (particularly) local leaders' lukewarm reaction to Nixon's proposal. First, the modest $500 million first-year allocation left them cold. Second, local leaders felt shortchanged by the proposed distribution formula, which allocated only 27 percent of the funds to localities, with the rest going to states (Thompson 1973, 61–62). Third, leaders of small cities and towns were miffed at the proposal to target monies to large urban areas, and thus to distribute funds only to localities with populations over 50,000. Finally, the resistance of local officials also had a partisan tinge to it. In 1969–1970, most big city mayors were Democrats while two-thirds of the nation's governors were Republicans. Some mayors thus saw revenue sharing as a proposal by a Republican president to provide direct aid to Republican governors, shortchanging the cities and their Democratic leaders (Haider 1974, 66–67).

Only a handful of state and local officials testified before Congress on revenue sharing at the time. Although Republican Governor Daniel Evans of Washington and Democratic Governor Kenneth Curtis of Maine offered mild statements of support, local leaders expressed reservations. Democratic Mayor Alfonso Cervantes of St. Louis, Missouri, complained that his city would receive only $750,000 in the program's first year, which he called "utterly inadequate to cope with the urban crisis. In order to avoid bankruptcy, St. Louis needs $10 million more revenue by May 1, 1970, and it has no feasible way to raise such revenue."[4] Edward Henry, the Democratic mayor of St. Cloud, Minnesota, complained that the typical city was "considerably under 50,000 in size" and would therefore be excluded from the program.[5] The mayors had strong allies in the Democratically controlled Congress, and their concerns fell on sympathetic ears. Eventually it became clear that Congress would not pass

---

[4] Senate Subcommittee on Intergovernmental Relations of the Committee on Government Operations, *Intergovernmental Revenue Act of 1969 and Related Legislation: Hearing on S. 2483 and S. 2048*, 91st Cong., 1st sess., October 7, 1969, 220.

[5] Senate Subcommittee on Intergovernmental Relations of the Committee on Government Operations, *Intergovernmental Revenue Act of 1969 and Related Legislation: Hearing on S. 2483 and S. 2048*, 91st Cong., 1st sess., October 7, 1969, 226.

revenue sharing legislation, and supporters' attention turned to putting together a new proposal to send to Congress in 1971.

Nixon's Second Proposal (1971–1972)

The failure of Nixon's first revenue sharing proposal demonstrated the need for a forceful lobbying campaign by a united coalition of state and local leaders. To this end, Rockefeller set out to convince Nixon to greatly expand the program's size. First, he convinced all 32 Republican governors to endorse a resolution calling for a $10 billion initial allocation, and he personally delivered the resolution to Nixon in January 1971. Rockefeller argued that an expanded revenue sharing plan, supported by the governors and mayors and opposed by the Democratic Congress, could help Nixon win the 1972 election (Haider 1974, 68). Although Nixon initially balked at the cost, Vice President Spiro Agnew – a former governor and county executive – later convinced the president to accept a compromise of $5 billion. To make sure the president lived up to this promise, Rockefeller told the administration that without revenue sharing, Nixon could not count on New York's 41 electoral votes in 1972 (Cannon 1986).

In addition, Rockefeller convinced the administration and his fellow governors that a substantial share of the monies should go to local governments. At a summit of the Advisory Commission on Intergovernmental Relations, Governor Rockefeller acknowledged: "If we're going to get [revenue sharing], we need a large slice to flow directly to local governments ... We [governors] can stop anything in the Senate, but the mayors can stop anything in the House." Rockefeller proposed the 1/3 state, 2/3 local split of funds that was ultimately included in the law, "apparently with no basis other than a desire to gain and motivate local support" (Wallin 1998, 37). Under the revised proposal, every city, town, and county would be eligible to receive funding, regardless of population size. Funds would be allocated to 38,000 jurisdictions according to a formula based on population, tax effort, and personal income. A significant side effect of these political maneuvers to secure passage was that the program's benefits were becoming increasingly diffuse.

A final sticking point was the fear among some state and local officials, particularly Democrats, that revenue sharing was a Trojan horse of sorts, designed to replace existing categorical grant programs instead of injecting new funds into state and local coffers. Democratic Mayor John Lindsay of New York City warned, "That would be one of the greatest shell games in history if they do that." The mayors collectively released a statement cautioning, "We will seek assurances that all monies appropriated for this fiscal year will be released for use this year and existing program levels will at the very least be maintained" (Herbers 1971, 1). The Nixon administration repeatedly reassured state and local officials that revenue sharing represented new money and would not substitute for the full funding of existing programs.

Thus, "a durable alliance was consummated between the White House and the government interest groups over revenue sharing which, in spite of obvious partisan tensions and periodic cleavages within and between the groups, persisted through revenue sharing's passage in late 1972" (Haider 1974, 67). The lure of $5 billion in the first year was "an impetus to cooperation" because it was "sizeable enough to diffuse prolonged disputes" and smooth over the "traditionally rancorous relations of state, county and city officials" (Thompson 1973, 122). The national recession intensified, and the worsening financial condition of state and local governments served to strengthen their determination and cohesion as advocates. As Congress considered revenue sharing legislation anew in 1971, Agnew told the administration's new allies that success on Capitol Hill would require a "unified massive effort" (Chapman 1971, A2).

In one of the most coordinated lobbying efforts ever undertaken by states and localities, "delegations of mayors, governors, and county officials swarmed over Capitol Hill demanding congressional passage of this program throughout the spring and summer of 1971" (Haider 1974, 252). Marvin Mandel, Chairman of the NGC, told Congress that the program was the governors' highest priority:

I want to state bluntly and without reservation that for the states there is no more vital and critical issue before the Congress than the promise of fiscal relief. I would even go so far as to say that in many cases it's a matter of life and death ... Congress has not only a financial obligation, but also a moral responsibility to provide fiscal relief to the people it is elected to serve.[6]

Rockefeller spoke in urgent terms of the fiscal crisis faced by state and local governments, with expenditures growing three to four times as fast as revenues from existing sources. He warned that without revenue sharing "this country is going to experience a domino wave of bankruptcies spreading from cities to states all over the nation during the next 5 years."[7] Lindsay, struggling to manage New York City's "tightest budget since the depression," told the Ways and Means Committee: "We seek assistance based on desperate need, proven effort, and demonstrated ability to manage our own affairs."[8]

Winning congressional approval was not an easy task, however, as many lawmakers were reluctant to hand over federal monies with virtually no federal oversight over their use. Some were concerned about retaining their ability to

---

[6] Senate Subcommittee on Intergovernmental Relations of the Committee on Government Operations, *Intergovernmental Revenue Act of 1971 and Related Legislation: Hearing on S. 1770 and S. 241*, 92nd Cong., 1st sess., June 8, 1971, 171.

[7] House Committee on Ways and Means, *General Revenue Sharing: Part 5*, 92nd Cong., 1st sess., June 15, 1971, 797. Rockefeller appeared as part of a panel of six governors.

[8] House Committee on Ways and Means, *General Revenue Sharing: Part 4*, 92nd Cong., 1st sess., June 11, 1971, 641. Lindsay chaired the Legislative Action Committee of the US Conference of Mayors at the time.

claim credit for public projects; others believed that from an accountability standpoint, revenue should be raised by the level of government that spends it (Conlan 1998, 65). Committee leaders saw revenue sharing as a threat to their authority and prerogatives. Conservatives were opposed to spending additional federal monies. Liberals worried about the implications of no-strings federal grants for the protection of civil rights and fair labor practices; they were also concerned that revenue sharing might ultimately replace categorical grants targeted to vulnerable populations. Partisans within the Democratic majority did not wish to hand Nixon a policy victory as the election approached.

Powerful House Ways and Means Chairman Wilbur Mills (D-AR) was a particularly vocal critic of revenue sharing and its circumvention of the regular appropriations process. When it was first introduced in 1969, Mills refused to even hold hearings on the measure. However, Mills suddenly did an about-face in late 1971, when he announced that revenue sharing would be his top priority in the coming legislative session. Mills explained, "Nelson talked me into it. Nelson and a few Democratic mayors" (Cannon 1986). His change of heart reportedly reflected his aspirations for the 1972 presidential nomination and his need to build support among state and local leaders (Thompson 1973). It also reflected growing support for revenue sharing among his committee's members, as they came under intense pressure from local officials in their jurisdictions. However, Mills only agreed to authorize the program for five years, not wanting to commit the national government to a permanent outlay without periodic review.

Both chambers of Congress passed the measure with bipartisan support and by wide margins. The final votes were 274–122 in the House and 64–20 in the Senate. A majority of Republicans and rank-and-file Democrats voted in favor, while committee and subcommittee chairs opposed it almost two to one (Beer 1976, 178). The nearly unanimous support of the New York delegation was particularly noteworthy: "In this one must see the influence of two leaders of the intergovernmental lobby. Rockefeller, who had long favored revenue sharing, was the most active among the governors, whereas from the other party, Lindsay had taken the lead among the mayors" (Beer 1976, 178). When asked why so many lawmakers voted for the bill, House Majority Whip Tip O'Neill (D-MA) replied, "Well, I guess we just gave in to all that pressure from the mayors and the governors" (Beer 1976, 190). Another member explained, "Although I was not a proponent of it and didn't like the idea very much, my governor, my mayor, and other state officials leaned very heavily on me. They thought it was a great panacea to all of their problems. I reluctantly voted aye for it."[9] Waning party discipline had created a power vacuum into which the intergovernmental lobby eagerly stepped. Members of the House were

[9] House Committee on Government Operations, *State and Local Fiscal Assistance Act (General Revenue Sharing, Part 2): Hearing on H.R. 6558 and Related Bills,* 94th Cong., 1st sess., November 5, 1975, 1118. This comment was made by Representative Parren Mitchell (D-MD).

especially vulnerable to pressure from state leaders at the time because reapportionment was under consideration in many state capitals (Thompson 1973).

REAUTHORIZATION AND RETRENCHMENT

Revenue sharing came up for reauthorization after five years, providing an opportunity to examine whether policy feedback occurred. Did state and local leaders mobilize to preserve the program? Did the creation of revenue sharing reshape their incentives, perceptions, and resources in ways that helped perpetuate the program? At first, it seems the answer was yes, as governors, mayors, and other state and local officials mobilized and narrowly succeeded in getting the program reauthorized in 1976 despite much congressional resistance. However, the story was quite different when it came up for reauthorization again in 1980. The second time around, state leaders largely stood on the sidelines with apparent indifference as Congress removed the states from the program.

What accounts for state leaders' activism in 1976 and demobilization in 1980? The rest of this chapter argues that two central features of the program interacted with key elements of its environment in ways that were not conducive to self-reinforcing feedback. In terms of policy design, the temporary authorization of general revenue sharing made it vulnerable to changes in the economic and political environment. Moreover, the program offered nontargeted benefits that reduced its coalition potential and resulted in a striking lack of state-level interest group support. In terms of timing, three developments during the 1970s reduced the feedback potential of the program. First, the budgetary environment was characterized by a rising national deficit and emergent state surpluses; these trends were nascent during the first reauthorization debate but dominant during the second. Second, the political environment was characterized by dramatic partisan turnover, largely as a result of the 1974 Watergate scandal, with Democrats gaining ground in state capitals and on Capitol Hill alike, particularly after 1977. Third, the late 1970s were characterized by the deterioration of intergovernmental relations due to a dispute between national lawmakers and state leaders over federal budget policy. These three inhospitable aspects of the program's timing interacted with its temporary authorization and nontargeted benefits to prevent strong, lasting feedback effects from occurring.

1976: Reauthorization

When Congress began to consider the future of revenue sharing in 1974 and 1975, the intergovernmental lobby – termed "the old general-revenue sharing steamroller" by one congressional aide – pushed hard for reauthorization (Wallin 1998, 102). The NGA, National Conference of State Legislatures

(NCSL), and several groups representing local leaders passed "strongly worded resolutions urging the Congress to take early and favorable action."[10] Numerous state and local officials submitted congressional testimony. Governor Patrick Lucey (D-WI) testified that "states and their local governments have their share of differences [but] are of one mind when it comes to revenue sharing." He urged lawmakers to "reenact promptly what we believe to be the single most useful and successful of all the federal grant programs."[11]

By this time the program had grown increasingly unpopular in Congress, however. The concerns many members had expressed during the debate over enactment had, in the program's first few years, been realized; not surprisingly, national lawmakers found they did not like handing over large sums of money to state and local governments with little oversight and few opportunities for credit-claiming. One member complained of state and local officials who financed projects with revenue-sharing funds: "They don't even ask us to the ribbon-cutting ceremonies" (Beer 1976, 185). The mounting federal deficit, illustrated in Figure 2, contributed to many members' disdain for the costly program. And in the wake of Nixon's scandal and resignation, power had shifted from the White House to Congress, emboldening lawmakers in their quest to dismantle Nixon's pet program.

Moreover, national lawmakers were beginning to feel that the states no longer needed the money. As the national economy recovered from the 1969–1970 recession, the financial condition of most states improved dramatically. Indeed, as Figure 3 displays, in fiscal years 1973 and 1974 the states ran a sizeable aggregate surplus. One representative called it "patently ridiculous for the Federal Government, which is expected to roll up a $70 billion deficit this year, to be handing out money carte blanche to state governments, most of which are operating with a surplus."[12] Moreover, half the states reported that, since the program's inception, they had been able to use revenue sharing funds to reduce their taxes. A senator lamented: "That means that we get the job of being the tax collectors and they are the heroes in handing out money ... I can see a lot of people getting reelected on that kind of spiel, particularly state governors."[13]

---

[10] Senate Subcommittee on Revenue Sharing of the Committee on Finance, *General Revenue Sharing*, 94th Cong., 1st sess., April 16, 1975, 13.

[11] Senate Committee on Finance, *General Revenue Sharing: Hearing on H.R. 13367*, 94th Cong., 2nd sess., August 25, 1976, 87. At the time, Lucey chaired the Committee on Executive Management and Fiscal Affairs of the National Governors' Conference.

[12] House Committee on Government Operations, *State and Local Fiscal Assistance Act (General Revenue Sharing, Part 1): Hearing on H.R. 6558 and Related Bills*, 94th Cong., 1st sess., September 30, 1975, 79.

[13] Senate Subcommittee on Revenue Sharing of the Committee on Finance, *General Revenue Sharing*, 94th Cong., 1st sess., April 16, 1975, 19.

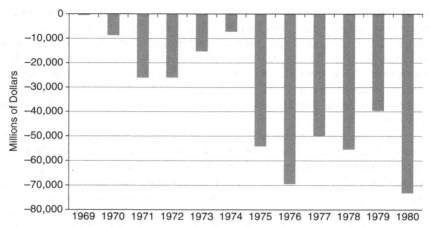

FIGURE 2 Federal On-Budget Deficit, 1969–1980
Source: US Office of Management and Budget, "Budget of the United States: Historical
Tables" (www.whitehouse.gov/omb/historical-tables/).

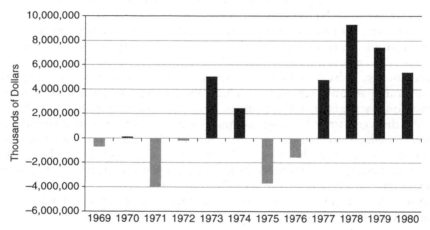

FIGURE 3 Aggregate State Surplus or Deficit, Fiscal Years 1969–1980
Source: US Census Bureau, "Annual Survey of State and Local Government
Finances: Historical Data" (www.census.gov/programs-surveys/gov-finances/data/
historical-data.html).

Although state finances were sound in 1973–1974, the plight of the cities
remained dire. Newspaper headlines screamed about the urban crisis, and
stories told of garbage piling up on streets and dangerous police force layoffs.
In a particularly high-profile case, New York City ran out of money to pay its
operating expenses and nearly went bankrupt. Numerous mayors and other

local officials testified before Congress in graphic detail about their cities' hardships. Keenly aware of the problems that continued to plague cities, congressional leaders remained committed to continuing revenue sharing for local governments, at least for the time being.

Given the states' improved financial condition and the cities' ongoing woes, some national lawmakers favored eliminating the states from the program and redirecting their funds to cities. Wilbur Mills first introduced such a bill in the summer of 1974. From a policy standpoint, it made sense to target funds to the cities, where the need was greater. From a political standpoint, however, removing the states would not be easy. "How much support do you think we will get for dropping the states?" asked Representative Barbara Jordan (D-TX) during congressional hearings. Answered Representative Jim Oberstar (D-MN): "Probably not very much; the governors collectively have a strong lobby, and a rather large, active organization here in Washington."[14]

Indeed, state leaders pushed hard to remain in the program, with governors and members engaging in heated exchanges during congressional hearings. When a member asked him pointedly: "Governor Lucey, your state had a surplus of $174 million at the end of 1973. Do you think that poses a problem for me and others in Congress when we give out revenue sharing?" Lucey retorted that, unlike the federal government, "We don't have the luxury of deficit spending. We have to have a balanced budget and we have to increase taxes if need be." Other state leaders, when confronted with evidence that the states no longer needed revenue sharing, protested that although the states had done well in 1973 and 1974, 1975 was "disastrous for state budgets" due to the 1974–1975 national economic recession.[15] Indeed, as shown in Figure 3, states were back in the red by fiscal year 1975. States won the day and remained in the program, at least temporarily.

Another point of contention was whether the program should be renewed annually, reauthorized for several years, or made permanent. During congressional hearings, one state and local leader after another asked Congress to give the program a permanent authorization to facilitate long-range budgeting and planning. However, one Democratic representative observed that there was "great opposition in the Congress ... to a permanent program" and a desire to keep a "flexible position, particularly in view of the deficit we have ... so that if at some time in the future the Congress decided it didn't want to continue the program in some form, there would be no damage to

---

[14] House Committee on Government Operations, *State and Local Fiscal Assistance Act (General Revenue Sharing, Part 2): Hearing on H.R. 6558 and Related Bills,* 94th Cong., 1st sess., November 5, 1975, 1132.

[15] House Committee on Government Operations, *State and Local Fiscal Assistance Act (General Revenue Sharing, Part 1): Hearing on H.R. 6558 and Related Bills,* 94th Cong., 1st sess., October 7, 1975, 346.

our state and local governments."[16] Nixon's successor and fellow supporter of revenue sharing, Republican Gerald Ford, proposed renewing the program for another five years, but this too proved unacceptable to the Democratic Congress. Ultimately, lawmakers reached a compromise, reauthorizing the program for three and three-quarter years, until September 30, 1980 (Wallin 1998, 102). This clearly fell short of the permanent authorization state and local leaders had wanted, reflecting a lack of long-term support for the program among national lawmakers. Congress also cracked down on the use of funds, adding provisions requiring periodic audits of state and local expenditures as well as nondiscrimination and citizen participation requirements.

Thus, while revenue sharing survived in 1976, the writing was on the wall: the Democratic Congress did not look favorably on the program – particularly the state portion. Absent a dramatic change in economic and political conditions, revenue sharing was on shaky political ground.

1980: Retrenchment

When revenue sharing came up for reauthorization again in 1980, the state leaders' reaction was quite different. Puzzlingly, as an increasingly critical Congress contemplated discontinuing the program, the governors hardly put up a fight. One observer marveled at "the meekness with which the nation's governors have taken the news," labeling the official state response "almost inaudible" (Peirce 1980, F5). Indeed, some Democratic governors expressed acquiescence bordering on support for the elimination of revenue sharing. Speaking on behalf of the Democratic governors in the spring of 1980, Governor Bill Clinton of Arkansas testified, "Our position is that if it's gone, it's gone" ("Fund Sharing Cutoff" 1980).

The governors' submission paved the way for Congress to eliminate revenue sharing for state governments, starting in fiscal year 1981. The legislation specified that the states could be included again in fiscal years 1982 and 1983, subject to future congressional approval, but with the proviso that for each revenue sharing dollar a state received, it would have to give up a dollar in categorical aid so as to achieve budget neutrality. When the time came, however, Congress did not approve the return of revenue sharing for state governments, and the program was gone for good.

What explains this surprising turn of events? Why did state leaders, who had worked so hard to get revenue sharing enacted in 1972 and reauthorized in 1976, stand by idly as Congress dismantled the program in 1980? The demise of revenue sharing can be traced to the interactive effects of the timing of its adoption – on the cusp of rising federal budget deficits, emergent state budget

---

[16] House Committee on Government Operations, *State and Local Fiscal Assistance Act (General Revenue Sharing, Part 2): Hearing on H.R. 6558 and Related Bills*, 94th Cong., 1st sess., November 5, 1975, 1148.

surpluses, partisan turnover, and souring intergovernmental relations – and policy design – both the program's temporary authorization and the noncategorical nature of the grants and the resulting absence of strong state-level interest-group pressure to retain the program.

TIMING

Revenue sharing was, in many respects, a victim of the shifting budgetary climate of the 1970s. It had been conceived in an environment of federal budget surpluses and fiscal drag, which had provided a rationale for its creation. By the time it was enacted years later, however, the surpluses had been replaced with large and growing deficits. Increased federal spending during the 1970s also contributed to rapidly rising prices; by 1980, the inflation rate was approaching 14 percent. These developments put pressure on national lawmakers to cut spending on programs like revenue sharing. Throughout the 1970s, "the choir of deficit-reduction hawks was growing," and by the end of the decade Washington was gripped by "near-hysteria over the deficit" (Wallin 1998, 112).

As the national budget situation deteriorated, state leaders' perceptions of the program began to shift. "What had been looked on in 1964 as an additional infusion of federal aid, and with good reason, suddenly began to appear more and more as a substitute for existing aid funds" (Break 1980, 146). The presumption that the program would inject new federal money had been essential to state and local leaders' support. As then-Governor Jimmy Carter (D-GA) observed:

Although the concept of revenue sharing was very good, I had great concern that there was no additional revenue to share. Despite the fact that the President ... assured the Congress and the public that existing funds would not be used to finance revenue sharing, I was fearful that this would be the case. (ACIR 1974, 47)

State leaders' fears were confirmed in 1973–1974, when the newly reelected president turned his attention to expenditure control and began to use his impoundment powers to slash categorical grant funding. Their worst suspicions were borne out when the White House repeatedly suggested that states and localities could use their new revenue sharing funds to make up for federal cuts in antipoverty and social service programs (Haider 1974, 272). Irked by the president's "bad faith," state and local leaders withdrew their support from his New Federalism agenda, marking "an abrupt turnabout in the relations between the Nixon administration and the government interest groups" (Haider 1974, 275–276).

Democratic governors were particularly dismayed by the Nixon administration's reversal, and, unlike the program's early years, by this time there was a sizeable majority of Democratic governors. When faced with a choice between revenue sharing and categorical grant programs – which were largely targeted to vulnerable populations – liberal leaders tended to prefer the latter. As Carter explained: "When these funds are taken away from the poor and put into general revenue sharing ... even the most enlightened legislature is not going to take these funds and put them back exclusively into programs that benefit the poor" (ACIR 1974, 47). Indeed, a 1974 analysis by the US Government Accountability Office (GAO) suggested that a negligible share of the funds distributed in the program's first year were used for social services for children, the elderly, or the handicapped (GAO 1974). Instead many state and local lawmakers reportedly used the grants to finance infrastructure improvements and general government operations, contributing to the program's declining popularity among the nation's overwhelmingly Democratic governors (Peirce 1980).

The 1970s also witnessed a dramatic transformation in the budget condition of the states, further contributing to the demise of revenue sharing. The program had been conceived in part to address the problem of "fiscal mismatch" – service demands outpacing revenues at the state and local level – but soon after it was enacted, this problem began to dissipate through a combination of tax reforms and economic recovery following the 1969–1970 recession. Many state governments responded to rising demand for services by increasing their income and sales taxes during the 1970s, resulting in stronger, more responsive tax systems and, in many cases, budget surpluses. During the 1976 reauthorization debate, these surpluses had disappeared temporarily due to the 1974–1975 recession. As Figure 3 shows, however, by the time of the 1980 reauthorization debate they had returned in full force.

The states' improved budget condition changed perceptions of revenue sharing among both federal and state leaders. First, it contributed to growing disdain for the program in Congress, particularly as lawmakers struggled to rein in the federal deficit. Senator Jim Sasser (D-TN) noted:

The idea of revenue sharing was born in the late 1960s when many lawmakers realized that state and local governments did not have the fiscal ability to meet their mounting service needs. Between 1967 and 1972, for example, state and local governments ran a combined operating deficit ... of $22 billion ... [But] times have changed for the states. In 1978 and 1979, for example, state governments ran surpluses totaling $14 billion ... We should not have a governmental system where one government raises taxes and runs monumental deficits while the other spends and runs budgetary surpluses.[17]

There was a growing perception in Congress that not only could the federal budget no longer support revenue sharing, but the states no longer needed it. A 1980 GAO study affirmed that although the loss of revenue sharing funds

---

[17] Senate Subcommittee on Intergovernmental Relations of the Committee on Governmental Affairs, *General Revenue Sharing – The Issues before Us*, 96th Cong., 1st sess., September 20, 1979, 58–59.

would create difficulties for the states, it would not cause them severe hardship (GAO 1980). In sum, "By being fiscally responsible, states had ironically put themselves in the position of losing support from a federal government that was becoming increasingly fiscally irresponsible" (Wallin 1998, 104).

The improvement in states' finances also changed state officials' perceptions of revenue sharing and weakened their incentives to protect the program against retrenchment. By the late 1970s most states were in excellent fiscal condition, and their prosperity "may have taken some of the fight out of them" (Wallin 1998, 110). State leaders also grew weary of the uncertainty around the program, as national lawmakers repeatedly threatened to eliminate or cut it. One state official explained, "Frankly, we've been whipsawed around this thing so much – one week we had it, the next week we didn't – after a while we realized we could do quite well without it" (Herbers 1980).

Moreover, increases in state and local taxes during the 1970s contributed to a surge of antitax sentiment among the electorate in the late 1970s, which in turn fanned the flames of congressional opposition. In a number of states, voters passed ballot measures like California's Proposition 13, barring further tax increases. As the public mood became more fiscally conservative, national lawmakers sensed the shift and adjusted accordingly. They began to take on more fiscally conservative positions and to call for the elimination of programs like revenue sharing (Swartz and Peck 1990, 10).

Despite this general ideological shift, revenue sharing remained fairly popular with not only state and local officials but also the public. Throughout the 1970s, when asked whether they favored or opposed general revenue sharing with state and local governments, a majority of Americans said they favored the program. As Figure 4 indicates, despite a slight downtick in favorability throughout the decade, the share who opposed the program never

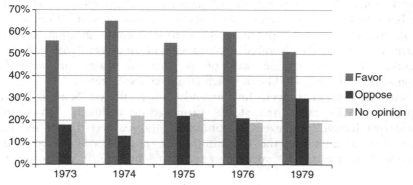

FIGURE 4 Public Attitudes toward Revenue Sharing
Source: The Roper Center for Public Opinion Research, "Changing Public Attitudes on Government and Taxes," various years.

exceeded 30 percent. Thus, it is important to note that the demobilization of state officials during the reauthorization debate of 1980 was not a response to the changing views of their constituents. It was instead a reflection of the shifting economic and political environment and how those shifts interacted with key features of the existing policy. Just as public opinion cannot account for the enactment of general revenue sharing, it does not explain the program's failure to generate self-reinforcing policy feedback or its ultimate demise.

In addition to these changes in the budgetary climate, the 1970s were also characterized by political changes that proved inhospitable to revenue sharing. Nixon's Watergate scandal and resignation reduced the political efficacy of virtually all of the Republican president's policy initiatives, and revenue sharing was no exception (Swartz and Peck 1990, 7). The balance of budgetary power shifted from the White House to the Democratic Congress, which had never looked favorably on the program. Following the scandal, the Democratic Party increased its margins in both the House and the Senate as well as in state capitals; Figure 1 indicates that roughly two-thirds of governors were Democrats in the late 1970s. While Nixon's Republican successor, Gerald Ford, supported revenue sharing, the program lost presidential support once Democrat Jimmy Carter – who had been skeptical of the program even as a governor – took office in 1977.

Against this backdrop of federal deficits, state surpluses, and an increasingly hostile political climate, a dramatic intergovernmental confrontation led to a souring of federal-state relations and sealed the program's fate. In the late 1970s, a growing number of states began to call on national lawmakers to rein in the federal deficit. By 1979, 28 state legislatures had passed measures calling for a constitutional amendment mandating a balanced federal budget.[18] Many governors vocally supported the proposal and spoke critically of Congress in so doing. In a televised speech, Democrat Jerry Brown of California argued that "the nation, no less than the individual states, must eventually balance its books" and called on lawmakers to "manifest a self-discipline ... so that we can begin to work for the future, not just consume the present" (Skelton 1979, A10). At the National Governors Association's winter meeting, Governor Pierre du Pont (R-DE) lectured a congressional attendee: "Don't make the mistake of thwarting the will of the several states or we'll have a constitutional crisis, the like of which we haven't seen before."[19]

National lawmakers were furious and soon retaliated. Senator Edmund Muskie (D-ME) called the states' proposed amendment "unworkable, counterproductive, and even irresponsible"; he warned that if the states succeeded in amending the Constitution to require a balanced budget, Congress's first target for spending cuts would be federal aid to the states

---

[18] The number eventually rose to 31.

[19] Transcript of Proceedings, National Governors Association 1979 Winter Meeting: Open Plenary Session, Washington, DC, February 25, 1979, 91.

(Ayres 1979, A17). Seizing on the amendment effort as an opportunity to dismantle a program they had never been fond of, national lawmakers zeroed in on revenue sharing in particular. Senator Lloyd Bentsen (D-TX) introduced legislation in February to eliminate the states' share of revenue sharing when the program came up for renewal in 1980. During congressional hearings, one member after another lambasted state leaders for their hypocrisy. Senator Sasser said pointedly: "we have been asked by state legislatures all across the nation ... to balance the budget ... No program, not even revenue sharing, is sacrosanct and can be immune to the national call for austerity."[20]

State leaders, realizing their tactical error, expressed remorse and began to backpedal. During a congressional hearing on revenue sharing, NGA chairman Lamar Alexander (R-TN) lamented the "stick it to the states syndrome that exists among some Members of Congress" but admitted that "perhaps the Governors and the State legislatures brought a lot of that on themselves. There may have been a little excessive chest-beating."[21] But efforts to smooth over the rift were futile; the damage to intergovernmental relations had been done, and the prospects for reauthorization of revenue sharing were bleak.

POLICY DESIGN

Thus, shortly after revenue sharing's inception, a series of inhospitable events, both budgetary and political, reduced the potential for self-reinforcing policy feedback. These dynamics did not singlehandedly sink the program, however. Rather, it was the interaction of the program's timing with two key features of its design. First, the program's temporary authorization made it vulnerable to retrenchment, giving an increasingly hostile and powerful Congress an easy opportunity to vote it down. Second, the non-targeted nature of the benefits ultimately led state leaders to abandon revenue sharing. As Congress began to press state leaders to choose between revenue sharing and categorical grants, the former's lack of state-level interest group support became a major liability.

In a last-ditch, half-hearted effort to save revenue sharing in the spring of 1979, Alexander urged Congress not to single out revenue sharing for disproportionate cuts. He clarified the states' evolving position, noting that "we are willing to accept cuts" but "we believe, as governors, that the state and local revenue-sharing funds help better than any other programs."[22]

[20] Senate Subcommittee on Intergovernmental Relations of the Committee on Governmental Affairs, *General Revenue Sharing – The Issues before Us*, 96th Cong., 1st sess., September 20, 1979, 58.

[21] House Subcommittee of the Committee on Government Operations, *Intergovernmental Fiscal Assistance Amendments of 1979 and Termination of General Revenue Sharing to State Governments: Hearing on H.R. 3198 and H.R. 2698*, 96th Cong., 1st sess., June 28, 1979, 126.

[22] House Subcommittee of the Committee on Government Operations, *Intergovernmental Fiscal Assistance Amendments of 1979 and Termination of General Revenue Sharing to State*

National lawmakers called the states' bluff, however, repeatedly demanding to know which grant programs to cut, if not revenue sharing. Bentsen recounted:

I said "Gentlemen, name me one of those categorical grants that you want cut. Which ones?" For two hours I asked them that, and at the end of two hours, [they] had not named one – not one categorical grant that they thought that the Federal Government ought to cut.[23]

If state leaders had not already come to view revenue sharing and categorical grant programs as substitutes, by this time the trade-off was crystal clear. Governor Lee Dreyfus (R-WI) lamented to his colleagues during an NGA meeting in the winter of 1980:

We have got to be prepared, at least those of us who have been arguing for a balanced federal budget, knowing what we don't want cut in the federal revenue sharing, to indicate where it is going to be cut in categorical aid. And if you aren't prepared for that, your Congressional Delegation is going to hit you back with it.[24]

Changes in the economic environment, including heightened intergovernmental conflict over the national budget and the sudden emergence of a fiscal regime of austerity (Pierson 2001), placed general revenue sharing in an increasingly vulnerable political position.

When state leaders, who had initially perceived revenue sharing as an infusion of new funds, came to perceive it as a substitute for existing categorical funds, they were unprepared to shield the program from retrenchment. Since categorical aid is visibly targeted to specific individuals or groups, threats of cuts tend to elicit strong political backlash among the state-level interest groups that benefit from such programs (Wallin 1998, 111). Indeed, the strong coalition potential of unemployment insurance and Medicaid enabled state leaders to work in concert with employer groups and the health care industry to preserve those programs. By contrast, revenue sharing funds simply went into the recipient government's general fund, meaning that alliances with other stakeholders did not materialize. As noted earlier, many state and local governments reportedly used the funds to finance general government operations and infrastructure improvements – expenditure items with fewer well-identified interest groups than, say, categorical grants targeted at transportation or health care.

Governments: Hearing on H.R. 3198 and H.R. 2698, 96th Cong., 1st sess., June 28, 1979, 125–127.

[23] Senate Subcommittee on Intergovernmental Relations of the Committee on Governmental Affairs, *General Revenue Sharing – The Issues before Us*, 96th Cong., 1st sess., September 20, 1979, 51.

[24] Transcript of Proceedings, National Governors Association 1980 Winter Meeting: Open Plenary Session, Washington, DC, February 25, 1980, 19–20.

Moreover, the fungibility of revenue sharing funds with other revenue sources made it difficult to discern exactly how they were used and to whose benefit. As the GAO reported to Congress in 1975:

A state government can use the funds for any purpose ... This creates a situation where funds are easily displaced or substituted ... Thus, there are a variety of fiscal consequences which can result from the application of revenue sharing funds which are not necessarily reflected by the designated uses of the funds. The funds might actually permit a recipient government to do such things as ... increase its spending levels in programs other than those in which revenue sharing funds were designated for use. (GAO 1975, 3)

For example, a state's accounting records might report that revenue sharing funds were used to pay the salaries of construction workers, but the net effect of this designation was that the state was able to use its own funds, which otherwise would have been used to pay those salaries, for another purpose such as acquisition of construction equipment. As a result, even the GAO had "difficulties in isolating what is actually being accomplished with revenue sharing" (GAO 1975, 7). This lack of transparency meant that few state-level interest groups perceived the program as beneficial to their narrowly defined interests.

Members of Congress surely understood that, for these reasons, state leaders would not put specific categorical grant programs on the chopping block to save revenue sharing. As one Democratic senator observed: "special interest groups ... promote those categorical grant programs. We haven't found many people at the state level that have said 'cut this one' or 'we can stand a little cut in this one,' because no one wants to stand up and have those special interest groups center in."[25] In contrast, the benefits of general revenue sharing were too diffuse to elicit protests from specialized interests when the program came under fire. State leaders may have preferred revenue sharing to the relatively circumscribed categorical grant programs from a policy standpoint, but from a political standpoint, protecting categorical grants – even at the expense of revenue sharing – proved expedient.

The states were not alone in this regard. Categorical grant programs also enjoyed the support of the congressional committees and subcommittees that oversaw them, and the federal bureaucrats who administered them, filling out the classic iron triangle (Wallin 1998, 124). During a meeting of the National Governors Association, Governor James Thompson (R-IL) questioned why the administration and Congress were singling out revenue sharing for cuts when categorical grant spending was growing five times faster: "If nothing else, these numbers say that 300 committees and subcommittees of the Congress find it hard to say no to the 492 special interests that their grant programs have

---

[25] Senate Subcommittee on Intergovernmental Relations of the Committee on Governmental Affairs, *General Revenue Sharing – The Issues before Us*, 96th Cong., 1st sess., September 20, 1979, 74. This observation was made by Lawton Chiles (D-FL).

created."[26] By contrast, revenue sharing lacked a similarly broad base of support. As Dreyfus explained, "Congress will cut where it gets the least screaming, and there are only 50 voices – the state governors – interested in preserving general revenue sharing" (Wallin 1998, 108). Once the governors stopped screaming, revenue sharing had no one left to protect it.

After hobbling along for a few years, the local portion of revenue sharing met its demise in 1985, as Congress voted to discontinue the program altogether when it was set to expire the following year. As with the state portion, the local portion was dismantled amidst a large and rapidly growing federal deficit and marked improvements in the financial condition of the recipient governments. President Ronald Reagan's stated rationale for signing the legislation reflected these developments: "How can we afford revenue sharing when we have no revenues to share? How can the Federal Government justify, strapped as it is with a deficit, borrowing money to be spent by . . . local governments, some of which are running surpluses?"[27] The local portion of revenue sharing – like the state portion before it – was eliminated because its diffuse benefits, combined with its temporary authorization, made it an easy target in an environment of scarce resources and deficit reduction (Wallin 1998, 120).

CONCLUSION

In summary, revenue sharing was a victim of both the timing of its enactment and a design that did not lend itself to self-reinforcing policy feedback despite its financial generosity and unprecedented level of state administrative discretion. The program's non-targeted benefits meant that it had weak state-level special interest group support. Whereas state leaders joined with business groups to fight the (perceived) federalization of the UI program and enjoyed the support of key constituencies such as hospitals and nursing homes in their efforts to preserve and expand Medicaid, governors found themselves with few powerful allies as general revenue sharing came under repeated congressional attacks. Together with its temporary authorization, its weak coalition potential made the program vulnerable to inhospitable changes in the political and budgetary climate during the 1970s. Party turnover at both the national and state levels and major short- and long-term economic shifts meant that general revenue sharing came up for renewal in an environment that differed greatly from the one in which it had been developed.

In this case, the interaction of policy design and timing facilitated one of the most surprising developments in the history of American intergovernmental

[26] Transcript of Proceedings, National Governors Association 1979 Winter Meeting: Open Plenary Session, Washington, DC, February 25, 1979, 20.

[27] Ronald Reagan, "Remarks at the Annual Legislative Conference of the National Association of Counties," Washington, DC, March 4, 1985, Ronald Reagan Presidential Library, www .reaganlibrary.archives.gov/archives/speeches/1985/30485c.htm.

relations. Less than a decade after the creation of general revenue sharing, state leaders quietly watched Congress dismantle a program they had once overwhelmingly supported, and whose enactment they had once identified as their single highest national policy priority. In the words of Bruce Wallin (1998, 120), "There are few programs of the magnitude of general revenue sharing of which it can be said that it was remarkable that it was enacted at all and remarkable that it was ended. But such is the unique history of the federal revenue sharing."

6

How Superfund Sowed the Seeds of Its Own Instability

Signed into law during a lame-duck session of the 96th Congress, the Comprehensive Environmental Response, Compensation, and Liability Act (CERCLA) established a tax on the chemical and petroleum industries that was dedicated to a trust fund for cleaning up abandoned or uncontrolled hazardous waste sites. Known colloquially as Superfund, CERCLA received strong bipartisan support in the Senate and in the House, partly due to a series of high-profile incidents at places like Love Canal in New York and Valley of the Drums in Kentucky.[1] Since its adoption in 1980, however, Superfund has been the subject of considerable controversy, so much so that its dedicated taxes have lapsed twice and its operations came to a "virtual standstill for more than a year" (Patashnik 2000, 162). In addition to being politically unstable, Superfund has been characterized as ineffective, with one observer describing it as "notorious for fostering too much litigation and too little actual cleanup" (Babich 1995, 1520). Others have portrayed the hazardous waste cleanup program as "an implementation nightmare" and a "Superfailure" (Mazmanian and Morell 1992, 18).

This chapter examines the developmental trajectory of Superfund, emphasizing the critical role of intergovernmental relations. The program has been described as an example of "contentious federalism" (Bowman 1985, 135) that "created what was often an explicitly antagonistic pattern of intergovernmental relations" (Hula 2001, 182). In other words, it generated mostly self-undermining policy feedback among state government elites. Operating through professional associations like the National Governors Association (NGA), the National Association of Attorneys General (NAAG), and the Association of State and Territorial Solid Waste Management Officials

---

[1] The Senate endorsed the final version of CERCLA in a 78–9 vote; the vote in the House was 274–94.

(ASTSWMO), state leaders lobbied for fundamental changes to Superfund. Their efforts to increase the generosity of the program and eliminate the financial incentives that put the states at odds with the national government have been mildly successful. Moreover, in legislative and judicial settings they pressed repeatedly, and often successfully, for greater state administrative control and for the elimination of provisions that seemed to preempt existing state policies. Ironically, certain features of Superfund helped state governments build the administrative capacity necessary to confront the problem of hazardous waste cleanup. By capping the number of sites for which the national government would be responsible, Superfund effectively forced the states to build the necessary expertise to clean up hundreds of sites on their own. Combined with continued frustration over the slow progress of the national program, these experiences caused state officials' complaints about duplication and potential preemption to grow stronger over time. Superfund therefore inadvertently spurred additional intergovernmental conflict: "as states passed legislation and developed infrastructures to meet their financial responsibilities under CERCLA, they inevitably sought greater control over hazardous waste cleanup" (Young 1990, 993). Thus the program sowed the seeds of its own political instability.

A combination of policy design, timing, and their interaction led to great dissatisfaction among state officials and other groups. Key provisions of the program affected its ability to take root and flourish. Initially Superfund received an authorization that was both temporary rather than permanent and was viewed almost universally as insufficient, with most observers believing that it would cost far more to clean up abandoned waste sites nationwide. The program also centralized authority at the national level, granting state governments only limited input, and had limited coalition potential. The impact of these design features was exacerbated by Superfund's inauspicious economic and political timing. It was enacted at "a time of severe budgetary stringency" (Landy, Roberts, and Thomas 1990, 144), which limited state governments' ability to devote financial resources to the cleanup of abandoned hazardous waste sites, a relatively new administrative task with which most of them lacked experience. Its adoption occurred one month prior to the inauguration of Republican President Ronald Reagan, and his administration, especially under Environmental Protection Agency (EPA) Administrator Anne Gorsuch, did not evince a strong commitment to the program. Due to their general interest in hazardous waste cleanup, state lawmakers did not seek to terminate Superfund despite their reservations about the program. Since its inception, however, they have contributed to its political instability by lobbying for major changes to its structure and operations.

SUPERFUND: AN OVERVIEW

In terms of its structure, Superfund differs from both traditional environmental programs and the other intergovernmental initiatives featured in this book.

Most environmental programs are regulatory initiatives "in which EPA sets standards, issues permits based on those standards, and then takes enforcement actions for failure to comply with permits" (Cohen and Tipermas 1983, 44). They are forward-looking initiatives that address the current or future generation of pollution. Consider, for instance, one of Superfund's predecessors, the Toxic Substances Control Act of 1976 (TSCA). The law granted EPA the authority to impose reporting, recordkeeping, and testing requirements related to chemical substances. In managing programs under the TSCA and related laws, the national agency "evaluates new and existing chemicals and their risks, and finds ways to prevent or reduce pollution before it gets into the environment."[2] This preventative style is typical of environmental legislation.

In contrast, Superfund is primarily a reactive program that responds to past actions that had deleterious environmental or public health consequences. Its centerpiece is the Hazardous Substance Trust Fund that gave the program its popular name and can be used to clean up hazardous waste sites and respond to emergency incidents. When it was created by CERCLA in 1980, the $1.6 billion fund was financed largely by taxes on petroleum and chemicals. CERCLA also included liability provisions that sought to compel the parties responsible for producing hazardous wastes to finance cleanup costs. This combination of taxes and liability provisions explains why Superfund is often described as following the twin principles of "polluters pay" and "shovels first, lawyers later." Its taxes are premised on the idea that "those who pollute an area and/or that gain from the use of hazardous materials should be responsible for its cleanup" (Haggerty and Welcomer 2003, 34). Superfund monies can be used for reimbursement; the national government can pay to clean up a hazardous waste site and then pursue legal action against the parties it deems responsible to attempt to recoup those costs (Bowman 1985, 134). If the legally responsible party cannot be found or is not financially solvent, the hazardous waste site is considered an "orphan site" and funds from the trust fund are used to pay for its cleanup.

The standard Superfund cleanup proceeds through a complex series of steps.[3] It begins when a potential site is brought to the attention of the EPA, after which the site undergoes a prescreening to determine whether the Superfund site assessment process is appropriate; if so, the site is added to the agency's database. Then a preliminary assessment is conducted. If warranted, a site inspection or other more in-depth assessment is then conducted to assess whether the site requires short- or long-term cleanup

---

[2] United States Environmental Protection Agency, "Summary of the Toxic Substances Control Act," accessed March 16, 2017 (www.epa.gov/laws-regulations/summary-toxic-substances-control-act).

[3] This summary is based on United States Environmental Protection Agency, "Cleaning up Superfund Sites," accessed March 16, 2017 (www.epa.gov/superfund/cleaning-superfund-sites). The process differs slightly for national government facilities.

attention. At the end of each assessment, the EPA uses its Hazard Ranking System (HRS) to give the site a score that measures its relative potential to pose a threat to human health or the environment. A site that falls below the traditional cutoff of 28.5 generally requires no further remedial attention from the national government, but a site that exceeds this score is placed on the National Priority List (NPL). When a site is listed on the NPL, a remedial investigation and feasibility study are conducted to ascertain site conditions and evaluate alternative remedial actions. A remedy is then selected, designed, and constructed. After construction is complete, a site may require additional operations and maintenance over the medium to long term.

Unlike many of the intergovernmental initiatives analyzed in this book, which feature grants-in-aid through which the national government distributes money to the states, Superfund contains regulatory and public works components. It "operates much like a regulatory program" by spurring hazardous waste producers to dispose of their products carefully to avoid creating a Superfund site, and its requirement that private parties remediate existing waste sites "makes it essentially a public works project that is privately financed" (Hird 1994, 6). Conservatives have criticized the public works component of the program, with some claiming that members of Congress tend to view its monies as "funds with great pork barrel potential" (Burford 1986, 106).

Since its inception, state governments have played an important yet contested role in this regulatory-public works hybrid. In its original form, CERCLA provided "several opportunities for state involvement" throughout the cleanup process (Florini 1982, 320), yet state officials nevertheless viewed their role as excessively circumscribed. Moreover, state governments also found themselves partly responsible for the cost of cleaning up and then maintaining remediated sites. Finally, state officials frequently felt intense political pressure to do something about waste sites that ultimately were not placed on the NPL but were nonetheless viewed as potential threats to public health. Several states therefore established "their own administrative mechanisms to carry out their new federal and state responsibilities" and "develop[ed] their own programs to clean up the many hazardous waste sites not likely to be covered under the federal legislation" (Mazmanian and Morell 1992, 30). Their actions effectively created a parallel hazardous waste cleanup program. The scope of these parallel programs grew over time, and state officials frequently pointed to their accomplishments to claim that they deserved more authority in the cleanup process. As will be explained in the sections that follow, states' administrative discretion and financial responsibilities have been an ongoing source of intergovernmental tension. Before examining these tensions, the next section describes how CERCLA came into existence and the role of state officials in its creation.

THE ORIGINS AND ENACTMENT OF SUPERFUND

The 1970s are known as the "environmental decade," and as the decade progressed, the issue of hazardous waste gained increased prominence. In 1976, President Gerald Ford signed the Resource Conservation and Recovery Act (RCRA), which gave the EPA the authority to control the generation, transportation, treatment, storage, and disposal of hazardous waste. The RCRA represented a "cradle-to-grave" approach that soon came to be viewed as inadequate. The Love Canal saga in upstate New York "alerted the U.S. public to the ticking time bomb called hazardous waste [through its] images of lime-green chemical slime oozing into the basement of houses close to the canal" (Rahm 1998a, 719). Most Americans were familiar with Love Canal by July 1980,[4] and 76 percent of the respondents to an ABC News-Harris Poll of likely voters described "the dumping of toxic chemicals in the country today" as a "very serious" problem.[5] Thanks to Love Canal and similar incidents, members of Congress faced increasing pressure to address the issue of hazardous waste disposal.

CERCLA was a "drastically scaled-down" version of a Carter administration proposal that had been introduced in 1979.[6] At a subcommittee hearing on the more ambitious legislation, state officials expressed two major concerns that came to define the intergovernmental dynamics of Superfund. First, they worried that the proposal did not provide sufficient funds. Recognizing that government officials and the public were still gaining an appreciation of the scope of the problem, they pressed Congress to allocate more money to it. One Kentucky official said the problem was "staggering in size" and that "we are probably grossly underestimating the cost."[7] A state legislator from New York complained that the funds would cover only a small portion of the cleanup costs: "the proposed superfund just isn't 'super' enough to handle the problem."[8] These complaints persisted after Superfund's enactment.

[4] In a survey conducted by Cambridge Reports/Research International in July 1980, 69 percent of respondents answered "Yes" when asked, "Have you heard about the Love Canal incident, or not?" Only 22 percent answered "No," while 10 percent answered "Not sure." The survey was based on personal interviews with a national adult sample of 1,500.

[5] The survey was conducted by ABC News/Louis Harris and Associates from June 5 to June 9, 1980. It was based on telephone interviews with a sample of 1,493 likely voters. The other responses were "Only somewhat serious" (20 percent of respondents), "Hardly serious at all" (2 percent), and "Not sure" (2 percent).

[6] This description comes from "Congress Clears 'Superfund' Legislation." In *CQ Almanac 1980*, 36th ed., 584–593. Washington, DC: Congressional Quarterly, 1981. The article provides an excellent summary of the legislation's path through Congress. For more on these congressional developments see Landy, Roberts, and Thomas (1990).

[7] House Subcommittee on Transportation and Commerce of the Committee on Interstate and Foreign Commerce, *Superfund: Hearings on H.R. 4571, H.R. 4566, and H.R. 5290*, 96th Cong., 2nd sess., October 11, 1979, 556.

[8] House Subcommittee on Transportation and Commerce of the Committee on Interstate and Foreign Commerce, *Superfund: Hearings on H.R. 4571, H.R. 4566, and H.R. 5290*, 96th Cong., 2nd sess., October 11, 1979, 528.

State lawmakers' second major concern had to do with the respective roles of the national government and the states. Arkansas Governor Bill Clinton, then the chair of the NGA's Subcommittee on Environmental Management, used the experiences of his home state to contend that the states "should initially take the lead, with the federal government providing advice and financial assistance."[9] State officials were dissatisfied with the administration proposal because they felt that it centralized too much authority in the national government. They called for the states to be given more control over the cleanup process. Many national policymakers, however, questioned whether the states were capable of effectively carrying out a hazardous waste cleanup program (Hird 1994, 227).

The chemical industry also objected to the creation of a trust fund devoted to cleaning up toxic contaminants, mostly because of its proposed funding mechanism. The political agenda of the late 1970s was affected by the transition from an expansionary fiscal regime to a regime of austerity (Pierson 2001). With growing national government deficits and limited congressional appetite for new spending commitments, EPA staff sought to fund hazardous waste cleanups by levying a fee against chemical manufacturers rather than by imposing broad tax increases.[10] The symbolic implications of the fee, rather than its financial consequences, spurred the Chemical Manufacturers Association (CMA) to lobby vociferously against the proposed Superfund. The CMA decried the fee's reputational impact, arguing that it would give "the public the impression that the industry was to blame for the problem of hazardous waste sites and would fan the flames of public hostility toward it" (Landy, Roberts, and Thomas 1990, 145).

For various reasons, including industry opposition and tepid enthusiasm from subnational officials, the Superfund proposal made limited legislative progress during the 96th Congress. The resounding Republican victory in the November 1980 elections, rather than sounding the death knell for the legislation, actually revived it. Advocates of more ambitious legislation, particularly in the Senate that was soon to be under Republican control, cast aside their reservations about the existing options in order to do something before Ronald Reagan's inauguration.[11] The version of CERCLA that President Carter then signed into law on December 31, 1980 was "the product of a hastily

---

[9] House Subcommittee on Transportation and Commerce of the Committee on Interstate and Foreign Commerce, *Superfund: Hearings on H.R. 4571, H.R. 4566, and H.R. 5290*, 96th Cong., 2nd sess., October 11, 1979, 537.

[10] Under fire for the agency's response to the hazardous waste issue, EPA "staff conceptualized and wrote the initial hazardous waste Superfund bill and the agency eventually became the prime mover behind the legislation" (Cohen and Tipermas 1983, 48).

[11] The president-elect indicated to Senate Minority Leader Howard Baker (R-TN) that "he would not object to the lame-duck Congress finishing up the controversial bill before he took office." See "Congress Clears 'Superfund' Legislation." In *CQ Almanac 1980*, 36th ed., 584–593. Washington, DC: Congressional Quarterly, 1981.

worked-out compromise [that] was passed with almost no debate and under a suspension of the rules" (Young 1990, 987–988).

The expedited procedure through which CERCLA gained enactment was only possible because the Senate made several changes to the original proposal. The law retained the central features of the Carter administration proposal, but it embraced a "less exhaustive approach than was formerly sought" (Berger 1986, vi). Perhaps the most important change was a sharp drop in the size of the fund itself, from $4.1 billion in an earlier Senate version of the bill to $1.6 billion. The final legislation also eliminated a victims compensation provision for individuals injured by chemical accidents, included weaker liability standards than many House Democrats favored, and – largely due to a threatened filibuster by Senate Republicans – failed to cover oil spills (Hird 1994, 10).

The hasty adoption of CERCLA in December 1980 has been criticized by scholars who note that many crucial policy issues were barely addressed during the flurry of activity that led to its final passage. According to John Hird (1994, ix), the program "was hurriedly pieced together with little apparent concern for important policy issues such as fairness, the appropriate level of government to implement the cleanup program, acceptable site cleanup levels, and so on." Even though Congress devoted little time to intergovernmental relations in the immediate prelude to Superfund's adoption, the law had important federalism-related implications that interacted with the economic, political, and administrative environment to shape state officials' reactions.

POLICY DESIGN, TIMING, AND ELITE FEEDBACK POTENTIAL

When CERCLA was enacted in 1980, many of its provisions seemed likely to generate at least mild resistance from state officials. Many state leaders, environmental groups, and others viewed its trust fund as inadequate. One observer critiqued "the misnomer of a Superfund, which clearly lacks funding adequate to clean up more than a fraction of the abandoned hazardous waste sites" (Lieber 1983, 72). The number of sites that required remediation was unknown, but many speculated that the scope of the problem was so great that significantly more funds would be needed. The states "perceive[d] the extent of the problem to be considerably broader than what can be addressed" by Superfund; the program was expected to place 1,800 sites on the NPL, and the states estimated that over 7,000 sites required remediation (EPA 1984, 2–8). If state governments wished to clean up the additional sites, they would be responsible for obtaining the funds and developing the capacity to do so. Concerns about insufficient funding also reflected a belief that not enough money would be collected from private actors to obviate the need for considerable spending by the national government. The limited size of the trust fund seemed to constrain its feedback potential, and it has been a point of contention throughout the program's history.

Moreover, certain fiscal provisions of the law seemed likely to lead to intergovernmental conflict and self-undermining feedback effects. The national government and state governments faced irreconcilable financial incentives that made their preferences incompatible. Superfund held state governments responsible for 10 percent of the capital costs of hazardous waste cleanup and all operating costs beyond the first year (CBO 1985, 1). Before any cleanup could begin, state governments had to certify that they would provide the required funds. Because of the way Superfund distributed financial responsibility for distinct stages of the cleanup process, states tended to prefer capital-intensive cleanup strategies with low operations and maintenance costs, while the national government favored approaches involving less capital spending but higher operations and maintenance costs. Thus the financial structure of Superfund created "a major source of tension between EPA and the states" (Markell 1993, 61). For decades, state leaders pressed unsuccessfully for major changes to this feature of the program.

The inadequacy of the trust fund and its cost-sharing provisions were of particular concern to state leaders due to the economic context in which CERCLA was enacted. A brief recession in 1980, followed quickly by a deeper recession in 1981–1982, "severely constrained" state governments' finances, limiting their ability to "establish or enlarge their capabilities to respond to hazardous substance releases" (EPA 1984, 3–8). State governments found it difficult, at least temporarily, to meet their fiscal responsibilities under CERCLA and to develop the administrative capacity to clean up sites that were not placed on the NPL. Budgetary pressures, combined with various legal and institutional restrictions on the allocation of state funds, made it difficult to "marshal resources for cleanup efforts ... additional staff, and ... needed equipment and services" (EPA 1984, 3–8).

In terms of administrative discretion, Superfund concentrated authority in the national government. The program's supporters justified this centralization by highlighting the national scope of the hazardous waste problem, the fact that the effects of some sites allegedly crossed state lines, the need for a comprehensive legal framework rather than a patchwork that varied across the states, and the states' limited bureaucratic capacity to implement a Superfund-type program (Hird 1994, 227). CERCLA called for the national government to consult with the states at each step of the cleanup process, but most observers viewed this requirement as toothless. Most other environmental programs included a "state grant" provision, but Superfund favored contracts or cooperative agreements that permitted "a greater measure" of national government control (Cohen and Tipermas 1983, 57). The states' secondary role fostered intergovernmental tensions. In the words of Richard Hula (2001, 185), "Rather than promoting cooperation and flexibility, the EPA is seen as trying to impose a centralized vision of toxic waste policy."

In addition to having general concerns about their limited administrative discretion, state officials soon found themselves enmeshed in a legal controversy over whether Section 114(c) of CERCLA preempted existing state policies. At issue were the state-level "superfunds" that had been created both before and after the enactment of the national legislation. The precise statutory language in Section 114(c) outlined that "no person may be required to contribute to any fund, the purpose of which is to pay compensation for claims for any costs of response or damages or claims which may be compensated under this subchapter." This language sparked a legal dispute that eventually went to the Supreme Court.[12] The case, *Exxon Corporation* v. *Hunt*,[13] centered on the Spill Act, a 1977 New Jersey law "which, much like CERCLA, created a fund from taxes levied on major chemical facilities in the state" (Regas 1986, 536). Exxon sued New Jersey in federal and state court, pressing for the application of a total preemption standard that would override the state tax provision.[14] State attorneys general from California, Connecticut, Ohio, Maine, New Hampshire, New York, Texas, and Vermont submitted an *amici curiae* brief supporting the argument that the national statute did not preempt the New Jersey tax. In a split decision in 1986, the Court endorsed a compromise that invalidated specific parts of the state taxing scheme (Cooke 1987, 255). Although the Supreme Court ruling was rendered irrelevant when Congress amended CERCLA, the legal dispute highlights the intergovernmental tensions built into the original law. These tensions were particularly significant given state lawmakers' concerns about its fiscal inadequacy and their capability to marshal the necessary resources to address the hazardous waste problem.

The temporary authorization of Superfund was another feature of its design that hindered its ability to generate self-reinforcing feedback. Scheduled to expire after five years, the trust fund was vulnerable to changes in the political environment. Indeed, at the moment CERCLA was enacted, such a shift was about to take place. The Reagan administration had little interest in Superfund, which was reflected in the management styles of the two main political appointees with jurisdiction over the program: EPA Administrator Anne Gorsuch and Superfund Program Administrator Rita Lavelle. Although the two officials did not care for one another,[15] their combined leadership defined

---

[12] This paragraph relies on three legal analyses that examine the 1986 Supreme Court decision in *Exxon Corporation* v. *Hunt* in more detail (Cooke 1987; Regas 1986; Freeman 1986).

[13] 475 US 355 (1986).

[14] At the same time that Exxon sued New Jersey, the state "initiated two suits against the federal government" in an attempt "to clarify existing law so that the state could efficiently operate its cleanup and removal programs" (Cooke 1987, 251–252). Thus the uncertain implications of Section 114(c) worried corporations and state governments alike.

[15] In her autobiography Gorsuch pointedly notes, "The person in charge of the waste office, Rita Lavelle, was not my choice" (Burford 1986, 89). In addition, she devotes an entire chapter to Lavelle's shortcomings and disparages her in many other contexts. Despite their personal animosity, however, the two officials are indelibly linked by the fact that both of them ultimately

the early years of Superfund until they resigned (separately) in 1983. Political scientist John Hird (1994, 201) notes, "It is difficult to overestimate the impact the Burford-Lavelle years at EPA had on the progress (or degeneration) of Superfund." With respect to the program's temporary authorization, Gorsuch "enraged the environmental lobby by stating that she saw no need for Superfund to continue beyond its initial five-year authorization" (Patashnik 2000, 162). With its temporary authorization and its inauspicious political timing, Superfund seemed to be on perilous political footing.

Finally, Superfund possessed relatively weak coalition potential. Most importantly, its main provisions alienated the business community. The program's "polluters pay" principle put "state and local governments in an awkward position, for they may be forced to trade off the need for economic development, job creation, and retention as the EPA attempts to recover the cost of cleanup from companies even to the point of bankruptcy" (Rahm 1998a, 725). Moreover, interstate economic competition seemed likely to render the states "averse to imposing stringent hazardous waste controls because such action could dispel efforts to project a 'favorable business climate'" (Bowman 1985, 139). To be sure, there were others who seemed likely to develop a stake in Superfund's continuation. Its public works component represented a potential financial windfall for those involved in mitigating the harmful impact of hazardous waste, including environmental contractors and construction firms (Hird 1994; Patashnik 2000). Similarly, the process of identifying polluters and determining their obligations was notorious for sparking long-running legal battles, and trial attorneys serving the business community welcomed the legal fees that accrued as a result. However, they were unlikely to come to Superfund's defense since their clients generally maintained an adversarial posture toward the program. State officials and other political actors who supported the goals of the program but hoped to amend it therefore found themselves with few potential allies who felt the same way about what should be done.[16]

With its stingy temporary funding, its centralization of administrative discretion in the national government, and its limited coalition potential, Superfund seemed unlikely to generate self-reinforcing feedback effects among state government leaders. In fact, certain features of the program, such as its preemption clause and its provisions for financial responsibility, seemed likely to spur intergovernmental conflict. Moreover, the timing of Superfund's enactment, at a moment characterized by economic duress and a conservative

resigned over their mismanagement of Superfund. Gorsuch's resignation defined her legacy; indeed, the opening line of her obituary in the *Washington Post* describes her as the "EPA director who resigned under fire in 1983 during a scandal over mismanagement of a $1.6 billion program to clean up hazardous waste dumps" (Sullivan 2004).

[16] The program also seemed unlikely to generate mass-level feedback effects since "most citizens' reliance on the continuity of Superfund spending is extremely modest relative to their dependence on programs like Social Security and Medicare" (Patashnik 2000, 162).

turn in the political environment, looked likely to exacerbate rather than ameliorate this potential state-level resistance. Perhaps it is unsurprising that, as the next section describes, "the first six years of the program were marked by a lack of state participation" (Cline 2010, 118).

STATE GOVERNMENTS' INITIAL RESPONSE TO SUPERFUND

In the early 1980s, a combination of economic and political constraints prevented most state governments from implementing the new Superfund program effectively. An early survey of state efforts revealed a "striking" concentration of funds and staff in a group of active states that included New York, Minnesota, New Jersey, California, Pennsylvania, Michigan, Florida, and New Hampshire (EPA 1984, 2–34). However, the vast majority of states lacked the funds, personnel, or technical expertise to address the hazardous waste problem. National government agencies issued reports that were "severely critical" of the states' response, and one observer described the adequacy of state resources to deal with hazardous wastes as "perhaps the most crucial issue" facing the program (Lieber 1983, 69).

The states' inability to devote significant funds to Superfund implementation reflected both the general economic environment and various state-specific constraints. The recessions of the early 1980s had a profound effect on state government finances. In 1983, the ASTSWMO conducted a survey on state Superfund-related activity that formed the basis for a report issued the following year by the EPA. Of the 43 states that responded to the survey, 30 (70 percent) reported that they had a hiring freeze in place during the 1983 fiscal year, illustrating the widespread nature of the states' fiscal travails (EPA 1984, 3–15). The EPA cited hiring freezes, salary limitations for technical personnel, and procurement restrictions as factors that "impeded the progress of many state cleanup programs" (EPA 1984, ES-2). These financial constraints help explain why seventeen states reported no money available for Superfund cost sharing in 1983 and why four states (Colorado, Delaware, Louisiana, and Ohio) experienced a $3.4 million temporary shortfall in February 1985 (CBO 1985, 6). Even states that managed to budget funds for hazardous waste cleanup did not always make this money available for cost sharing under the Superfund program. Some states reserved the funds for the cleanup of sites that were not listed on the NPL or gave broad discretion to governors and other officials to use the funds for non-Superfund-related actions (EPA 1984, 3–7). By prioritizing independent cleanup activities that were not under the auspices of the national program, these states enhanced their administrative capacities and laid the foundation for hazardous waste cleanup programs that operated parallel to Superfund. These independent activities exemplify self-undermining feedback effects.

In addition to operating under economic and institutional constraints that hindered their ability to implement Superfund, some state leaders were reluctant to begin cleaning up hazardous waste sites until the EPA issued specific guidelines and standards (Berger 1986, 58). There was a lack of clarity about the operational requirements of the new program. CERCLA's centralization was a source of this uncertainty, and it was exacerbated by specific actions and inactions of the Reagan administration. The 1980 law had enabled the revision of the National Contingency Plan (NCP) that "provided the guidelines and procedures needed to respond to releases and threatened releases of hazardous substances, pollutants, or contaminants."[17] That revision was supposed to occur by June 1981. When the deadline passed without EPA action it drew condemnation from members of Congress, the NGA, the National League of Cities, and environmental groups. In September, the state of New Jersey sued the national agency, seeking an injunction ordering the revised NCP to be in effect by the following February (Berger 1986).

The administration's failure to revise the NCP epitomized its reluctance to act forcefully to implement Superfund. Under Gorsuch and Lavelle, the program "suffered from neglect and outright mismanagement" in its early years (Rahm 1998b, 76). The EPA administrator claimed that her Superfund "philosophy was to conserve the fund, to make it go as far as it could with that five-year revenue [and] to get more state money in instead of relying solely on the fund itself for cleanup" (Burford 1986, 106). Critics accused Gorsuch of settling for inadequate levels of cleanup and using her "legal discretion to shape a Superfund program based on conciliation with private industry" (Church and Nakamura 1993, 9). Congressional investigators and members of the environmental community described many of the agreements that the EPA negotiated as "sweetheart deals" that were overly generous to hazardous waste producers. They also alleged that Superfund money had been used for political purposes. Charges of mismanagement and political manipulation came to a head when the EPA refused to turn over its enforcement files to a congressional subcommittee, citing executive privilege. The ensuing conflict eventually led to the resignation of the EPA administrator.[18]

In sum, several factors conspired to limit Superfund-related activity by state governments in the early 1980s. Various fiscal and institutional constraints limited the states' capacity to act, and some active states focused their limited resources on hazardous waste sites that did not fall under the purview of the national program. Testifying before a congressional subcommittee in 1984, the executive director of the ASTSWMO explained, "States are operating under severe resource constraints. Both funding and staffing levels are inadequate to

---

[17] United States Environmental Protection Agency, "Superfund: CERCLA Overview," accessed April 17, 2017 (www.epa.gov/superfund/superfund-cercla-overview).

[18] Despite having reservations about the executive privilege claim, Gorsuch advanced it on the advice of the Justice Department. A few months after her resignation, the Justice Department "announced it would no longer represent her because it was involved in investigations into corruption at the EPA"; this move struck Gorsuch's allies as cold-blooded and callous (Sullivan 2004).

address fully the environmental problems facing the states."[19] Moreover, state leaders and many others were frustrated by the Reagan administration's unwillingness to implement Superfund forcefully. Although CERCLA had been signed into law with high hopes, by the mid 1980s there was widespread frustration with its implementation. As a result, the temporary authorization of the program proved especially impactful. The reauthorization process provided state officials and other critics with a "window of opportunity" to press their case for revisiting its central provisions. State officials played a key role during the reauthorization debate, lobbying for major revisions as Congress sought to address the "enormous gap between the promise and the performance of the original Superfund act" (Mazmanian and Morell 1992, 18).

THE SUPERFUND AMENDMENTS AND REAUTHORIZATION ACT (SARA) OF 1986

Congress began to consider the reauthorization of Superfund in 1984. Democrats argued that early action was necessary because the trust fund's taxing authority was due to expire late the next year. They also viewed reauthorization as a way to prod the EPA into acting more forcefully. In contrast, the Reagan administration and most congressional Republicans wanted to wait until the following year. A renewal bill was adopted in the Democratic House. It would have increased the size of the trust fund, broadened the reach of its taxing provisions, established a mandatory schedule for the EPA to clean up priority sites, and set uniform national standards for site cleanup. A Senate measure cleared the Committee on Environment and Public Works; the Finance Committee held hearings on the bill but took no action on it.[20]

The debate over the reauthorization of Superfund continued for two more years. In 1985, both the House and the Senate passed legislation to expand and reauthorize the program, but the two versions included conflicting financial provisions and differed significantly in their cleanup standards and schedules.[21] As the two chambers struggled to resolve these differences and the reauthorization effort stalled, Superfund's taxing authority expired on September 30, 1985. The Senate refused to approve a temporary extension, forcing the EPA to slow action on cleanups to conserve the $130 million

---

[19] House Subcommittee on Water Resources of the Committee on Public Works and Transportation, *Reauthorization of and Possible Amendments to the Comprehensive Environmental Response, Compensation, and Liability Act of 1980 (Superfund): Hearings on H.R. 5640*, 98th Cong., 2nd sess., May 16, 1984, 74.

[20] For more information about congressional developments in 1984, see "Superfund Reauthorization Passed by House." In *CQ Almanac 1984*, 40th ed., 309–313. Washington, DC: Congressional Quarterly, 1985.

[21] For a more detailed account of developments in 1985 see "House, Senate Pass Superfund Authorization." In *CQ Almanac 1985*, 41st ed., 191–198. Washington, DC: Congressional Quarterly, 1986.

remaining in the trust fund at that time. Eventually the two chambers agreed on a conference report that made $8.5 billion available to the program over the next five years and was endorsed by large margins.[22] President Reagan threatened to veto the conference report based on its cost and the additional taxes it imposed, but he changed course and signed the Superfund Amendments and Reauthorization Act (SARA) on October 17, 1986.[23] In addition to increasing Superfund's financial generosity, SARA set strict standards for cleaning up hazardous waste sites, required the EPA to begin work at 375 sites within five years, emphasized the use of permanent cleanup methods, extended the timeframe for dumping victims to sue responsible parties, and required companies to provide local communities with more information about the materials they handled and dumped.[24] The ambitiousness of SARA was a byproduct of the controversy that dominated Superfund's early years and lingering congressional mistrust of the Reagan administration (Hird 1994, 201). Its provisions were also shaped by the lobbying efforts of state officials, which will be the focus of the rest of this section.

The mobilization and legislative successes of professional associations like the NGA, the NAAG, and the ASTSWMO illustrate how Superfund generated self-undermining feedback effects. State officials who appeared before congressional committees pressed for three major changes to the program and achieved many of their goals. First, they argued that the states should be given a stronger administrative role; the reauthorized program included several

[22] The Senate adopted the conference report on October 3, 1986 in an 88–8 vote; five days later the House endorsed it in a 386–27 vote. The final measure featured $2.75 billion in petroleum taxes, $1.4 billion in feedstock taxes, a $1.25 billion general fund subsidy, and a controversial broad-based "corporate environmental income tax" that was expected to generate $2.5 billion. More than 500 corporations and trade associations lobbied against the broad-based tax, claiming that it violated the "polluter pays" principle on which Superfund was based. However, the tax appealed to Congress because it guaranteed "stable financing without antagonizing general taxpayers" and "avoided the need for even higher taxes on the petroleum and (especially) the chemical industries" (Patashnik 2000, 166).

[23] Kincaid (1987) traces the president's change of heart to the high likelihood of a veto override and to the fact that many congressional Republicans felt that a veto would hurt them in the November elections. Superfund retained strong public support despite its checkered early years. In a July 1986 poll, almost two-thirds of respondents said that the program should be "kept and funded at the same level" (31 percent) or "kept and funded at a higher level" (34 percent), while only 13 percent of respondents said that Superfund should be "kept but funded at a lower level" and only 6 percent of respondents said the program "should be eliminated." The other participants responded "Don't know" (16 percent). The survey was conducted by Cambridge Reports/Research International in July 1986 and was based on personal interviews with a national adult sample of 1,500. An identical survey fielded by the same group a year earlier produced very similar results: "Should be eliminated" (4 percent); "Kept but funded at a lower level (9 percent); "Kept and funded at the same level" (36 percent); "Kept and funded at a higher level" (35 percent); and "Don't know" (15 percent).

[24] This summary comes from "Reagan Signs 'Superfund' Waste-Cleanup Bill." In *CQ Almanac 1986*, 42nd ed., 111–120. Washington, DC: Congressional Quarterly, 1987. The article provides additional details about the politics and final provisions of SARA.

changes to that effect. In contrast to the UI and Medicaid cases, where state officials lobbied to preserve the status quo and hold on to policymaking authority that they already possessed, they pressed for a major restructuring of Superfund. State officials' second objective was to recalibrate Superfund's cost-sharing formula so that the national government and the states did not face competing financial incentives. This shift was not included, but SARA included a subtler change that attempted to alleviate state concerns. Third, state officials successfully lobbied for the repeal of the so-called "preemption clause" that limited their taxing options.

Many state officials who appeared at congressional hearings focused on the CERCLA provisions and EPA decisions that hamstrung the states' administrative discretion. A New York official pinned Superfund's limited accomplishments on its centralization: "Too much depends upon EPA policy and EPA's interpretation of congressional intent . . . [T]oo much depends on the whims and policies of the administration."[25] Several state officials made similar claims, like a New Jersey official who said,

We concur with the National Governors Association's position that the current centralized decision making process in Washington has unnecessarily delayed the Superfund program. The program would operate much more efficiently if the Regions and states were provided more authority in remedial action planning and implementation decisions.[26]

Witnesses appearing on behalf of the ASTSWMO described its position paper, which had been endorsed by all 50 states and contained 12 recommendations. Its overarching goal "was to streamline the Superfund cleanup process by involving the States more in this area of hazardous waste."[27] The NGA felt that state governments should be responsible for "establishing priorities, undertaking remedial investigations and feasibility studies, [and] selecting contractors," and it also asserted that they should have the "option to take the lead role in planning and implementing Superfund response actions, with a right of first refusal to assume the lead at particular sites."[28] Simply put, state officials wanted a stronger administrative role.

[25] Senate Committee on Environment and Public Works, *Amending and Extending the Comprehensive Environmental Response, Compensation, and Liability Act of 1980 (Superfund)*, 98th Cong., 2nd sess., April 25, 1984, 109–110.
[26] Senate Committee on Environment and Public Works, *Amending and Extending the Comprehensive Environmental Response, Compensation, and Liability Act of 1980 (Superfund)*, 98th Cong., 2nd sess., April 25, 1984, 154.
[27] House Subcommittee on Water Resources of the Committee on Public Works and Transportation, *Reauthorization of and Possible Amendments to the Comprehensive Environmental Response, Compensation, and Liability Act of 1980 (Superfund): Hearings on H.R. 5640*, 98th Cong., 2nd sess., May 16, 1984, 70.
[28] Senate Committee on Environment and Public Works, *Amending and Extending the Comprehensive Environmental Response, Compensation, and Liability Act of 1980 (Superfund)*, 98th Cong., 2nd sess., May 16, 1984, 222.

SARA was responsive to state officials' desire for more control over the cleanup process. Many members of Congress recognized that Superfund would be successful only if the states were willing to participate. In the words of Superfund advocate James Florio (D-NJ), "Many states have yet to either fund their own programs or sign the cooperative agreements with EPA which are the predicate for cleanup action within their borders. We must act to address the states' concerns or risk a fundamental breakdown of the program in the years ahead."[29] As a result, SARA included many provisions that altered intergovernmental relations during the cleanup of hazardous waste sites, and it expanded the prerogatives of state governments considerably. One key phrase in the amendments guaranteed states a "substantial and meaningful role" in all aspects of program implementation, although the precise meaning of the phrase was not defined in statute. The amendments required "state agency and regional EPA officials [to] negotiate the level of state involvement at all NPL sites"; it also allowed state governments to apply to the agency to carry out cleanup actions under Superfund (Cline 2010, 119). This final provision implied that states could, with EPA approval, effectively assert control over particular sites. Moreover, SARA permitted states to impose their own standards on Superfund cleanups. States' standards could be more restrictive than existing national requirements as long as they were formally adopted and generally applicable and as long as the state was willing to pay the incremental costs associated with meeting the more stringent requirements (Hird 1994, 20).

State leaders also sought to alleviate the financial constraints under which the states operated. They pressed for the national government and the states to face the same financial incentives, with the executive director of the ASTSWMO explaining that many states had been "very uncomfortable" with the remedial actions chosen for some hazardous waste sites because their "long-term costs would really be in the operations and maintenance area where we are the ones that would be carrying the full burden."[30] Finally, Congress heard repeatedly from state officials who lobbied for the complete repeal of Section 114(c), the so-called "preemption clause" that severely limited the taxing options available to states as they funded their share of the Superfund program. Robert Stafford (R-VT), chair of the Senate Committee on Environment and Public Works, agreed that states should have the ability to establish their own taxing laws and insisted that the goal of the section had not been to subvert state authority. He conceded, however, that "despite our good intentions, the presence of the

---

[29] House Subcommittee on Water Resources of the Committee on Public Works and Transportation, *Reauthorization of and Possible Amendments to the Comprehensive Environmental Response, Compensation, and Liability Act of 1980 (Superfund): Hearings on H.R. 5640*, 98th Cong., 2nd sess., May 15, 1984, 5.

[30] House Subcommittee on Water Resources of the Committee on Public Works and Transportation, *Reauthorization of and Possible Amendments to the Comprehensive Environmental Response, Compensation, and Liability Act of 1980 (Superfund): Hearings on H.R. 5640*, 98th Cong., 2nd sess., May 16, 1984, 77.

preemption clause is casting a shadow over the right of State and local governments to respond to Superfund problems."[31] Some members of Congress disagreed,[32] but in general the states' claims found a receptive audience.

Indeed, the amendments included several legal and financial provisions for which state leaders had lobbied. The states gained the ability to sue the EPA in federal court to force it to choose a remedial action that complied with applicable state or federal requirements, and the agency was required to issue regulations providing for state involvement in the cleanup process. SARA also directed the EPA to grant states a credit against their share of cleanup costs for any money they spent at a site before it was placed on the NPL. The amendments delayed for up to 10 years the time when states would be responsible for all operations and maintenance costs, a shift that did not go as far as state leaders had hoped but sought to relieve some of the pressure they felt due to the conflicting financial incentives embedded in Superfund.[33] Finally, SARA removed the preemption clause in Section 114(c) of CERCLA. During the contentious interchamber negotiations over reauthorization, "preemption was one of the few issues upon which the conferees immediately agreed" (Regas 1986, 536). Thus national legislators sided with state officials and endorsed one of their major priorities, effectively contradicting the nation's highest court in the process.

The reauthorization of CERCLA was a contentious process that pushed Superfund to the brink of expiration, yet ultimately the program emerged intact. Lobbying by state officials contributed to programmatic changes that restructured Superfund to align more closely with their financial and institutional interests, including both the addition of language guaranteeing states a "substantial and meaningful role" and the removal of the preemption clause. According to one observer, these changes reflected the Reagan administration's discovery "that the states were a powerful force in the

---

[31] Senate Committee on Environment and Public Works, *Amending and Extending the Comprehensive Environmental Response, Compensation, and Liability Act of 1980 (Superfund)*, 98th Cong., 2nd sess., May 16, 1984, 174.

[32] Legislators who wished to preserve the preemption clause often portrayed it as a provision that protected business interests and worried that its elimination would have a detrimental effect on chemical manufacturers. Representative John Breaux (D-LA) explained, "There is nothing in the bill that would prohibit the States from duplicating the fund from the Federal level or doubling the fund. What assurances do we have that we are not going to create a situation where everybody is going to get into the Superfund act, everybody is going to pass the same type of tax?" House Subcommittee on Water Resources of the Committee on Public Works and Transportation, *Reauthorization of and Possible Amendments to the Comprehensive Environmental Response, Compensation, and Liability Act of 1980 (Superfund): Hearings on H.R. 5640*, 98th Cong., 2nd sess., May 16, 1984, 94.

[33] This list is not exhaustive. For more on the intergovernmental implications of SARA and other central provisions of the amendments see "Reagan Signs 'Superfund' Waste-Cleanup Bill." In *CQ Almanac 1986*, 42nd ed., 111–120. Washington, DC: Congressional Quarterly, 1987.

lobbying over CERCLA authorization" (Light 1987, 647). Members of Congress also recognized state officials' power and expressed a willingness to accommodate the states' top reform priorities. During one committee hearing, Senator Frank Lautenberg (D-NJ) repeatedly urged state officials to make their views known and assured them that they had his backing. He told three witnesses appearing on behalf of the ASTSWMO that he was interested in their concerns, was impressed with and persuaded by their unanimity, and wanted them to know "that you have support in the Congress because every State has a threatened community. We know the States want to move ahead now."[34] He later urged New Jersey Governor Thomas H. Kean, who was representing the National Governors Association, to "encourage [the governors] to continue to put the pressure on wherever they can. This is not a partisan issue at all, but the weight of 50 states calling for help is indeed impressive."[35] Congress's receptivity to the states' concerns resulted in major changes to the Superfund program. As a result, SARA "marked a potential turn in the program from one dominated by the federal government to one characterized by a more equal partnership" (Cline 2003, 73). This "potential turn" never materialized, however. As states took advantage of their expanded prerogatives and built their administrative capacities to clean up hazardous waste sites, their concerns about duplication only grew more pronounced, fostering more self-undermining feedback and ongoing intergovernmental conflict.

CONTINUED INTERGOVERNMENTAL TENSIONS AND GROWING STATE CAPACITY

The controversy surrounding Superfund did not abate after the bruising 1986 fight for reauthorization. The program continued to make limited progress in cleaning up hazardous waste sites, due partly to a challenging economic environment. As the national budget deficit grew in the 1980s, the Reagan administration pressed the EPA to limit its Superfund spending and to rely more heavily on payments from private parties. State governments also faced fiscal pressures as reduced tax revenues, slow economic growth, regional economic troubles, and minimal growth in aid from the national government "all combined to put a squeeze on revenues and expenditures in many states" (Kincaid 1987, 19). Although state officials generally were pleased that SARA granted them greater administrative discretion, their struggle to make headway

---

[34] Senate Committee on Environment and Public Works, *Amending and Extending the Comprehensive Environmental Response, Compensation, and Liability Act of 1980 (Superfund)*, 98th Cong., 2nd sess., April 25, 1984, 111.

[35] Senate Committee on Environment and Public Works, *Amending and Extending the Comprehensive Environmental Response, Compensation, and Liability Act of 1980 (Superfund)*, 98th Cong., 2nd sess., May 16, 1984, 178.

on the hazardous waste cleanup problem continued. As Superfund's first decade drew to a close, one observer noted, "CERCLA is not working as well as its drafters had hoped or intended" (Young 1990, 1002).

Even though one of the goals of SARA had been to facilitate improved intergovernmental relations, disputes between state officials and the EPA continued. The existence and nature of these tensions varied across states and regions in the late 1980s and early 1990s. Sometimes the cleanup process slowed because state agencies and the EPA disagreed about which applicable or relevant and appropriate requirements (ARARs) should apply to a particular site. At other sites, such as Laskin Poplar in Ohio and Cliffs Dow in Michigan, state agencies and the EPA engaged in parallel activities. This redundancy created intergovernmental friction "over which standards are applicable [and] disputes over the extent to which the states should contribute matching funds or take on risks as the final custodians of sites" (Church and Nakamura 1993, 148). These conflicts were even more contentious when the site in question involved a national government facility. For instance, the Departments of Energy and Defense served as "lead agencies" at the Weldon Spring site in Missouri and Reese Air Force Base in Texas, respectively. The two departments "generally frustrated active participation by state environment regulatory agencies in the federal cleanup process," forcing state officials to work with the appropriate regional office of the EPA as they sought to gain authority over the sites (Davis and Puro 1999, 33).

In addition, a small provision of SARA added a new wrinkle to the intergovernmental tension surrounding Superfund by subjecting state and local governments to the severe liability regime that was one of the program's most controversial elements. Although it was not an explicit part of CERCLA or its reauthorization, a series of federal court decisions established a regime under which liability was retroactive, strict, joint, and several. In practice, this meant that a party found responsible for contributing to the contamination of a site was technically liable for the full cost of cleaning that site, no matter their overall contribution and regardless of whether they acted legally at the time. Businesses railed at the unfairness of this system; initially it had virtually no effect on subnational governments. SARA, however, contained a section clarifying that a state "shall be subject to the provisions of this Act in the same manner and [to] the same extent" as any nongovernmental entity. In 1989, the Supreme Court ruled that this language withdrew any state immunity that may have been previously implied (O'Leary 1990, 86).[36] As a result, states and localities increasingly found themselves targeted by the EPA as polluters and had Superfund liabilities imposed on them based on their roles as generators or transporters of hazardous wastes or as the owners

[36] For an excellent summary of the Supreme Court ruling in *Pennsylvania* v. *Union Gas Co.* (491 US 1[1989]) and the legal and oversight expenses faced by state and local governments see O'Leary (1990).

or operators of facilities that receive hazardous wastes. The fiscal uncertainty of this process caused significant anxiety for state officials, who found themselves "in a role that pits them against the EPA" (Rahm 1998b, 82). This provision of SARA exacerbated the intergovernmental tensions that had characterized Superfund since its creation.

As intergovernmental tensions continued to influence Superfund implementation, many states sought to increase their capacity to conduct hazardous waste cleanups. A 1989 EPA report emphasized the importance of this trend for intergovernmental relations and the program more generally when it noted that the "prospects for increasing state involvement at both NPL and non-NPL sites depends on the willingness and capacity of states to develop effective programs, supported by adequate resources to fund cleanups, pursue enforcement to obtain private cleanups, and conduct oversight activities" (EPA 1989, 1). Even though fiscal challenges limited the amount of Superfund-related activity in which the average state could engage, it did not stop the states from making policy changes. By 1990, 41 states had adopted a state Superfund law based on some form of liability while 44 states had developed funding authorities; these provisions were described as "two essential components to implementing an effective state cleanup program."[37]

Significant variation across states remained, and the patchwork nature of state programs was perhaps their most noteworthy quality. Strong programs existed in states like Minnesota, New Jersey, and New York; other states' initiatives paled in comparison, lacking the necessary administrative or financial resources. According to the EPA's 1989 report, five states did not have Superfund programs, six states had limited remedial action authorities or capabilities due to severely limited funds, and fourteen states were engaged in limited Superfund activities because of either insignificant fund balances or inadequate staffing levels. Four small state cleanup programs depended entirely on financial support from the national government. While the combined balance of existing state funds was approximately $415 million, nearly 80 percent of those funds were concentrated in only nine states (EPA 1989, 20).[38]

Facing financial and institutional limitations, some states gravitated toward "voluntary programs" for the contaminated sites under their jurisdiction. These programs, which were often used in tandem with more traditional mandatory initiatives modeled on CERCLA, emphasized "less complex administrative organization and partial liability relief from cleanup costs if

---

[37] House Subcommittee on Transportation and Hazardous Materials of the Committee on Energy and Commerce, *Hearing on H.R. 3800: Superfund Program (Part 3)*, 103rd Cong., 2nd sess., February 10, 1994, 567.

[38] Including the $1.981 billion authorized in bonds in 4 states rendered this financial imbalance even starker, as 96 percent of the available funds were concentrated in only 11 states.

private parties would take the initiative to sufficiently rehabilitate such properties and return them to productive economic use" (Hula 2001, 192). The first voluntary programs were adopted in the early 1980s as state leaders realized that there were potentially thousands of hazardous sites that would not fall under the jurisdiction of Superfund but still required investigation and potential cleanups. In the early and mid 1990s, this approach spread like wildfire. Only 14 states operated voluntary programs in 1993; this number rose to 35 in 1995 and 44 in 1998 (Hula 2001, 192). The diffusion of the voluntary approach reflected state officials' continued interest in the issue of hazardous waste cleanup and their ongoing dissatisfaction with the national Superfund program. They continued searching for ways to improve their administrative capacity, with a majority of the states effectively creating hazardous waste cleanup programs that competed with Superfund. Thus the reauthorization of the program did not clarify the balance of responsibility between the national government and the states. Instead, state government activities continued to blur the lines of bureaucratic authority and essentially created administrative duplication.[39] These state-level initiatives and their successes undermined state officials' willingness to view themselves as stakeholders in the national program.

Despite ongoing reservations about its effectiveness, Congress endorsed a "hurried and unheralded four-year extension" of Superfund in 1990 (Church and Nakamura 1993, x). The low visibility and uncontroversial nature of the reauthorization was reassuring for the industry and environmental organizations which had participated in the debate surrounding SARA (Hird 1994, 252). However, it neither ushered in a new era for the program nor reflected a newfound consensus about how to make it more successful.[40] Key stakeholders remained divided about several issues that had dogged Superfund since its inception, including the appropriate role of state governments. When the imminent expiration of SARA and the taxes supporting the trust fund placed Superfund reauthorization on the congressional agenda in the mid 1990s, state officials once again pressed their national colleagues for greater administrative authority. They argued that the states had the laws, trust funds, and technical expertise that they lacked when CERCLA was adopted in 1980. Congressional debates therefore featured several discussions of intergovernmental relations. In fact, partisan disagreements about the appropriate state role in Superfund helped make reauthorization even more challenging than it had been in the past.

---

[39] The administrative duplication that flowered during the 1990s is the opposite of the "creative destruction" that Patashnik (2008) associates with the durability of general interest reforms.

[40] Church and Nakamura (1993, x) argue that the 1990 reauthorization of Superfund reflected "political exhaustion after the acrimony accompanying passage of the Clean Air Act of that same year, and a desire to postpone a serious evaluation of Superfund until energy levels in the environmental policy community could be restored."

PARTY POLARIZATION AND CONGRESSIONAL INACTION

When Democrat Bill Clinton became president in 1993, the EPA made a concerted effort to address the intergovernmental tensions that bedeviled environmental policy. It sought to address "long-standing complaints of poor federal-state relationships" through various initiatives that had "the potential to foster a new, more cooperative era of intergovernmental relations" (Kraft and Scheberle 1998, 114). There seemed to be public support for including Superfund reform as part of its effort. In an October 1993 poll, 60 percent of respondents said Superfund should be "extended with changes," while only 16 percent said it should be "extended in its present form" and 8 percent said it should be "allowed to expire."[41] The EPA announced three rounds of Superfund reforms between June 1993 and October 1995. The first round tried to "expedite cleanups and help resolve disputes over liability," the second round "was described as testing key components of the administration's proposed reauthorization plan for CERCLA," and the third round concentrated on "identifying cost-effective cleanup strategies, reducing litigation and transactions costs, and increasing involvement of state and community actors in cleanup decisions" (Hula 2001, 186). State officials generally welcomed these executive branch efforts but recognized that congressional action was needed as well.

Congress considered numerous Superfund proposals during the 1990s.[42] While none of them was enacted into law, they spurred debates that highlighted continued controversies over who should be responsible for the cost of cleaning contaminated sites, the standards that should be imposed, and the states' role in the cleanup process. Initially the congressional debate focused on the Clinton administration's reauthorization proposal, which limited the liability of polluters who had contributed incidentally to a hazardous waste site and incentivized other polluters to join an arbitration process to determine how to allocate costs.[43] Five congressional committees endorsed a version of the Superfund overhaul, but it did not make it to the floor of either chamber by the time Congress adjourned in 1994.

When Congress reconvened in 1995, the taxes that supported the trust fund were scheduled to expire at the end of the year and Republicans exercised majority control of the House and the Senate for the first time in decades. The

---

[41] The remaining participants in the survey (16 percent) responded "Don't know." The survey was conducted by Cambridge Reports/Research International in October 1993 and was based on telephone interviews with a national sample of 1,250 adults.

[42] According to Rahm (1998a, 728), the 103rd Congress (1993–1994) introduced 34 bills concerned with Superfund, the 104th Congress (1995–1996) introduced 57 Superfund-related bills, and the 105th Congress (1997–1998) introduced 50 bills with a reference to Superfund.

[43] For more on the Clinton administration proposal and its reception see "No Floor Action on Superfund Bill." In *CQ Almanac 1994*, 50th ed., 231–236. Washington, DC: Congressional Quarterly, 1995.

new majority targeted Superfund's retroactive liability provisions, arguing that it was unfair to hold polluters responsible for legal dumping that had occurred before the adoption of CERCLA in 1980. Its reform effort made it no further than a congressional subcommittee, and at the end of the year "the existing trust fund's taxing authority expired yet again, the second such lapse in a decade" (Patashnik 2000, 170).[44] For the rest of the decade the Clinton administration made annual requests that Congress reinstate the taxes that supported Superfund, but the Republican-controlled legislature refused to take action without a broader program overhaul.[45] The resulting partisan dispute over taxes, liability, and the role of state governments prevented any reauthorization measure from gaining enactment. Reauthorizing Superfund had never been an easy task, but the obstacles to reaching an agreement became even more formidable in an era of growing partisan polarization.

As national officials considered changes to the Superfund program, intergovernmental relations were a prominent and increasingly divisive topic. In some respects, the debates of the 1990s echoed those of the previous decade. State officials continued to express concern about the financial sufficiency of the program. They lobbied their national counterparts for the elimination of provisions that had the potential to preempt state government authority and for greater administrative discretion. As the legislative proposals were reviewed, however, the problem of intergovernmental duplication and overlap took on heightened importance. State leaders and their congressional supporters cited the states' increased cleanup capacity and recent history of making more progress than the national program as reasons to decentralize Superfund. Moreover, these federalism-related disputes occurred as the ideological distance between Republicans and Democrats increased, and this polarization left the program in a state of legislative limbo as the decade came to an end.

State officials continued to complain about the financial provisions of Superfund. They claimed the states' responsibility for operation and maintenance costs "not only imposes an unreasonable burden on the states, but also provides an inappropriate incentive for the federal government to select lower capital cost remedies that are not permanent."[46] Even though SARA had moved in state officials' preferred direction on this issue by delaying the point at which the states became responsible for these costs, it remained a prominent source of intergovernmental tension. State leaders also lobbied for more generous authorizations, noting their beneficial impact on the states' ability to

---

[44] For more on developments in 1995 see "No Progress on Superfund Overhaul." In *CQ Almanac 1995*, 51st ed., 5–11, 5–13. Washington, DC: Congressional Quarterly, 1996.

[45] Even though the trust fund's taxing authority had expired, it had a surplus that the Congressional Budget Office (CBO) estimated could fund the program through the 2000 fiscal year.

[46] House Subcommittee on Transportation and Hazardous Materials of the Committee on Energy and Commerce, *Superfund Program (Part 3): Hearing on H.R. 3800*, 103rd Cong., 2nd sess., February 10, 1994, 483.

address the hazardous waste issue. In the words of a New Jersey official, "state programs have developed significantly since the inception of Superfund in 1980 and will continue to do so, but only if sufficient resources are allocated."[47] Concerns about program generosity had dogged the Superfund program since its inception and continued to be a sticking point. However, state leaders were increasingly inclined to view additional funds as a way to build state capacity rather than a way to improve the functionality of the national program. This shift illustrates the generation of self-undermining feedback as state governments took on a more active role in cleaning up hazardous waste sites. Well-established programs in a growing number of states, a development encouraged by the law itself, helped undercut state officials' support of the national initiative.

The potential preemption of state policies was a prominent discussion topic throughout the 1990s. Witnesses appearing on behalf of the NGA, the ASTSWMO, and the NAAG repeatedly attacked Section 127 of the Clinton administration's reauthorization proposal, which would have relieved responsible parties from any additional cost imposed by more stringent state cleanup requirements. Colorado Attorney General Gale Norton described the states as "very troubled" by this component of the proposal, taking it as an indication of "the administration's apparent goal of total preemption of state environmental laws."[48] The ASTSWMO "strongly recommend[ed the] deletion" of Section 127, characterizing it as "a preemption of State law [that] may even be a constitutional issue."[49] These organizations continued to raise concerns about preemption once the congressional focus turned to the initiatives put forward by Republican legislators. In 1998, a witness representing the NAAG cited its June 1997 resolution calling for a reauthorization bill that "reaffirms that CERCLA does not preempt state law."[50] The National Conference of State Legislatures (NCSL) used similar language in a letter to Representative Thomas J. Manton (D-NY): "No state laws or regulations should be preempted or infringed."[51]

---

[47] House Subcommittee on Transportation and Hazardous Materials of the Committee on Energy and Commerce, *Superfund Program (Part 3): Hearing on H.R. 3800*, 103rd Cong., 2nd sess., February 10, 1994, 584.

[48] House Subcommittee on Transportation and Hazardous Materials of the Committee on Energy and Commerce, *Superfund Program (Part 3): Hearing on H.R. 3800*, 103rd Cong., 2nd sess., February 10, 1994, 468.

[49] House Subcommittee on Transportation and Hazardous Materials of the Committee on Energy and Commerce, *Superfund Program (Part 3): Hearing on H.R. 3800*, 103rd Cong., 2nd sess., February 24, 1994, 762, 776.

[50] House Subcommittee on Finance and Hazardous Materials of the Committee on Commerce, *The Superfund Reform Act: Hearings on H.R. 3000*, 105th Cong., 2nd sess., March 26, 1998, 196.

[51] House Subcommittee on Finance and Hazardous Materials of the Committee on Commerce, *The Superfund Reform Act, Addendum: Hearings on H.R. 3000*, 105th Cong., 2nd sess., March 10, 1998, 14.

State officials' concerns about preemption merged with a broader debate about program duplication that took on heightened importance as the capacity of state governments to clean up hazardous waste sites increased. The states had long chafed at the centralization of Superfund, so their efforts to acquire more administrative discretion were not new. However, there was a subtle shift in the arguments that state officials advanced. Many of them contrasted the limited progress of the national Superfund program with the achievements of state governments. "The states are responsible for clean-up of tens of thousands of sites that are not on NPL,"[52] explained a state official appearing on behalf of the NGA, arguing that the states' voluntary cleanup programs had contributed to a record of more efficient and successful cleanups. Another witness highlighted site cleanup trends and the fact that 30 states were in the process of developing cleanup standards as the drive for national cleanup standards languished in Congress: "The states have leaped out in front of the federal government, and if you don't catch up, NPL sites will continue to drag behind."[53]

With the states playing a more active role in cleaning up hazardous waste sites, program overlap took on heightened importance. One of the chief arguments in favor of delegating more authority to state governments was that it "would eliminate duplication of effort and, thus, the possible time consuming conflicts that have existed between the state and federal agencies."[54] State officials offered many suggestions that they believed would increase the efficiency of the Superfund program and took aim at provisions that they thought would have the opposite effect. They felt that the Clinton administration proposal was a mixed bag, praising its delegation of more authority to the states but lamenting its inclusion of a site-by-site review of state plans. One witness explained, "That is simply delegating with one hand and taking it back with the other. That's not delegation. That's probably worse than the present system."[55] Testifying at a hearing in 1998, a Massachusetts official appearing on behalf of the ASTSWMO stated, "Our main goal is to avoid duplication as much as possible and [we] therefore believe that if a state is capable of addressing the emergency then there is no need to utilize EPA's resources."[56]

---

[52] House Subcommittee on Finance and Hazardous Materials of the Committee on Commerce, *The Superfund Reform Act: Hearings on H.R. 3000*, 105th Cong., 2nd sess., March 26, 1998, 163.

[53] House Subcommittee on Finance and Hazardous Materials of the Committee on Commerce, *The Superfund Reform Act: Hearings on H.R. 3000*, 105th Cong., 2nd sess., March 26, 1998, 167.

[54] House Subcommittee on Transportation and Hazardous Materials of the Committee on Energy and Commerce, *Superfund Program (Part 3): Hearing on H.R. 3800*, 103rd Cong., 2nd sess., February 10, 1994, 563.

[55] Senate Subcommittee on Superfund, Recycling, and Solid Waste Management of the Committee on Environment and Public Works, *Superfund Reform Act of 1994: Hearings on S. 1834*, 103rd Cong., 2nd sess., March 2, 1994, 245.

[56] House Subcommittee on Finance and Hazardous Materials of the Committee on Commerce, *The Superfund Reform Act: Hearings on H.R. 3000*, 105th Cong., 2nd sess., March 26, 1998, 171.

State officials' push for administrative discretion reflected preferences that had existed since CERCLA had been enacted in 1980. At that time, however, the states had little experience cleaning up hazardous waste sites and lacked the financial wherewithal to make large investments in building that capacity. Nearly two decades later, the situation had changed. While advancing a similar set of arguments, state officials could point to a record of accomplishments that, they contended, exceeded that of the national Superfund program. They could claim, in the words of a NAAG resolution, "Many state cleanup programs have proven effective in achieving cleanup, yet the CERCLA program fails to use state resources effectively."[57] The gist of their administrative argument was summarized by J. Winston Porter, president of the Waste Policy Institute, who told a Senate subcommittee in 1994, "The only way I know to fix Superfund is to delegate most of the action to the states ... If you want to get this program moving, let the states do it."[58] Such a policy prescription would have been unthinkable during the early years of the program, when various economic and institutional constraints limited states' efforts to clean up hazardous waste sites.

Democrats and Republicans in Congress recognized the need for Superfund reform and described the program's performance as unacceptable, but their conflicting opinions about the appropriate role of state governments helped stall every piece of legislation that was considered in the 1990s. These partisan differences hardened as the decade progressed. EPA Administrator Carol Browner faced hostile questioning from members of both parties when she defended the Clinton administration's Superfund reauthorization plan at a 1994 hearing. Senator Max Baucus (D-MT) expressed concerns about whether the plan would "sufficiently limit EPA's interference with states so that states will want to seek authorization and run the Superfund program."[59] His Republican colleagues pressed this issue more aggressively. Senator Robert Smith (R-NH) said that the administration's proposal included several provisions that would inhibit the use of state authority and would give "the federal government too much room to interfere with state and local decisions [even though the] states ... are asking for and crying out for more flexibility in dealing with these problems."[60] Senator Alan Simpson (R-WY) insisted that the

---

[57] House Subcommittee on Finance and Hazardous Materials of the Committee on Commerce, *The Superfund Reform Act: Hearings on H.R. 3000*, 105th Cong., 2nd sess., March 26, 1998, 193.

[58] Senate Subcommittee on Superfund, Recycling, and Solid Waste Management of the Committee on Environment and Public Works, *Superfund Reform Act of 1994: Hearings on S. 1834*, 103rd Cong., 2nd sess., March 2, 1994, 244–245.

[59] Senate Subcommittee on Superfund, Recycling, and Solid Waste Management of the Committee on Environment and Public Works, *Superfund Reform Act of 1994: Hearings on S. 1834*, 103rd Cong., 2nd sess., February 10, 1994, 3.

[60] Senate Subcommittee on Superfund, Recycling, and Solid Waste Management of the Committee on Environment and Public Works, *Superfund Reform Act of 1994: Hearings on S. 1834*, 103rd Cong., 2nd sess., February 10, 1994, 5–6.

administration's proposal did not go far enough in giving state governments more authority. Echoing the claims of state officials, he argued that it "kind of 'giveth and taketh away' at the same time" and asked pointedly, "Why doesn't the EPA trust the states, with their own approved Superfund programs in place, to do the adequate clean-up?"[61]

The partisan dispute over Superfund intensified after the midterm elections gave Republicans control of the congressional agenda. The majority continued to argue that devolution would improve the program's performance. Some Republicans justified this change by pointing to state governments' enhanced capacities and recent accomplishments. As he described his proposal to allow states to accept full delegation of the Superfund program or the partial delegation of up to six categories of delegable authorities, Smith explained, "state programs clean up similar sites three times as fast at one-fifth the cost of the federal program."[62] His colleague James Inhofe (R-OK) praised the bill for providing states "with the technical knowledge and the programmatic ability to take full charge of their own Superfund program, while reassuring critics that every state will not be forced to assume more authority than they are capable of handling."[63] Democrats were skeptical of this delegation. In addition to warning that the effort to make Superfund fairer and more efficient should not come at the expense of cutting corners or stopping cleanup, Lautenberg contended that "we shouldn't just shift burdens to states and local governments who could be left literally dumped on as we stand stuck in the mud."[64] This line of attack undercut a House effort to repeal the program's retroactive liability provisions, and it was especially potent at a time when the Republican majority was committed both to reducing the budget deficit and to unfunded mandate reform.[65]

In 1998, partisan differences sank two further efforts to reform the Superfund program. A bill cleared the Water Resources and Environment Subcommittee of the House Transportation Committee in an 18–12 vote in which only two Democrats joined Republicans in support. This outcome fell far short of the bipartisan support that committee chair Bud Shuster (R-PA) said was required for the bill to move forward. The Senate Committee on Environment and Public Works also endorsed a Superfund bill along largely

---

[61] Senate Subcommittee on Superfund, Recycling, and Solid Waste Management of the Committee on Environment and Public Works, *Superfund Reform Act of 1994: Hearings on S. 1834*, 103rd Cong., 2nd sess., February 10, 1994, 23.

[62] Senate Committee on Environment and Public Works, *Accelerated Cleanup and Environmental Restoration Act: Hearing on S. 1285*, 104th Cong., 2nd sess., April 23, 1996, 5.

[63] Senate Committee on Environment and Public Works, *Accelerated Cleanup and Environmental Restoration Act: Hearing on S. 1285*, 104th Cong., 2nd sess., April 23, 1996, 32.

[64] Senate Committee on Environment and Public Works, *Accelerated Cleanup and Environmental Restoration Act: Hearing on S. 1285*, 104th Cong., 2nd sess., April 23, 1996, 8.

[65] "No Progress on Superfund Overhaul." In *CQ Almanac 1995*, 51st ed., 5–11, 5–13. Washington, DC: Congressional Quarterly, 1996.

partisan lines, but the bill went no further. Federalism ranked "among the most difficult issues" the committee considered, as Republicans hoped to cede more authority to the states and Democrats wanted the EPA to have the leading role.[66] The Senate bill allowed the EPA to delegate responsibility for the Superfund program to a requesting state or to authorize the state program to operate in lieu of the national program, based on the recognition that "many states now have both the resources and the technical expertise necessary to conduct and oversee remedial actions at NPL and NPL-caliber sites."[67] During its discussions the committee took eight votes, some of which had federalism-related implications, and only a single Democrat voted with his Republican colleagues.[68]

As Superfund's second decade drew to a close, state officials' ambivalence toward the program epitomized its public standing. Most observers agreed that the program had not lived up to the high hopes expressed at its adoption and that it had not made enough progress in cleaning up hazardous waste sites. One state official said of this consensus, "the governors, Congress, the administration, and almost all parties have stated that the Superfund law is unworkable and unnecessarily costly."[69] Making major changes to CERCLA proved to be a heavy legislative lift, however, as stakeholders of all sorts – including state leaders – advanced different reform visions based on their experiences and self-interest. Intergovernmental relations helped stall Superfund reform in two ways. First, the growing administrative capacities of state governments represented a form of self-undermining feedback that caused issues of duplication to rise to the fore and limited state officials' stake in the national program. By creating what was effectively a competing program at the state level, Superfund undercut its own long-term political prospects, especially as states showed signs of cleaning up hazardous waste sites more effectively. Second, increasingly heated partisan disputes over the appropriate role of the states – themselves an outgrowth of partisan polarization in American politics – made Superfund reform even more difficult than it had been during the 1980s. Members of Congress could not surmount these obstacles to reform, leaving the program in a state of legislative limbo.

[66] "Congress Unable to Resolve Differences on Superfund Overhaul." In *CQ Almanac 1998*, 54th ed., 11–15, 11–16. Washington, DC: Congressional Quarterly, 1999.
[67] Senate Committee on Environment and Public Works. *Report to Accompany S. 8: Superfund Cleanup Acceleration Act of 1998*, 105th Cong., 2nd sess., Report 105–192, 1998, 10.
[68] Senator Bob Graham (D-FL) sided with his fellow Democrats on a single amendment dealing with the community role in decision-making but otherwise supported the Republican majority. Senator Max Baucus (D-MT), who had offered comments that seemed to support additional state government discretion in 1994, voted with his Democratic colleagues on all eight amendments. Senate Committee on Environment and Public Works. *Report to Accompany S. 8: Superfund Cleanup Acceleration Act of 1998*, 105th Cong., 2nd sess., Report 105–192, 1998, 97–98.
[69] House Subcommittee on Finance and Hazardous Materials of the Committee on Commerce, *The Superfund Reform Act: Hearings on H.R. 3000*, 105th Cong., 2nd sess., March 26, 1998, 164.

CONCLUSION

In the early twenty-first century, the politics of Superfund are largely the same as they were in the 1990s. Widespread dissatisfaction with the program persists. In a report that marked Superfund's 35th anniversary in 2015, one environmental interest group summarized the situation with a simple claim: "Superfund is struggling" (Beins and Lester 2015, 4).[70] Its travails are both programmatic and political. The widespread sense that Superfund has made insufficient progress in cleaning up hazardous waste sites has contributed to a shaky political foundation that has kept the national program in something of a holding pattern since the mid 1990s. Although reauthorizing legislation has been introduced several times in Congress, the taxing authority of the Superfund program has not been renewed since its expiration over two decades ago. The trust fund's balance remained positive until the 2003 fiscal year (CRS 2007, 9), and as the remaining funds were spent, "Congress increased the contribution of general Treasury revenues in an effort to make up for the shortfall from the expired industry taxes" (Bearden 2012, 1). Any additions to the trust fund are now subject to the congressional appropriations process; annual appropriations declined over 26 percent in nominal terms from the 1999 fiscal year through the 2013 fiscal year, and EPA expenditures of site-specific funds on remedial cleanup activities also decreased (GAO 2015, 12).[71] In addition to allowing the program to wither financially, over the past two decades Congress has taken only very limited steps to alter Superfund's administrative operations despite persistent dissatisfaction with its accomplishments.[72]

State officials' reservations about the Superfund program are one important source of both its current political instability and its uneven developmental trajectory over the long term. Their misgivings can be attributed to certain features of Superfund's design, the timing of its adoption, and the interaction of these two factors. When the program was enacted in 1980, state officials felt that its temporary authorization was insufficient to address the emerging challenge of cleaning up contaminated sites. They chafed at its centralized administrative discretion and at specific provisions that seemed to preempt

---

[70] The report was published by the Center for Health, Environment & Justice, which "was founded in 1981 by Lois Gibbs, the community leader who led the successful fight to relocate over 800 families away from the Love Canal toxic waste dump in Niagara Falls, NY" (Beins and Lester 2015, 2).

[71] Under the American Recovery and Reinvestment Act, Superfund received an additional $639 million during fiscal year 2009. At the time, its annual appropriation was approximately $1.4 billion (GAO 2015, 12–13).

[72] Since the adoption of SARA in 1986, various statutes have protected certain fiduciaries and financial lenders from liability, exempted generators and transporters of recyclable scrap materials from liability, provided financial assistance for the cleanup of "brownfields" properties, and made other changes to the Superfund program (Bearden 2012). While these amendments are certainly important to the various actors they affect, they did not alter the basic structure of Superfund, either generally or in terms of intergovernmental relations.

state policies. The enactment of CERCLA in an unfavorable economic environment weeks before the inauguration of a conservative president simultaneously constrained state governments' ability to implement Superfund effectively and limited the program's ability to take root and flourish.

Moreover, certain features of the Superfund program generated self-undermining policy feedback effects that contributed to its programmatic and political dysfunction. CERCLA sought to enhance the states' ability to clean up contaminated sites, and the cap it placed on the number of NPL sites inadvertently facilitated the growth of state administrative capacity in a way that undercut state leaders' support. The cap left thousands of sites beyond the reach of the national government, forcing the states to remediate these sites on their own and effectively creating a program that sometimes competed with Superfund for scarce financial and administrative resources. As officials in many states gained more expertise in this policy area, they eventually began to claim that their record was stronger than that of the national Superfund program. State leaders remained committed to addressing the problem of hazardous waste, but increasingly they became convinced that they could do so independently of the national government.

Not only did Superfund fail to galvanize the political support of subnational lawmakers; those officials actively worked to move the program in a wholly new direction. In contrast to the political dynamics surrounding both the Sheppard–Towner Act and general revenue sharing, state officials did not stand by idly during subsequent congressional debates about Superfund's future. Instead, they actively pursued structural changes to the program. Their lobbying efforts produced important successes during the first reauthorization of the program in 1986, such as SARA's "minimum requirements for state participation at virtually every phase of decision-making, from site assessment to enforcement and actively managing site cleanup" (CRS 2007, 8). More recently, state governments' increased administrative capacity reinforced the partisan polarization that stymied major structural reforms. The combative nature of intergovernmental relations in the Superfund program helps explain why this attempt to clean up hazardous waste sites remains trapped in a state of legislative limbo.

7

No Child Left Behind and the Politics of State Resistance

When President George W. Bush signed the No Child Left Behind Act (NCLB) into law on January 8, 2002, he was joined by a bipartisan group of officials that included liberal stalwarts Edward Kennedy (D-MA) and George Miller (D-CA) as well as conservatives like John Boehner (R-OH). This political diversity reflected the overwhelming support with which the measure had cleared both chambers of Congress.[1] Republicans and Democrats alike hoped that NCLB would improve the American education system, leading to stronger academic performances by students of diverse backgrounds. This bipartisan enthusiasm dissipated remarkably quickly, however, and the effort to reauthorize NCLB eventually led to the passage of a law that was widely viewed as a repudiation of its central provisions.

This chapter traces the developmental trajectory of NCLB, emphasizing its recalibration of the national government's role in education policy and how those changes were received by state officials and other affected parties. Even though NCLB built on earlier national government initiatives and endorsed a standards-based vision of education reform that many states had begun to implement, organizations representing state officials had a surprisingly limited impact on its initial design. As the law was implemented, however, it placed national and state officials on a "collision course" (Manna 2011). Intergovernmental conflicts arose because the US Department of Education "took a rigid approach to enforcing the NCLB requirements that did not recognize the complexity of state responsibilities" (Sunderman and Orfield 2006, 535). State officials, in turn, chafed at the prescriptive nature of the law and its rigid enforcement and complained that it was insufficiently funded. Political opposition to the law arose in several states, intensified over time, and took various forms. The virulent opposition of state lawmakers, who

[1] The House agreed to the conference report in a 381–41 vote, while the Senate vote was 87–10.

historically have exercised considerable discretion over education policy, prevented NCLB from taking root and rendered it unstable.

Policy design, timing, and their interaction spurred NCLB to generate self-undermining feedback effects among state officials and other groups. The education law's "highly qualified" teacher requirements, strict testing regime, and rigid sequence of interventions for schools and districts that failed to make adequate yearly progress limited state governments' administrative discretion. These mandates took effect "at a time when the financial resources available to fund needed programs [were] sorely lacking" due to an economic recession and increased spending on public safety following the attacks of September 11, 2001 (Goertz 2005, 86). NCLB included a temporary infusion of additional funding, but it neither kept pace with inflation nor headed off concerns that the law represented an unfunded mandate. Other key constituencies, particularly teacher unions, shared state officials' reservations about NCLB's fiscal impact, establishing a coalition that was united by its interest in challenging, and not preserving, the law. Importantly, NCLB was itself a reauthorization of the Elementary and Secondary Education Act (ESEA), and it was scheduled to expire on September 30, 2007. This temporary authorization encouraged policy updating and opened up a window for policy change that state officials and other constituencies attempted to exploit (Adler and Wilkerson 2012; Kingdon 1995). As their frustration rose, state officials proposed major changes to NCLB and actively worked to undermine it through the passage of state legislation, lawsuits, and the development of the Common Core State Standards Initiative. This panoply of state-led efforts helped prevent NCLB from becoming an entrenched component of American education policy.

STANDARDS-BASED REFORM AND THE ORIGINS OF NCLB

Dissatisfaction with the American education system, epitomized by the publication of *A Nation at Risk* in 1983, helped put education reform on the national political agenda. Proponents of standards-based reform argued that student achievement would improve if education officials clearly specified what students should know at various points of their academic careers and then assessed whether those expectations were being met. As applied to education policy, a "standard is both a *goal* (what should be done) and a *measure* of progress toward that goal (how well it was done)" (Ravitch 1995, 7, emphasis in original). In the 1980s and 1990s, "standards-based reform took hold as the dominant policy idea" in discussions of education reform (DeBray, McDermott, and Wohlstetter 2005, 3). With its testing requirements and its effort to hold schools and districts accountable for student performance, NCLB adhered to the basic philosophy of standards-based reform.

The passage of NCLB was not the first time, however, that a national law tried to move the American education system in the direction of assessment and accountability. President Bill Clinton signed two pieces of legislation in 1994 that established the foundation for NCLB.[2] The first, Goals 2000, was "a revolutionary attempt to promote education reform on a national scale" by providing grants to states to develop their own standards and standards-linked assessments and offering increased financial flexibility "in exchange for submitting to certain accountability measures" (Superfine 2005, 10). The statute provided $700 million for states and districts that adhered to the federal guidelines, but the grants were optional and states were not required to participate in Goals 2000. The second law, the Improving America's Schools Act (IASA), was a reauthorization of the ESEA. It conditioned receipt of Title I funds on the enactment of standards-based assessments but preserved "considerable [state] discretion over how to define annual yearly progress and what to do if schools or districts failed to achieve it" (DeBray, McDermott, and Wohlstetter 2005, 6). The reforms embodied in the IASA were an important development, but they also were "largely toothless and unenforced" (McGuinn 2005, 45). State governments took advantage of the statute's inherent flexibility and weak enforcement to mold "the requirements to fit their own policy priorities and the capacity of their state agencies" (Sunderman and Orfield 2006, 532). By the time that President Bush signed NCLB eight years later, fewer than half of the states were in compliance with the IASA.

Even though the impact of Goals 2000 and the IASA was not as profound as their supporters had hoped, state officials did not object to the thrust of the reforms. Their general acceptance of the laws is illustrated by the fact that "only two states vigorously objected" to Goals 2000 (Wong and Sunderman 2007, 348). Content standards in the core subject areas of English, mathematics, science, and social studies proved quite popular, and most states had them in place by the end of the decade. However, states were slower to develop the assessments and performance standards that would determine whether students, schools, and districts were making adequate academic progress. Although change was not occurring as quickly as proponents of standards-based reform wanted, clearly the states were moving in the desired direction.

The election of President Bush, who had made education reform a top priority during the 2000 campaign, galvanized the standards movement. At a press conference three days after his inauguration, the president presented a 30-page blueprint for education reform that focused on mandatory testing, state and local flexibility, assisting low-performing schools, and choice. Even though federalism was a crucial issue as this blueprint transformed into NCLB and made its way through Congress, and despite the states' experience with standards and the presence of a former governor in the White House, the intergovernmental lobby had a surprisingly limited impact on the legislative process. Organizations like the National Governors Association (NGA), the Council of Chief State School Officers (CCSSO), and the National Conference

---

[2] See Fuhrman (1994) for a more detailed examination of the Clinton administration's education agenda.

of State Legislatures (NCSL) did not mobilize to express their concerns until relatively late in the legislative process. As a conference committee began its work in mid July, state education superintendents and commissioners expressed fears "that the legislation will not fully pay for the new tests it requires; that the timetables for proficiency by all students within twelve years are unrealistic, and that they lack the staff to enforce its prescription for punishing low-performing schools and districts" (Wilgoren 2001). In September and October, the CCSSO sent letters to conference members and congressional appropriators calling for increased flexibility with respect to accountability and teacher qualifications. In early October, the NGA sent "a relatively lukewarm letter" to the conference leaders reminding them to consider the governors' views if they hoped to produce a workable solution. In contrast, only the NCSL "became a vocal critic" of the legislation; it argued that NCLB was a "one-size-fits-all" reform that did not properly account for demographic and programmatic differences at the state level (Manna 2006, 121–130). NCLB supporters nonetheless continued to contend that the measure enhanced subnational flexibility, and the protests of state and local officials had a limited impact on the final legislation. One account of the late and ineffective mobilization of the intergovernmental lobby contends that "many officials were not privy to the law's details until after both chambers had extensively debated its preliminary versions, and Congress never scaled back the problematic provisions due to local concern" (*Harvard Law Review* 2006, 896).

TIMING, POLICY DESIGN, AND FEEDBACK POTENTIAL

The enactment of NCLB occurred at a complicated moment with mixed implications for the law's long-term trajectory. The early 2000s featured close presidential elections and narrow congressional majorities as Republicans and Democrats battled for control of national political institutions. Republicans controlled the House and, for the most part, the Senate until the 2006 elections swept Democrats into the majority in both congressional chambers. The absence of a major shift in partisan fortunes during the early years of NCLB's implementation boded well for its potential to take root and flourish, as did the ongoing enthusiasm of the Bush administration and the bipartisan support the law received upon its adoption. At the same time, the early twenty-first century was a period of intense partisan polarization in Congress (Theriault 2008). The vast and growing ideological gap between Republicans and Democrats seemed likely to complicate efforts to reauthorize NCLB as its expiration date approached.

The economic context was less auspicious. Following 10 years of growth, the American economy sank into a recession. Thus the adoption of NCLB occurred at a time when state governments faced an increasingly bleak fiscal environment. Their tax bases deteriorated, and they experienced major drops in capital gains and corporate profit tax revenues. At the same time that the states struggled to generate the financial resources to fund essential programs, they confronted exploding health care costs and the need for greater spending on public safety in the aftermath of the attacks of September 11, 2001. A combination of declining revenues and rising expenditures put state officials in a major bind, forcing them to balance their budgets through a mix of budget cuts, tax increases, and other strategies that included spending down "rainy day" funds and borrowing against tobacco settlements and pension funds. State government spending on education was one casualty of this fiscal environment, as real per-pupil aid to school districts declined in 34 states between 2002 and 2004 (Goertz 2005, 86). State officials struggled to invest in the implementation of NCLB as they faced their most challenging fiscal situation in decades.

Moreover, the economic context had an especially profound impact because NCLB relied heavily on state government administrative systems. The states played a central role in the law's "theory of administration" (Manna 2011); key provisions of NCLB imposed new requirements on state governments at a moment when many of them seemed to lack "the necessary human and financial resources or organizational capacity to adequately meet their increased responsibilities" (Sunderman and Orfield 2006, 526). It was not simply an issue of financial capacity; it was also a matter of reorienting state education agencies to perform tasks that had previously been beyond their purview. Prior to the enactment of NCLB, these agencies had primarily been responsible for distributing funds and conducting oversight to ensure those funds were spent appropriately. Now they were required to make substantive policy decisions about program design. Their capacity to innovate was fairly limited, however, because state policies had to cohere to specific guidelines laid out by the national government. Although the states were already moving in the direction of standards-based education reform, the law "pushed them into adopting particular kinds of testing and accountability policies" (DeBray, McDermott, and Wohlstetter 2005, 10).

In terms of policy design, then, the federalism-related implications of NCLB were mixed. Bush administration officials constantly characterized the law as enhancing the role of the states in education policy, while critics countered that it represented "a major programmatic expansion of federal authority over education" (Wong and Sunderman 2007, 334). These contrasting views reflected how NCLB "contained provisions that both centralized and decentralized authority over public elementary and secondary education" (McDermott and Jensen 2005, 40). This complexity nevertheless represented a somewhat novel approach to national education legislation. Even as the role of the national government expanded in the 1960s and the 1970s, its capacity to "assert direct control over states and localities was limited" (Elmore and Fuhrman 1990, 151). National government intervention was confined to select areas. Early iterations of standards-based reform, like the legislation of the 1990s, were "meant to be inspiring rather than controlling" (Fuhrman

1994, 90). They sought to encourage the states to build upon existing activities. NCLB contained elements of this approach, but it was far more prescriptive than its predecessors.

The central pillars of NCLB illustrate state governments' paradoxical combination of increased responsibility and limited discretion. For instance, the national law imposed a strict regime of student testing linked to state-defined standards in mathematics, reading, and science. It called for student assessments every year in grades 3 through 8 and at least once afterward, a requirement that obliged the states to develop standards and the associated exams. This posed an implementation challenge nationwide, particularly in the 18 states that needed to design at least 10 new exams to comply with NCLB requirements (Manna 2011). Moreover, states had to define the levels of student achievement that would constitute proficiency. This critical decision was linked to a second central pillar of NCLB that imposed new burdens on state governments – the notion of Adequate Yearly Progress (AYP). The national law incorporated an ambitious goal of 100 percent student proficiency by 2014, and AYP required them to make steady gains toward that objective. In addition, NCLB required state governments to disaggregate student data based on various demographic characteristics to ensure that all students were making the needed gains in terms of student achievement, test participation, attendance, and graduation rates. Many state officials "cited data integrity as a major challenge in meeting the NCLB reporting requirement" since "many [school] districts simply lacked the infrastructure necessary to collect the required data" (Sunderman and Orfield 2006, 547). Some states had already devised their own measures of AYP, and discrepancies between national and state metrics would become a major source of contention during the implementation of NCLB.

The measurement and transparency requirements of NCLB, according to its supporters, were insufficient to improve student learning. Thus a third central pillar of the national law was its highly prescriptive series of strict and escalating consequences for schools and districts that received Title I funds but failed to meet NCLB's performance goals. Students in low-performing schools and districts would gain access to supplemental educational services, which imposed yet another administrative burden on the state governments that would need to certify and oversee these service providers. Students would also be allowed to transfer out of schools that repeatedly failed to meet their AYP objectives. Thus, in addition to forcing state education agencies to focus more of their energy on curriculum development and assessment, NCLB gave them heightened responsibility for school organization and management. The agencies generally lacked capacity in those areas. Only one year into NCLB implementation, officials in half the states reported that "they did not have sufficient in-house expertise to provide technical assistance to all the schools and districts that had been identified for improvement" (DeBray, McDermott, and Wohlstetter 2005, 11). Moreover, in some states a combination of economic duress and the "antibureaucratic assumptions" of conservative policymakers contributed "to slashes in professional staff, even as the responsibilities for complex educational intervention soared" (Sunderman and Orfield 2006, 536).

Teacher quality represented a fourth key pillar of NCLB. It too imposed administrative challenges, particularly in rural states. The law sought to ensure that a "highly qualified" teacher would be present in every classroom where core academic subjects were being taught. This requirement took effect during the 2005–2006 school year. It mandated that instructors should have at least a bachelor's degree, be competent in the academic subject they taught, and be fully certified either through passing a licensing exam or fulfilling the other requirements to receive a teaching license. This highly prescriptive definition of teacher quality did not sit well with veteran instructors or teacher unions, and it was especially difficult to implement in rural school districts, where single teachers are often responsible for multiple subjects. Even though the teacher quality initiative was not a major priority of the Bush administration, it was a source of consternation for the state governments charged with its implementation (Manna 2011).

Some designers of NCLB recognized that its provisions would impose an administrative and financial burden on state governments. In fact, during the congressional debate over the law, Republican officials consistently pressed for giving greater administrative responsibilities to state governments while their Democratic colleagues argued that such a change justified a substantial infusion of funds. For example, Representative George Miller (D-CA) said that meeting the lofty goals of NCLB would require the commitment of "significant new resources."[3] Other witnesses, such as American Federation of Teachers (AFT) Vice President Randi Weingarten, echoed this sentiment. She said, "But you cannot just lift the bar, as Diane Ravitch says. You have to put the ladder steps in there too ... we know how to turn around schools. You help us with the resources and with the accountability standards and the alignment, [and] we will do it."[4] Once NCLB was signed into law, estimates of the cost of developing and administering the new state assessments ranged from $1.9 billion to $7 billion (Goertz 2005, 75).[5] Meanwhile, some studies speculated that "the costs of providing administrative support and remedial instructional services to poorly performing districts and schools would be far greater" (Sunderman and

---

[3] House Committee on Education and the Workforce, *Transforming the Federal Role in Education for the 21st Century: Hearing on H.R. 1, H.R. 340, and H.R. 345,* 107th Cong., 1st sess., March 29, 2001, 3.

[4] House Committee on Education and the Workforce, *Transforming the Federal Role in Education for the 21st Century: Hearing on H.R. 1, H.R. 340, and H.R. 345,* 107th Cong., 1st sess., March 29, 2001, 13.

[5] The wide range of these estimates reflected methodological differences and divergent "assumptions about the mix of items on the assessments (multiple choice, open ended, essay), public release of test items, and the extent of test customization" (Goertz 2005, 75).

Orfield 2006, 540). The new national law seemed likely to impose a substantial financial burden on state governments.

The final version of NCLB included a temporary infusion of additional funds that helped consolidate Democratic support. This authorization was neither permanent nor generous. Instead, the national government increased its allocation in the Title I program by about 18 percent ($1.7 billion) and included an additional $900 million for early reading initiatives. These increases in appropriations were concentrated during the first year of NCLB's implementation and by 2005 they did not keep pace with inflation (Wong and Sunderman 2007, 338). These provisions were accompanied by "new flexibility" in how state governments could spend the education-related funds they received from the national government. School districts were permitted to "shift up to 50 percent of the federal funds they receive for teaching improvement, innovation, technology, and safe and drug-free schools among the different programs or into Title I," and NCLB allowed "some Title I schools to use federal funds for schoolwide projects rather than for low-achieving students and authorize[d] a number of demonstration projects that relax[ed] ... federal regulations in some states and school districts" (McGuinn 2005, 43). The increased funds were sufficient to prevent widespread Democratic defections, and the increased flexibility appealed to Republicans. As state governments implemented NCLB, however, congressional "disputes regarding funding levels broke out almost immediately" and undermined the bipartisan consensus that had briefly surrounded standards-based education reform (Superfine 2005, 30).

In sum, the state officials charged with implementing key provisions of NCLB seemed unlikely to become a strong source of political support for the law. Members of Congress chose not to address the objections of groups like the NCSL in drafting the legislation and, as a result, the final measure seemed to possess limited self-reinforcing feedback potential along virtually every dimension of policy design. Most importantly, NCLB required state education agencies to engage in several activities with which they generally had limited experience, constraining their options in the process. At the same time, the law provided a temporary and minimal infusion of additional funds to assist the states in fulfilling their new administrative responsibilities. Finally, NCLB was a reauthorization of the ESEA and would formally expire on September 30, 2007. This combination of limited financial generosity, constrained state discretion, and a temporary authorization was exacerbated by an economic downturn and other fiscal pressures that seemed to counteract the relatively strong bipartisan support that the measure received upon its adoption. Thus the long-term prognosis for NCLB was not promising.

THE STATES REACT: FROM TEPID SUPPORT TO GROWING RESISTANCE

The passage and early implementation of NCLB created a conundrum for state officials. Even though they supported the law's general objectives, they had strong reservations about the means through which it pursued those goals. NCLB embodied numerous core principles that had been a part of state-level systemic reforms for several years. Governors, state legislators, and other subnational officials were familiar with an approach to education reform that included more testing and greater accountability, expanded school choice, better teachers, and enhanced technology. The underlying goals of the law were unobjectionable. As one analysis of governors' attitudes noted, "After all, no governor is opposed to raising standards, closing the achievement gap, or holding schools accountable for student performance" (Fusarelli 2005, 124). Many state officials viewed the new NCLB mandates as consistent with what they were already doing. This basic overlap, in combination with other factors, led them to express at least tepid initial support for NCLB. However, as the administrative challenges embedded in the law gained force and the Bush administration proved unwilling to accommodate state concerns, state leaders became an increasingly vocal opposition force. This opposition, which took several different forms, helped prevent NCLB from taking root.

Implementing NCLB: Early Challenges

NCLB seemed to create new opportunities for some state and local officials, particularly "policy generalists" like governors and mayors, to play a more prominent role in public school reform (Wong and Sunderman 2007, 338). These officials, who generally supported the law's core principles, hoped to use NCLB to leverage change within the educational system. Although they had some reservations about its mandates, they refrained from being too outspoken out of a "fear that open, vocal opposition to NCLB will result in retribution from Washington, with loss of federal funds to states" (Fusarelli 2005, 125). The law had been a top priority of the president, and when he signed it into law in early 2002 his public approval rating hovered between 80 and 90 percent. Outright hostility to NCLB therefore seemed to be an unwise approach to modifying a law whose fundamental goals they shared.

The administrative challenges of implementing NCLB nevertheless remained cause for concern. State leaders fretted about the interaction of preexisting state policies and new NCLB requirements as well as their capacity to fulfill the law's demanding testing and accountability provisions. Paul Manna (2011, 43) explains, "Even early in 2002, state systems leaders worried that once they and their federal counterparts began implementing NCLB, the ensuing collisions would be counterproductive rather than transformative." Comments from Secretary of Education Rod Paige, who publicly declared that the administration would not be willing to accommodate any state waiver requests, seemed to foreshadow heightened intergovernmental tensions during the law's implementation.

State officials' concerns came to the fore in September when the Senate Committee on Health, Education, Labor, and Pensions held a hearing on the implementation of Title I. Subnational officials raised such issues as flexibility, capacity, and funding during their testimony. The Commissioner of Education from Colorado, a state which achieved "full implementation" of the IASA and had embraced standards-based reform, expressed his hope that national lawmakers would be flexible and work closely with states during the implementation process.[6] He also submitted a letter from his assistant commissioner; it advocated giving states flexibility "to develop AYP processes and procedures that are consistent with and philosophically aligned to the value-added, longitudinal approach to assessing student achievement."[7] Flexibility was a key concern for many state leaders whose "quarrel with NCLB was not that they were being forced to enact performance accountability policies for education but instead that they were being pressed to change their existing performance accountability policies, which they believed were better tailored to state conditions" (McDermott 2011, 8).

During their testimony, the Secretary of Education from Virginia and the Executive Director of the Council of Great City Schools emphasized capacity and funding. The former called capacity "the most significant" challenge to providing public school choice, particularly in urban and rural areas.[8] The city official explained that many "cities simply do not have the capacity [to provide public school choice] because so many of the schools are overcrowded already."[9] Both witnesses also asked the Bush administration and Congress to provide additional funds to ensure the success of NCLB, with the Virginia official pointing specifically to the three grades in which the state would have to develop new assessments. She noted that the need for additional national government funds was "especially critical in light of the current budget shortfalls we are facing at the State level."[10] Her colleague made a very similar point, explaining that the "extraordinary pressure" being placed on city officials through NCLB was being exacerbated by "the budgetary cutbacks that we have experienced over the last year or so ... [O]n overage, our cities have taken budget cuts of anywhere between 10 and 15 percent of their operating budgets."[11] These requests highlight the interactive impact of policy design and timing. Subnational lawmakers already had reservations

[6] Senate Committee on Health, Education, Labor, and Pensions, *Successful Implementation of Title I: State and Local Perspectives*, 107th Cong., 2nd sess., September 10, 2002, 8.
[7] Senate Committee on Health, Education, Labor, and Pensions, *Successful Implementation of Title I: State and Local Perspectives*, 107th Cong., 2nd sess., September 10, 2002, 36.
[8] Senate Committee on Health, Education, Labor, and Pensions, *Successful Implementation of Title I: State and Local Perspectives*, 107th Cong., 2nd sess., September 10, 2002, 5.
[9] Senate Committee on Health, Education, Labor, and Pensions, *Successful Implementation of Title I: State and Local Perspectives*, 107th Cong., 2nd sess., September 10, 2002, 76.
[10] Senate Committee on Health, Education, Labor, and Pensions, *Successful Implementation of Title I: State and Local Perspectives*, 107th Cong., 2nd sess., September 10, 2002, 6.
[11] Senate Committee on Health, Education, Labor, and Pensions, *Successful Implementation of Title I: State and Local Perspectives*, 107th Cong., 2nd sess., September 10, 2002, 76.

about the fiscal impact of NCLB's mandates, and those pressures only grew as their fiscal predicaments worsened. At least some members of the Senate committee were sympathetic to their plight. Committee Chair Edward Kennedy (D-MA) described the Bush administration's education budget proposal as "inadequate to today's challenges," noting that "even since it was submitted, State budget crises have forced over $10 billion in cuts in education."[12] Even though the testimony at this hearing did not represent a frontal assault on NCLB by subnational officials, it foreshadowed the stronger resistance that was to come.

Moreover, the congressional testimony cited in the previous paragraphs was emblematic of the general mobilization of the intergovernmental lobby. Different groups of state lawmakers, some working through professional associations, expressed deep concerns about NCLB and its implementation. In February 2003, only 13 months after the law had been signed, the NGA released a bipartisan policy statement that described it as an "unfunded mandate and called for greater flexibility and additional funding to support the program" (Wong and Sunderman 2007, 343). State legislators issued a similar call, arguing that the increased funds allocated by NCLB were insufficient to implement its numerous requirements or to meet its ambitious objective to bring all American schoolchildren to academic proficiency. State officials' financial concerns were not shared by their constituents, who continued to support the law.[13] Thus the growing opposition of state government elites cannot be attributed to electoral incentives.

Other constituencies agreed with state officials that NCLB was an unfunded mandate. As a result, the financial provisions of the law encouraged the formation of a coalition that sought to undermine, rather than reinforce, NCLB. The NCSL commissioned a law firm to investigate how states might challenge the measure as an unfunded mandate (McDermott and Jensen 2005,

---

[12] Senate Committee on Health, Education, Labor, and Pensions, *Successful Implementation of Title I: State and Local Perspectives*, 107th Cong., 2nd sess., September 10, 2002, 1.

[13] A January 2003 survey conducted by Lake Snell Perry & Associates on behalf of Public Education Network, Education Week revealed that public support for the law did not change when the funding issue was brought to respondents' attention. Approximately 75 percent of respondents said that schools would need "more money" to meet the requirements of NCLB. When asked whose responsibility this increased funding should be, 42 percent of respondents said "the federal government," 24 percent said "the state government," 12 percent said "the local government," and 18 percent said "all of the above." Half of the respondents were asked to characterize their support for NCLB after being informed that "the federal government did not provide full funding to the states for the law's requirements." The law retained strong support, with 28 percent of respondents saying they "strongly favor" the law, 30 percent saying they "not so strongly favor" the law, 12 percent saying they "not so strongly oppose" the law, and 11 percent saying they "strongly oppose" the law. The survey relied on a national sample of registered voters, was based on 1,050 telephone interviews, and included oversamples of African Americans and Latinos. The results reported here are "weighted to be representative of a national registered voter population."

51). Other stakeholder groups, most notably the National Education Association (NEA), were also interested in this possibility. The nation's largest teacher union, the NEA had remained neutral on NCLB as it was debated in Congress. However, its concerns about the underfunding of the law and about the law's overreliance on standardized testing as an accountability measure led the organization to oppose NCLB strongly and to become more outspoken in its opposition. At its national convention in the summer of 2003, NEA president Reg Weaver announced the organization's "intention to find a plaintiff state to sue the federal government, characterizing NCLB as an unfunded mandate" (DeBray, McDermott, and Wohlstetter 2005, 16).[14] Such a legal challenge did not occur until after the November 2004 presidential election, but open discussions of this possibility hinted at the growing coalition of professional associations with an interest in challenging the new statute. By bringing potential opponents together, NCLB undercut its own long-term political prospects.

State-level concern about the implementation of NCLB was not limited to its financial impact; it was also about flexibility and the application of particular provisions. For example, as NCLB was implemented, more schools were identified as falling short of its AYP standards. The standards applied to special needs students, such as English language learners and students with disabilities. During the 2003–2004 academic year, "nearly one fourth of school districts reported they had at least one school that did not make AYP on the basis of one subgroup" (Goertz 2005, 80). State officials therefore desired flexibility in the subgroup accountability provisions of the law, which was one component of their broader hope for less rigidity in both the measurement of student progress and the sanctions applied when such progress did not materialize. Even though NCLB advocates touted flexibility as one of its key features, many state officials felt that the law did not live up to its promise. Looking back on the early years of NCLB implementation, one of them complained: "We were soon to learn, however, that the flexibility existed more in theory than in application."[15]

Major change was not forthcoming, however, forcing state policymakers to express their frustration in numerous ways. In March 2004, the "chief state school officers from fifteen states sent Education Secretary Rod Paige a letter

[14] In May 2003, the NEA launched a new organization, called Communities for Quality Education, whose goal was to alter NCLB and secure additional funding for the law. A year later, the NEA began running public service announcements outlining its objections to the law's testing requirements (Koppich 2005). The nation's other major teacher union, the American Federation of Teachers (AFT), took a "more considered, and sometimes less predictable, approach" to express its discontent with NCLB, steering clear of the legal strategy (Koppich 2005, 137).

[15] Subcommittee on Early Childhood, Elementary and Secondary Education of the House Committee on Education and Labor, *Reauthorization of the Elementary and Secondary Education Act: Current and Prospective Flexibility under No Child Left Behind*, 110th Cong., 1st sess., June 7, 2007, 35.

asking for more flexibility in determining which schools were making adequate yearly progress" (Wong and Sunderman 2007, 344). At the same time, numerous state legislatures "debated resolutions that declared that NCLB was a violation of states' rights, was inadequately funded, and/or was being administered in an inflexible or unworkable manner" (McGuinn 2005, 59). The legislation appeared all over the country, in diverse states that included Illinois, Maine, Utah, and Virginia. Utah lawmakers ultimately endorsed a proposal that allowed state education officials to ignore provisions of NCLB that conflicted with state law, even though they were cautioned that the measure could cost the state as much as $76 million (Sack 2005). Other proposals exhibited an especially strong form of resistance to the national government that federalism scholar John Dinan (2011a) has labeled "non-acquiescence"; they prohibited states "from spending state funds to comply with NCLB or even participating in the NCLB program" (Wong and Sunderman 2007, 344).

At least initially, states' efforts to acquire relief from NCLB's fiscal and administrative mandates bore little fruit. One observer characterized these efforts as "political posturing about states' rights and unfunded mandates [that] appear to be little more than negotiating tactics to force compromise on NCLB" (Fusarelli 2005, 131). National officials were unenthusiastic about revisiting the terms of the education law. The Bush administration continued to adopt a "rigid approach" to enforcement (Sunderman and Orfield 2006, 535). Secretary Paige refused to take advantage of Section 9401 of the law, which gave him the authority to issue waivers from national regulations. Meanwhile Congress signaled that it was not inclined to act until after the November 2004 elections and that major change was unlikely. The states' unrequited frustration continued building, and it led them to take more forceful actions after the election.

Growing Resistance and a Shifting Response

The intergovernmental tension surrounding the implementation of NCLB escalated after President Bush won reelection in November 2004. One dramatic example occurred the following April, when school districts in three states (Michigan, Texas, and Vermont) joined forces with the NEA and filed a federal lawsuit claiming that the national government "could not force states to comply with NCLB's mandates unless more funding was forthcoming" (Manna 2011, 63). The NEA had hoped that a state, which seemed to offer stronger legal standing than that of school districts or a teacher union, would join the lawsuit. Ultimately, however, the plaintiffs included only the NEA, 10 of its affiliates, and the school districts (Keller 2005). Even so, the NEA's willingness to file and fund the suit highlighted growing and more aggressive resistance to NCLB among various stakeholders. The challenge was rejected in a federal district court in November, after which the school districts and the NEA appealed to the US Court of Appeals for the Sixth Circuit. This legal battle was not resolved for another three years. A three-judge panel issued a split decision endorsing the school districts' claims. However, the case was then reheard *en banc*, with an 8–8 split, before the Supreme Court announced that it would not hear the case. Its refusal to act left the original district court decision in force (Manna 2011, 63).

The state of Connecticut also sued the national government in a separate lawsuit. Filed in August 2005, the state's complaint asserted that NCLB "illegally imposed more than $50 million in unfunded mandates." In addition to illustrating dissatisfaction with the law's fiscal provisions, the Connecticut lawsuit highlights the challenge of integrating existing state policies with NCLB requirements as well as the rigidity of the Bush administration. Connecticut "consistently noted that it has maintained a successful assessment scheme for over 20 years that complies with the basic tenets" of NCLB and submitted a number of waiver requests to the national government. Connecticut wanted to continue its existing practice of alternate year testing, wait several years before administering the test to English language learners, and test special education students at their instructional level rather than their grade level. The state launched a lawsuit after its waiver requests were repeatedly denied. Its court filing blasted the US Department of Education for its "rigid, arbitrary, and capricious interpretation" of NCLB mandates and its failure to issue waivers.[16] Connecticut's legal challenge to NCLB ultimately proved unsuccessful; the lawsuit was labeled premature in district and circuit court, and the Supreme Court ruled against hearing the state's challenge to NCLB in February 2011 (Reitz 2011). Even though the two lawsuits did not force policy change, they nevertheless represent an especially dramatic manifestation of intergovernmental tension.

At the same time that the two lawsuits were filed, the impact of NCLB's strict sanctions regime was becoming increasingly apparent. The sanctions "rapidly deepened conflict over the law" by generating "embarrassing publicity about educational failure for not reaching goals, which many schools and districts soon learned they could not meet" (Sunderman and Orfield 2006, 552). As a result, "opposition to [NCLB was] extensive in its scope and depth" (Wong and Sunderman 2007, 334). Despite their growing frustration with the law's mandates about data collection, testing requirements, and market-based sanctions, however, state officials grudgingly proceeded with NCLB's implementation. A spring 2004 assessment of state implementation efforts based on a database developed by the Education Commission of the States (ECS) identified varied levels of progress across states and specific administrative tasks but ultimately concluded that "the overall picture is

---

[16] The information and quotations in this paragraph come from Soncia Coleman, "Background on Connecticut's No Child Left Behind Law Suit," Office of Legislative Research of the Connecticut General Assembly, July 6, 2006. In addition, the report includes a detailed timeline of the actions Connecticut took prior to filing the lawsuit.

encouraging" (Wanker and Christie 2005, 61). Another analysis used similar language, identifying "striking good faith at the administrative level" (Sunderman and Orfield 2006, 552). Perhaps because of their general approval of, and previous experience with, standards-based education reform, state officials focused more on altering the provisions of NCLB than ignoring its requirements entirely.[17]

The conflict between national and state officials caused some observers to conclude that "the administration was forced to accommodate state concerns or risk open rebellion among the states" (Wong and Sunderman 2007, 334). This assessment probably overstates the resistance among state leaders, as noted above, but it highlights an increased willingness among the Bush administration to move away from its initial rigidity. The first hints of change predated the 2004 elections. As more schools and districts were identified for improvement and political opposition to NCLB grew in late 2003, the US Department of Education began to give ground on NCLB's treatment of special needs students and its deadline for "highly qualified" teachers. Even though it did not change its policy toward state waivers, the department "loosened some of [the law's] key accountability requirements" (Superfine 2005, 31) and "entered into negotiations with states to change their accountability plans" (Wong and Sunderman 2007, 345). This shift began after the chief school officers of thirty-five states had a two-hour meeting with the president and his advisors in March 2004 (Hoff 2004),[18] and it accelerated once Margaret Spellings took over as secretary of the department in 2005. Spellings proved more willing than her predecessor to issue waivers from various aspects of the law. A combination of aggressive lobbying by the states and increased Bush administration receptivity led to a flurry of bargaining that did not characterize the law's early implementation. In the words of Patrick McGuinn (2006, 186), "Growing state opposition to NCLB ... clearly had an effect by 2005." In addition, state lawmakers grew more skilled at exploiting various NCLB loopholes to limit the law's impact.

Efforts to modify NCLB gained additional leverage by virtue of the fact that the law was due to be reauthorized. Indeed, its imminent expiration gave state officials and other dissatisfied parties a platform to voice their concerns that would not have existed had the law been permanent. Thus the developmental trajectory of NCLB illustrates yet again the profound importance of the duration of a law's authorization. As the formal expiration date of NCLB approached, Congress held several hearings on the law, its implementation,

[17] State officials might also have been reluctant to launch a frontal assault on NCLB because the education law still retained moderate public support. Surveys taken in August 2005 and March 2006 found that 52 and 53 percent of respondents, respectively, had a "favorable" impression of the law, with 38 and 39 percent of respondents holding "unfavorable" impressions. The surveys relied on a national sample of registered voters, were conducted by the Winston Group, and were based on 1,000 telephone interviews.

[18] For more on this meeting and its impact see McGuinn (2006, 186).

and potential changes. In contrast to its virtual absence from the discussions that led to the enactment of NCLB, the intergovernmental lobby participated actively in the lengthy debate to reauthorize the law. Organizations representing state officials sent numerous witnesses to testify at congressional hearings, where their concerns about funding and flexibility dominated the agenda. Moreover, many members of Congress signaled their openness to making changes that would accommodate state officials' concerns.

As the bipartisan consensus that characterized the adoption of NCLB frayed, the amount of money dedicated to the law became a key dividing line between Republicans and Democrats. At a special hearing on national government funding for NCLB, Senator Tom Harkin (D-IA) questioned the administration's financial commitment and flatly stated, "We in the Federal Government have not done our share. We put new demands on schools and States, but we have not given them the resources they need to meet those demands."[19] In defending the Bush administration and rejecting the charge that the law was an unfunded mandate, Secretary Spellings acknowledged, "But as a 9 percent investor in education, I do not think we will ever bear the full cost of meeting the requirements of grade-level proficiency by 2014. I do not think that was ever envisioned when No Child Left Behind was enacted. We are a minority investor in education and I suspect will remain so."[20] Her response frustrated state officials, who wanted the national government to spend considerably more money on longitudinal data systems, school improvement grants, and state assessments. The executive director of the CCSSO claimed that the "incredible transformation" sparked by NCLB "came at a sizable, and ongoing, cost to States at a time when many State budgets are strained and when staff within State education agencies has been reduced."[21] Another witness reported the results of a fall 2006 survey in which two-thirds of the states reported that they received insufficient funds to carry out their general responsibilities under NCLB or their duties of assisting schools in need of improvement.[22] NCLB strained state governments' administrative and fiscal capacities by requiring that they engage in new activities; one witness argued, "State departments of education are being converted into assistive agencies where they are starting to help local school districts more to bring about improvement and they need help with this transition."[23]

---

[19] Subcommittee of the Senate Committee on Appropriations, *Federal Funding for the No Child Left Behind Act*, 110th Cong., 1st sess., March 14, 2007, 2.

[20] Subcommittee of the Senate Committee on Appropriations, *Federal Funding for the No Child Left Behind Act*, 110th Cong., 1st sess., March 14, 2007, 22.

[21] Subcommittee of the Senate Committee on Appropriations, *Federal Funding for the No Child Left Behind Act*, 110th Cong., 1st sess., March 14, 2007, 74.

[22] Subcommittee of the Senate Committee on Appropriations, *Federal Funding for the No Child Left Behind Act*, 110th Cong., 1st sess., March 14, 2007, 65–66.

[23] Subcommittee on Early Childhood, Elementary and Secondary Education of the House Committee on Education and Labor, *Reauthorization of the Elementary and Secondary*

The possibility of increasing state governments' administrative discretion also received significant attention as NCLB's expiration date approached. For example, a House subcommittee devoted an entire hearing to "current and prospective flexibility" under the education law. Speaking on behalf of the National Association of State Boards of Education, a Michigan official described how her state's accountability workbook submissions initially earned positive feedback only to be rejected by the US Department of Education. She argued that states deserved "the latitude to address their unique circumstances [and] the freedom to develop and implement policies that meet their specific needs while remaining within the spirit of the law."[24] The President-Elect of the CCSSO issued a similar plea, outlining some of the "areas where rural states like South Dakota have felt most challenged by the rigidity of the current framework."[25] Calling for a "culture shift" that would allow states to base their decisions on sound evidence about best practices and adjust to the particularities of their environments, he argued, "Flexibility should not be understood as bending the rules, but should rather be available whenever it makes the best educational sense for students."[26]

When the presidency changed hands in 2009, the Obama administration seemed to embrace state officials' call for additional flexibility. It continued its predecessor's use of the waiver process to encourage the states to adopt policy changes. The waivers represented one component of the administration's "aggressive push on school reform" that included competitive grant programs, School Improvement Grants, and the Investing in Innovation program (McGuinn 2016, 394). Eventually the administration approved "quite ambitious" NCLB waiver applications from over 80 percent of the states (Wong 2015, 405). However, the waiver process proved controversial because the Obama administration took the unprecedented step of attaching conditions to the waivers that it granted. It released states from the most onerous requirements of NCLB when they agreed to make policy changes that the administration favored. This stance turned a tool that state leaders had previously viewed as a source of flexibility into another source of national

Education Act: Current and Prospective Flexibility under No Child Left Behind, 110th Cong., 1st sess., June 7, 2007, 50.

[24] Subcommittee on Early Childhood, Elementary and Secondary Education of the House Committee on Education and Labor, *Reauthorization of the Elementary and Secondary Education Act: Current and Prospective Flexibility under No Child Left Behind*, 110th Cong., 1st sess., June 7, 2007, 35.

[25] Subcommittee on Early Childhood, Elementary and Secondary Education of the House Committee on Education and Labor, *Reauthorization of the Elementary and Secondary Education Act: Current and Prospective Flexibility under No Child Left Behind*, 110th Cong., 1st sess., June 7, 2007, 33.

[26] Subcommittee on Early Childhood, Elementary and Secondary Education of the House Committee on Education and Labor, *Reauthorization of the Elementary and Secondary Education Act: Current and Prospective Flexibility under No Child Left Behind*, 110th Cong., 1st sess., June 7, 2007, 32.

government leverage over state education policy. The aggressiveness and scope of the reform effort was immensely controversial, as was its circumvention of the standard reauthorization process. Nevada Governor Brian Sandoval, a Republican who chaired the NGA Education and Workforce Committee, later explained, "While waivers are important tools that provide states with flexibility to innovate and to manage programs, government by waiver is a sign that underlying laws do not work and are in need of reform."[27]

Elected officials, the public, and various stakeholder groups shared the view that NCLB required major revisions. Congressional Republicans and Democrats put forward numerous plans to reauthorize the law, continuing discussions that had begun during the previous administration. Lawmakers from both major parties agreed that NCLB "was too prescriptive and had unintended consequences, such as lowering standards and allowing chronically failing schools to continue failing."[28] At the same time, there was strong public support for significant change. A January 2011 poll found that only 21 percent of respondents wanted to "keep the No Child Left Behind law basically as it is," whereas 41 percent of respondents wanted to "keep the law but with major revisions" and 16 percent of respondents wanted to "eliminate the ... law."[29] Meanwhile students, teachers, parents, and school administrators argued that NCLB encouraged "teaching to the test" and prioritized certain academic subjects at the expense of others. State government elites had raised concerns about the law for years; now they were joined by a growing chorus of voices.

Due in part to partisan polarization and the existence of divided government, various attempts to reauthorize NCLB made limited legislative progress despite general agreement that the time had come to make major changes to the law. In 2011 alone, the president issued a blueprint to overhaul the law, the House Education and the Workforce Committee approved three separate bills that rewrote portions of the law, and a Senate committee spent the entire year writing a bipartisan overhaul that it eventually endorsed in a 15–7 vote.[30] State leaders actively participated in the lawmaking process; the executive director of the CCSSO and two state superintendents of public instruction appeared before the House committee and pressed for additional flexibility in

---

[27] "NGA and NCSL Release Recommendations for ESEA Reauthorization," press release issued by the National Governors Association, Washington, DC, February 10, 2015.

[28] "Congress Stymied on Education Law." In *CQ Almanac 2011*, 67th ed., edited by Jan Austin, 8–6, 8–7. Washington, DC: CQ-Roll Call Group, 2012.

[29] The remaining respondents in the survey either responded "Don't know enough to say" (21 percent) or did not answer the question (1 percent). The survey was conducted by the Gallup Organization on behalf of *USA Today* in January 2011. It was based on telephone interviews with a national sample of 1,032 adults.

[30] For more on congressional developments in 2011 see "Congress Stymied on Education Law." In *CQ Almanac 2011*, 67th ed., edited by Jan Austin, 8–6, 8–7. Washington, DC: CQ-Roll Call Group, 2012.

NCLB's accountability provisions.[31] The hyperpartisanship that sank these proposals was even more pronounced after the presidential election of 2012. In 2013, the Republican House and the Democratic Senate advanced "separate, and very partisan, bills" that "were so radically different that the two chambers made no effort to find a compromise position that could be enacted."[32] The parties' reauthorization bills diverged in the three "key areas" of accountability for student achievement, teacher quality versus teacher effectiveness, and targeted support for elementary and secondary education versus a block grant (Skinner et al. 2013). They made no effort to reconcile these approaches, in part because the administration's waiver policy "took much of the pressure off lawmakers to act."[33]

Common Core and the Every Student Succeeds Act

As the effort to reauthorize NCLB foundered on the shoals of partisan polarization, leaving the future of the law uncertain and the states' concerns unaddressed, state officials made an attempt to reassert their traditional control over education policy. The Common Core State Standards Initiative, better known as Common Core, began as a state-led effort to develop a new set of standards for language arts and mathematics that were "fewer, clearer, and higher." Led by the NGA and the CCSSO, Common Core responded to the states' collective frustration with NCLB. During an appearance before Congress, the president of the CCSSO said, "To preserve the project's integrity, it is imperative that the common standards initiative remains a State-led process."[34] Members of Congress, particularly Republicans, seemed receptive to this request as they continued their efforts to reauthorize the ESEA. Senator Michael Enzi (R-WY) stated, "We should find ways to assist States, not require or coerce them with this difficult, but important, work. The development and adoption of these [Common Core] standards by the States are just the first steps in a very long process."[35]

The development of Common Core was a multiphase process during which the NGA and the CCSSO drew on the expertise of a wide range of individuals

---

[31] House Committee on Education and the Workforce, *State and Local Funding Flexibility Act*, 112th Cong., 1st sess., 2011, Report 112–180, 4–5. See also George Miller, "Real Relief for Schools: Accomplishing Effective Flexibility," July 2011.

[32] "No Deal on Renewing 'No Child' Law." In *CQ Almanac 2013*, 69th ed., 8–14, 8–16. Washington, DC: CQ-Roll Call Group, 2014. The article includes additional details about the legislative activity that occurred in 2013 and the specific areas of disagreement between Republicans and Democrats.

[33] "No Deal on Renewing 'No Child' Law." In *CQ Almanac 2013*, 69th ed., 8–14, 8–16. Washington, DC: CQ-Roll Call Group, 2014.

[34] Senate Committee on Health, Education, Labor, and Pensions, *ESEA Reauthorization: Standards and Assessments*, 111th Cong., 2nd sess., April 28, 2010, 10.

[35] Senate Committee on Health, Education, Labor, and Pensions, *ESEA Reauthorization: Standards and Assessments*, 111th Cong., 2nd sess., April 28, 2010, 3.

and organizations that included education researchers, principals, teachers, business representatives, and the College Board. An initial draft was released for public comment, and "nearly 10,000 people responded to an online survey over a one-month period" (Rothman 2012, 7). The final version of the standards was then unveiled in Georgia on June 2, 2010. Advocates praised the rigor of Common Core, emphasizing its ability to "spell out the academic knowledge and skills all students need at each grade level to be ready for college and careers by the time they leave high school" (Rothman 2012, 4).[36] Within 6 months of their release, 43 states and the District of Columbia had adopted the Common Core standards.

The rapid adoption of Common Core occurred as sharp partisan disagreements continued to undermine the reauthorization of NCLB. Members of Congress had been urged to put together a revised version of the law that would give the states flexibility in devising their accountability systems and codify "a new State-Federal partnership that does, in fact, promote innovation in alignment of practice to this set of Common Core standards."[37] Limited congressional progress on this task caused the Obama administration to take matters into its own hands. The provisions of its Race to the Top competitive grant program "all but required states to adopt [Common Core] to be eligible for a share of the $3.4 billion available to support education programs" (Jochim and Lavery 2015, 382). Funded through the American Recovery and Reinvestment Act, the so-called "stimulus" law that responded to the Great Recession, Race to the Top made funds available as state governments confronted a challenging fiscal environment. State officials claimed that the academic appeal of the standards outweighed the fiscal incentive as a source of Common Core's rapid diffusion (Rothman 2012, 8), but there is no doubt that the provisions of Race to the Top played an important role. The grant program awarded states 40 points out of a possible 500 if they adopted the Common Core standards or something like them; as a result, the vast majority of them did.[38]

Even though the Common Core standards began as a state-led initiative, their association with Race to the Top and the aggressive reform efforts of the Obama administration "eventually led to a political backlash ... against federal involvement in education more generally" (McGuinn 2016, 394). The November 2010 elections, in which the Democrats suffered a "shellacking" both at the national and the state level, played a key role because they meant that many of the officials who had signed on to Common Core were no longer in office. However, partisanship was not the only factor that contributed to

---

[36] See Rothman (2012) for more on the development of and initial response to the standards.
[37] Senate Committee on Health, Education, Labor, and Pensions, *ESEA Reauthorization: Standards and Assessments*, 111th Cong., 2nd sess., April 28, 2010, 45.
[38] For more on how Race to the Top shaped state education policy, see Howell and Magazinnik (2017).

dissatisfaction with Common Core. State-level legislation critical of the standards came from across the political spectrum, teacher unions objected to the pacing of the standards rollout and its potential negative implications for teachers and students, and public support dwindled as the standards had unanticipated effects on suburban schools that had historically been viewed as effective (Jochim and Lavery 2015). Legislation to limit or even forbid state participation in Common Core appeared all over the country, and several states rescinded their earlier support of the initiative.

As the optimism that initially surrounded Common Core faded, national officials finally came together to reauthorize NCLB in December 2015. State-level developments helped spark this successful reauthorization effort, which occurred "at a moment when backlash in the states has reached an all-time high, opening up new political windows to strip the federal role out of education" (Severns 2015). Moreover, the intergovernmental lobby actively sought to influence the congressional reauthorization debate. In February, the NGA and NCSL jointly released a set of recommendations that were designed to both "allow for more collaborative input at the state and local level" and "return control over K-12 education accountability and school improvement strategies back to states while providing high expectations for student success."[39] The plan called for major shifts in the governance of the ESEA. It advocated changes in the state plan approval process and the federal waiver process while also calling for improved funding flexibility. These changes aligned with previous policies endorsed by the two professional associations. However, the groups took a more aggressive posture in lobbying for them. As the reauthorization measure known as the Every Student Succeeds Act (ESSA) slowly made its way through Congress, the NGA "fully endorse[d]" it and "call[ed] on Congress to pass this landmark legislation before the end of the year." This formal endorsement showcased the governors' bipartisan unity and marked an "extraordinary step" for an organization that generally endorses broad policy positions and principles rather than specific congressional proposals.[40] It came

---

[39] "Governors' and State Legislatures' Plan to Reauthorize the Elementary and Secondary Education Act," released by the National Governors Association and the National Conference of State Legislatures on February 10, 2015.

[40] The endorsement took the form of a letter sent to the chair and ranking members of the education committees in the House and the Senate. The quotations cited in this paragraph came from the letter, which was dated December 2, 2015 and signed by Governors Gary Herbert (R-UT), Terry McAuliffe (D-VA), Jay Inslee (D-WA), and Robert Bentley (R-AL). The letter was accompanied by a press release from the NGA ("Nation's Governors Endorse Every Student Succeeds Act: National Governors Association Issues First Bill Endorsement in Nearly 20 Years") that was issued on November 30, 2015. The first paragraph of the press release read as follows: "In advance of the House and Senate votes on the Every Student Succeeds Act (ESSA), the National Governors Association (NGA) today announced its full endorsement of the bill. The endorsement is a unique move – one not taken in nearly 20 years – and demonstrates governors' strong bipartisan support for the legislation."

shortly before the ESSA received strong bipartisan support in both houses of Congress and was then signed into law by President Obama.[41]

The ESSA preserved several key features of NCLB while also making numerous changes with implications for intergovernmental relations.[42] Importantly, ESSA represented a continuation rather than a rejection of standards-based education reform because it preserved NCLB's annual testing and reporting provisions as well as the requirement that at least 95 percent of students participate in the tests. Moreover, it continued NCLB's mandate that student achievement data be disaggregated for different groups of students. In terms of the relationship between the national government and the states in the making of education policy, ESSA broke with NCLB in significant ways. Importantly, it was a "compromise package" that "gave states significantly more say in education policy" by "rolling back federal involvement in education policy and giving states greater control of systems for holding schools, teachers and districts accountable for their performance."[43] In its summary of the law, the National Conference of State Legislatures (2015) devoted an entire section to "prohibitions on federal influence" that cited both specific provisions of the law and several "Sense of Congress" passages. Among other things, the ESSA required the national government to cover the cost of all state activities mandated by the law and forbade the national government from endorsing any curriculum or encouraging the use of a national test in reading, mathematics, or another subject. Thus ESSA took away one of the tools that the Obama administration had used effectively in its push for education reform; the national government would no longer be able to attach conditions to any waivers that it granted (McGuinn 2016; Wong 2015). This prohibition had been one component of the NGA-NCSL reauthorization plan that the organizations released the previous February.

In addition to its proscriptions on national government activity, the ESSA included other provisions that represented a stark change from NCLB. The most significant changes centered on accountability, the "area where NCLB was most prescriptive and controversial" (McGuinn 2016, 405). The ESSA altered the process through which struggling schools would be identified, and it loosened the rigid sequence of interventions that states had been required to

---

[41] This statement is not meant to imply that the governors' endorsement is the ultimate cause of the lopsided votes. The internal dynamics of Congress, including the resignation of Speaker of the House John Boehner (R-OH) and his replacement by Paul Ryan (R-WI), played a more significant role in jumpstarting the reauthorization process in the fall of 2015 (Saultz, Fusarelli, and McEachin 2017). The House of Representatives endorsed the conference report on December 2 in a 359–64 vote, and one week later the Senate endorsed it in an 85–12 vote.

[42] See National Conference of State Legislatures (2015) for a comprehensive summary of the ESSA.

[43] "Frustrated with 'No Child Left Behind', Congress Takes a New Path on Schools." In *CQ Almanac 2015*, 71st ed., edited by CQ-Roll Call, 8–11, 8–15. Washington, DC: CQ-Roll Call, Inc., 2016. The article includes additional details about the content of the ESSA and the legislative maneuvering that led to its enactment.

impose on schools and districts that failed to make AYP. In the words of Patrick McGuinn (2016, 406), "The key takeaway here – and the big shift from NCLB – is that federal compliance monitoring of state accountability and school improvement efforts will be considerably reduced ... the feds will have to rely on guidance more than enforcement to steer state accountability and school improvement policies." Thus the ESSA granted state governments more administrative flexibility, addressing one of their central complaints about NCLB.

CONCLUSION

When a national law has intergovernmental implications, state officials' responses to it are shaped by its policy design, the timing of its enactment, and the interaction of these two factors. Like the other policies profiled in this book, NCLB illustrates this dynamic. It expanded the role of the national government in education policy, simultaneously demanding more of state governments and constraining their options as they fulfilled their new responsibilities. Thus NCLB strained the states' administrative capacities at the same time that an economic downturn and other developments caused the states to confront a challenging budgetary environment. Lacking financial resources to invest in NCLB implementation and underwhelmed by the small and temporary infusion of funds included in the national law, state officials repeatedly referred to NCLB as an unfunded mandate. State officials' concerns were among the main factors that helped stall the reauthorization debate as NCLB neared the end of its five-year authorization.

In addition to illustrating the destabilizing influence of a temporary authorization, the developmental trajectory of NCLB also showcases the importance of a law's coalition potential. Although state government elites raised some of the earliest and most consistent objections to NCLB, teacher unions and eventually the public came to share state officials' reservations. Thus the law generated self-undermining feedback, bringing together a coalition that called for major changes. School districts in three states were joined by the NEA as they filed suit against the law, and Connecticut filed a lawsuit of its own. This lawsuit was one of many actions state officials took in their efforts to challenge NCLB. The state-led effort that precipitated the Common Core State Standards Initiative, for instance, was an attempt to reassert state leadership in the making of education policy.

Partisan polarization stalled the reauthorization of NCLB for several years. Eventually, however, widespread dissatisfaction with the law and Common Core contributed to the passage of the ESSA, national legislation "that rolls back the federal role in K-12 schooling in important ways" (McGuinn 2016, 394). The ESSA represents a recalibration of intergovernmental relations in American education policy, but it does not represent a rejection of standards-based education reform. In fact, it retains the testing and reporting requirements that comprised a central feature of NCLB. The persistence of these requirements resonates with a somewhat puzzling feature of state officials' reaction to NCLB. Even as they took active steps to undercut the law and reassert control over education policy, state officials made a good-faith effort to implement NCLB. Their posture might be explained by their previous experiences with standards-based reform, favorable attitudes toward it, or something else. However, it showcases both the complex legacy of NCLB and the residual effects of laws that generate self-undermining feedback. State officials wanted to move education policy in a new direction. Just as their dissatisfaction with Superfund did not lead them to give up on efforts to clean up toxic waste sites, their reservations about NCLB and its implementation did not terminate interest in education standards. This complicated resolution speaks to the density of governing arrangements in the contemporary United States, a topic that will be addressed in the concluding chapter.

8

Policy Design, Polarization, and the Affordable Care Act

In 2010, the Democratic Congress narrowly passed and President Barack Obama signed into law the Patient Protection and Affordable Care Act (ACA) – the most significant expansion of health coverage since the enactment of Medicare and Medicaid in 1965. In addition to mandating that individuals have qualifying health coverage or pay a tax penalty, the law imposed a host of regulations on insurance companies concerning the plans offered, premiums charged, and denial of coverage. Two additional provisions directly implicated the states. First, the ACA expanded eligibility for Medicaid (the subject of Chapter 4) to include all able-bodied adults under the age of 65 up to 133 percent of the federal poverty level. Second, it called for the creation of health insurance marketplaces, also called health insurance exchanges – organizations in each state through which individuals and small businesses could purchase health insurance.

It is, of course, too soon to draw firm conclusions about the long-term trajectory of the ACA. As Paul Pierson (2004, 9) has observed, policy feedback involves "'slow-moving' processes that require attentiveness to extended periods of time." Nonetheless, it is possible to offer a preliminary analysis of developments to date. This chapter uses the book's analytical framework to illuminate the roles of timing and policy design in shaping the ACA's trajectory during the program's first decade.

The ACA did not come into being at a propitious moment for policy durability. With partisan polarization at its highest level since the Civil War (Barber and McCarty 2015), the measure passed despite scathing criticism from conservatives and unanimous Republican opposition. The Tea Party movement gained momentum, rallying to protest big government, mobilizing Republican voters around the country, and contributing to sizeable GOP gains on Capitol Hill and in state capitals. The economy was still reeling from the Great Recession; at the time of the ACA's passage, the unemployment rate hovered at around 10 percent and federal and state budgets faced gaping shortfalls. The Supreme Court – which would soon determine the law's fate – was ideologically conservative by historical standards. Timing alone would suggest that the law's long-term prospects were dim.

The ACA's policy design was more of a mixed bag, however, as certain provisions lent themselves to self-reinforcing feedback while others did not. The Medicaid expansion and the exchanges differed dramatically in their design and therefore evoked radically divergent responses from the states. The Medicaid expansion initially elicited vehement red state resistance, but the combination of generous financial incentives for state participation, lobbying by state-level private interests such as medical providers and business groups, the administrative ease of expanding an existing program, and the enhanced flexibility afforded by "waivers" ultimately led most states to accept it. Indeed, the ACA has yielded the single largest eligibility expansion in Medicaid's history, bringing approximately 17 million additional people into the program thus far.[1] In contrast, the market-oriented health insurance exchanges were relatively uncontroversial during enactment but quickly became a symbolic lightning rod for red state resistance to the ACA. Due in large part to the absence of both strong financial incentives and vested state-level interests, not to mention the administrative burden of creating a brand new policy instrument, very few Republican state officials consented to establish their own exchanges (Béland, Rocco, and Waddan 2016).

MEDICAID EXPANSION[*]

Medicaid emerged as a central component of national health care reform largely as a means of cutting and shifting costs. Indeed, the difficulty of finding a politically palatable way to fund the expansion of coverage had long been the primary obstacle to comprehensive health care reform in the United States (Oberlander 2008). The funding challenge was particularly acute in the economic and political climate of 2009–2010. As the national economy struggled to recover from the Great Recession and the budget deficit approached a record $1.4 trillion, or nearly 10 percent of GDP, health care reform had to compete with economic recovery and deficit reduction on the domestic policy agenda. Moreover, political resistance to the growth of the federal government had reached fever pitch with the emergence of the conservative Tea Party movement.

As policymakers searched for ways to lower the cost of reform, they found themselves turning to Medicaid. Despite covering a population that is less healthy than average, Medicaid is quite inexpensive relative to private health

---

[1] Kaiser Family Foundation, "Medicaid Expansion Enrollment: Timeframe FY 2017," accessed February 1, 2019 (www.kff.org/health-reform/state-indicator/medicaid-expansion-enrollment/).
[*] This section draws on Rose (2013) and Rose (2015).

insurance for several reasons. Its provider reimbursement rates and administrative costs are lower than private insurance, and it contains no profit component (Rosenbaum 2009). However, the single most attractive feature of Medicaid expansion is arguably the potential for cost-shifting embedded in the program's intergovernmental structure, which required the states to share the cost (Sparer 2009). For these reasons, the per capita federal cost of providing coverage through Medicaid is only about one-third of the cost of providing coverage through a private insurance exchange (Rosenbaum 2009).

In addition, Medicaid expansion is less politically costly than most alternatives. Hospitals and private insurers tend to be supportive because Medicaid provides funding for low-income populations that would otherwise have difficulty paying for care. As a state-administered program, Medicaid also has the advantage of provoking less political resistance to national government encroachment than alternative platforms such as the so-called "public option" – a government-run health insurance agency that would compete with private insurers – promoted (but eventually abandoned) by Obama.

Thus, to the extent that there was disagreement among policymakers during the health care reform debate of 2009–2010, it was not about whether to expand Medicaid but rather by how much. Prior to the ACA, eligibility standards varied widely across the states, from 11 percent of the federal policy level in Alabama – or $2,425.50 for a family of four – to 300 percent for certain populations in Massachusetts (Jacobs and Skocpol 2010, 92). Eligibility was also largely limited to specific categories of low-income individuals: children, parents, pregnant women, people with disabilities, and elderly persons. Early proposals floated federal minimum standards that ranged from 133 to 150 percent of the federal poverty level ($29,330 to $31,804 for a family of four). They also extended coverage to a group that had largely been excluded from Medicaid up until that point: able-bodied adults under the age of 65 without dependent children.

Policymakers also had to grapple with the question of how much of the cost to shift to the states. Requiring them to pay their customary share would clearly relieve pressure on Congress to raise taxes. On the other hand, the states were already struggling to balance their budgets in the wake of the Great Recession, and the stimulus funds for Medicaid under the American Recovery and Reinvestment Act of 2009 would soon expire. Moreover, since the states would be critical partners in the implementation of any health care reform package, their buy-in was viewed as essential. Congressional deliberations reflected this trade-off. For instance, the Senate Finance Committee's initial proposal had the national government picking up between 77 and 95 percent of the cost of newly eligible enrollees (more generous than the normal 50 to 83 percent) for the first five years, after which the matching rates would return to their usual levels.[2]

---

[2] Senate Finance Committee, *Chairman's Mark: America's Healthy Future Act of 2009*, 111th Cong., 1st sess., September 16, 2009.

As a general matter of principle, the nation's governors were divided on the issue of health care reform – as they were on most policy matters during this period of escalating partisan polarization. While congressional leaders struggled to hammer out the details of a deficit-neutral proposal, 22 of the nation's 28 Democratic governors signed a letter urging Congress to move forward, noting that "the status quo is no longer an option" – although the letter did not mention the proposed Medicaid expansion.[3] However, most Republican governors vehemently opposed the proposals being floated by the Democratic Congress and the White House. As a result of this internal partisan division, the National Governors Association (NGA) repeatedly found itself unable to achieve the two-thirds vote needed to issue a policy resolution.

However, there was one area in which the governors were in wholehearted agreement: if the national government was going to require states to expand Medicaid coverage, then it should pick up the tab. Indeed, the NGA's only letter to Congress throughout the entire debate declared that the governors were "steadfastly opposed to unfunded federal mandates and reforms that simply shift costs to states" and cautioned that "any unfunded expansions would be particularly troubling given that states face budget shortfalls of over $200 billion over the next three years."[4] Individual governors of both parties also lobbied Congress and the White House and made media appearances defending the states' collective financial interests. In letters to his state's congressional delegation, Haley Barbour (R-MS) complained that "the debate in Congress has shifted to finding ways to ... expand the Medicaid program at additional costs paid not by the federal government, but passed down to the states."[5] Similarly, Phil Bredesen (D-TN) protested: "Don't say, 'Well, I can't pass a tax, I'm going to find some way to lay it off on somebody else' ... The governors are obviously in open revolt about the notion of [Congress] just laying it on them, and rightly so" (Sher 2009).

In addition to their "universal interest" in maximizing federal financial assistance for all states, many governors also pursued "particularistic interests" by seeking additional funds for their own states (Dinan 2011b, 4). The leaders of "high-need states" with particularly high unemployment rates and low Medicaid enrollments claimed that they needed additional financial assistance. The governors of so-called expansion states, which had already voluntarily expanded coverage to adults up to 100 percent or more of the federal poverty level, complained that since the enhanced matching rate only

---

[3] Democratic Governors Association, "Democratic Governors Write Congress to Urge Health Care Reform," press release, October 2, 2009.

[4] National Governors Association, "Senate Medicaid," accessed May 21, 2018 (www.nga.org /cms/nga-letters/senate-medicaid). The letter was dated July 20, 2009 and signed by governors James H. Douglas (R-VT) and Joe Manchin III (D-WV).

[5] Representative Mike Rogers of Michigan, "Governors of Mississippi and Nebraska Express Concern with Unfunded Mandates in Health Reform," 111th Cong., 1st sess., *Congressional Record* 155 (October 8, 2009), 24506–24507.

applied to newly eligible enrollees, they would receive less federal financial assistance than states with less generous eligibility criteria. And swing states Louisiana and Nebraska held out for "sweetheart deals" in exchange for their senators' votes. As congressional leaders caved to these various demands and amended the law, other states grew increasingly outraged. In his State of the State address, Governor Arnold Schwarzenegger complained that "health care reform, which started as noble and needed legislation, has become a trough of bribes, deals and loopholes."[6] Attorneys general in more than a dozen states threatened to sue, alleging that preferential treatment for certain states was unconstitutional.

By the end of the summer, state officials' hostility to sharing the cost of the proposed Medicaid expansion was one of the biggest remaining obstacles to health care reform. Deluged by letters and phone calls from their states' governors, a growing number of senators began to express grave concerns about the potential financial impact on their states. Worried about the states' opposition to his top domestic policy initiative, President Obama acknowledged that state leaders had a "legitimate concern" and urged Congress to pursue Medicaid expansion "in a way that is coordinated carefully with the governors" (Young 2009).

Congress ultimately revised the bill to provide 100 percent federal funding for all newly eligible Medicaid recipients in 2014 through 2016 before gradually phasing down this matching rate to 90 percent in 2020 and thereafter. Relative to the early congressional proposals, the final provisions of the ACA represented an enormous victory for the states. State officials' "success in securing this added funding can be attributed primarily to their direct lobbying of members of their congressional delegation who were in a position to cast a pivotal vote on the bill" (Dinan 2011b, 17). Nonetheless, many cash-strapped governors remained "exercised about having to contribute more in due course" (Jacobs and Skocpol 2010, 163).

From Complaints to Compliance

Following the ACA's passage, Florida's Republican attorney general, Bill McCollum – with the backing of the state's Republican governor, Charlie Crist – filed a lawsuit seeking to overturn the new law. The Republican governors or attorneys general of 25 other states subsequently joined the lawsuit. The suit cited a variety of objections, among them the Medicaid expansion's "unprecedented encroachment on the sovereignty of the states." In particular, the suit claimed that it was unduly coercive to require states to expand coverage as a condition of continuing to participate in the voluntary Medicaid program. Refusing the Medicaid expansion not only implied that a state would forego the national funds devoted to insuring newly eligible

---

[6] Arnold Schwarzenegger, "2010 State of the State Address," January 6, 2010.

Medicaid recipients; it meant that a state would be ineligible to receive any Medicaid funds from the national government.

In contrast, Democratic state officials generally defended the law as a valid exercise of congressional authority. Thirteen Democrat-led states filed an *amici curiae* brief with the court arguing that "Medicaid has always been a cooperative partnership between the federal government and the states and the ACA does not change that." The brief observed that states would remain free to operate their programs and determine benefits as they saw fit, within broad federal guidelines, and would continue to be able to apply for waivers to federal law in order to experiment with different approaches and respond to local needs. The brief concluded that the ACA "strikes an appropriate, and constitutional, balance between national requirements that will expand access to affordable healthcare and State flexibility to design programs that achieve that goal."

Legal scholars cast doubt on the merits of the case against the Medicaid expansion. They argued that Medicaid funds essentially constitute a gift to the states, the national government is free to set the terms of that gift – as it does for countless other federal-state programs – and the states are free to decline that gift if they disapprove of those terms (Jacobs and Skocpol 2010). Nonetheless, the conservative-leaning Supreme Court, while upholding the rest of the ACA, struck down the Medicaid provision. Writing for a 7–2 Court majority, Chief Justice John Roberts described the expansion as a "gun to the head of the states"; the majority opinion implied that the states have grown so dependent on Medicaid funding that doing without it is not a legitimate option.[7]

The Supreme Court decision rendered the ACA's Medicaid expansion optional rather than mandatory. Initially, the decision to opt in or opt out was largely driven by a state's partisan composition (Rigby 2012; Jacobs and Callaghan 2013; Barrilleaux and Rainey 2014). Nearly all states with Democrat-controlled or divided governments quickly expanded Medicaid, while virtually all of the remaining holdouts have Republican-controlled governments. This partisan split at the state level is perhaps not surprising, given that not a single Republican in Congress voted for passage of the Affordable Care Act, while nearly every Democrat did (Jacobs and Skocpol 2010). In addition to a reluctance to support the signature domestic policy of the Obama administration, Republican leaders' resistance also reflects ideological disagreement about the appropriate size and scope of social programs.

However, the growing number of red expansion states suggests that partisanship is not the full story. By 2019, more than two-thirds of the states – 36 plus Washington, DC – had voluntarily expanded Medicaid, and the list is likely to continue growing.[8] Indeed, expansion states with Republican

---

[7] *National Federation of Independent Businesses* v. *Sebelius* (567 US 519 [2012]).

[8] Kaiser Family Foundation, "Status of State Action on the Medicaid Expansion Decision," accessed May 13, 2019 (www.kff.org/health-reform/state-indicator/state-activity-around-expanding-medicaid-under-the-affordable-care-act).

governors now outnumber those with Democratic governors.[9] In some cases, including Nevada, Arizona, and Ohio, Republican governors themselves opted into the Medicaid expansion. In other cases, such as Arkansas, Kentucky, and Massachusetts, Republican governors who inherited the policy from their Democratic predecessors chose not to dismantle it. Republican state leaders have been "crosspressured" by various political and practical dynamics that are pushing them toward adoption (Jacobs and Callaghan 2013). Specifically, they have found it difficult to ignore the compelling financial incentives built into the ACA as well as the demands of powerful interest groups (Rose 2015).

First, the ACA's Medicaid expansion gives the states even more powerful financial incentives for participation than the original Medicaid program. Since the national government pays 90 percent of the long-run cost of newly eligible enrollees, states that decline to expand Medicaid are forgoing hundreds of billions of dollars in federal funds (Dorn, McGrath, and Holahan 2014). Meanwhile, the state's taxpayers must continue to pay the federal income taxes that finance the cost of expansion in participating states and continue to bear the financial burden of a larger uninsured population within the state. These financial considerations are clearly compelling for state leaders. In a *New England Journal of Medicine* study of governors' stated rationales for their positions on the Medicaid expansion, one of the most commonly cited reasons for support was that it would save their states money by replacing state health care dollars with federal funds (Sommers and Epstein 2013).

Second, the Medicaid expansion has great coalition potential due to the benefits it confers on hospitals and businesses. With billions of dollars in federal funds at stake, health care providers – traditionally among the most powerful lobbies in state capitals – have pushed hard in states where lawmakers have resisted the Medicaid expansion. Hospitals stand to gain financially from the expansion of coverage because it reduces their burden of uncompensated care. Business groups such as state chambers of commerce have also strongly supported Medicaid expansion in many states despite continuing to oppose other parts of the ACA (Hertel-Fernandez, Skocpol, and Lynch 2016); they typically cite lower employer costs as a major reason for their position (see, for example, DuVal 2013). The preferences of these two stakeholder groups are linked. Hospitals' uncompensated care costs create a "hidden health care tax" that increases the costs that businesses pay to cover their workers; by reducing the number of uninsured in the state, the Medicaid expansion presumably alleviates this tax burden. In announcing their support, business groups have also noted that the Medicaid expansion would relieve some small employers from paying penalties for not covering their low-income workers and would bring billions of federal dollars into the state, creating jobs and consumer

[9] Kaiser Family Foundation, "Expansion States with Republican Governors Outnumber Expansion States with Democratic Governors, January 2018," accessed May 21, 2018 (www .kff.org/medicaid/slide/expansion-states-by-governor-party-affiliation).

spending (Rose 2015). Hospitals face particularly large uncompensated care burdens and business face especially high hidden health care costs in red states with higher uninsured rates, explaining why Republican officials often find themselves crosspressured on the issue of Medicaid expansion.

Indeed, a combination of financial incentives and interest group pressure has led a growing number of red states to expand Medicaid, starting with Nevada. In December 2012, Governor Brian Sandoval – an influential champion of the Medicaid expansion, as discussed in this book's introduction – became the first Republican governor to officially embrace the policy. Sandoval came under intense pressure from a united front of all of the states' major health care providers in the weeks leading up to his announcement. The president of the Southern Nevada Medical Industry Coalition told state leaders in November 2012:

It is not just that health care delivery would improve, but $300 million would come into the economy. Doctors would get paid, hospitals get paid, and we would hire more nurses. If you don't accept the money, then that money goes to another state. We in Nevada would be paying for it out of our taxes and our money would go to pay for Medicaid in other states. (Vogel 2012)

Budgetary considerations were also central to the governor's decision. Upon announcing his intentions, Sandoval told reporters that he continued to oppose the ACA but could no longer defend forgoing federal funds purely on the basis of principle, noting, "A lot of it had to really come down to, what would be the fiscal impacts? . . . I think, when you take the opportunity to look through all of this, at least the fiscal part of this, it makes perfect sense" (Sebelius 2012). Other red state governors such as Arizona's Jan Brewer followed suit, referring to the Medicaid expansion as a "strategic way to reduce Medicaid pressure on the State budget [and] protect rural and safety-net hospitals from being pushed to the brink by their growing costs in caring for the uninsured."[10]

In red states that have not expanded Medicaid thus far, the support of statewide business associations has been outweighed by the opposition of ideologically conservative organizations such as Americans for Prosperity (AFP) and the American Legislative Exchange Council (ALEC) (Hertel-Fernandez, Skocpol, and Lynch 2016). For example, pressure from conservative groups led Tennessee's Republican-controlled legislature to reject Governor Bill Haslam's expansion proposal, despite the strong support of state hospitals and the public. In the weeks leading up to the special legislative session, the Tennessee chapter of AFP ran radio ads warning the state's conservatives that some Republican lawmakers might "vote for Obamacare" (Bacon 2015). During a legislative hearing to debate the proposal, more than 100 members wearing red AFP T-shirts packed the chamber – crowding out

[10] "Arizona Gov. Jan Brewer's 2013 State of the State Speech," January 14, 2013, www .governing.com/news/state/arizona-brewer-2013-speech.html.

Tennessee Hospital Association officials, who had to stand in the back or wait outside. Craig Becker, president of the Tennessee Hospital Association, lamented: "The problem is not many in the public understand the program. They just hear from Americans for Prosperity, the Koch brothers, saying 'this is Obamacare' and they say, 'we don't like that'" (Bacon 2015).

Another factor that has led a growing number of red states to set aside partisan politics and embrace the Medicaid expansion is the enhanced state administrative flexibility afforded by waivers. Federal law permits the US Secretary of Health and Human Services to waive certain Medicaid requirements so as to allow state experimentation with new health care approaches as long as they promote the objectives of the Medicaid program. Since the 1990s, dozens of states have used waivers to expand eligibility to individuals who are otherwise ineligible for Medicaid, to provide services not typically covered by Medicaid, or to use alternative service delivery systems such as managed care.

In 2014, Arkansas became the first state to use a waiver to expand Medicaid eligibility under the ACA. For Governor Mike Beebe, a Democrat, the waiver solved a difficult political problem: how to get the Republican-controlled legislature to agree to expand Medicaid – particularly given that the state constitution requires the approval of a 75 percent supermajority to pass appropriations bills. Although the legislature rejected the idea of a straightforward expansion of Medicaid, legislative leaders told Beebe that they were open to a "private option" that used federal Medicaid funds to buy private health insurance for the state's low-income population (Khazan 2013). Substituting a private program for a public one made participation politically palatable for Republican lawmakers, as it reflected conservative principles, benefited private insurance companies, and distanced the policy from the stigma of Obamacare. A supermajority of the legislature narrowly approved the expansion, which enrolled more than 300,000 low-income adults by January 2019.

Since Arkansas took the lead, waivers have paved the otherwise rocky road to expansion in seven other Republican-led states: Arizona, Indiana, Iowa, Kentucky, Michigan, Montana, and New Hampshire. These states have added to the Arkansas "private-option" model a variety of new provisions, such as requirements that beneficiaries pay monthly premiums or make contributions to health savings accounts, and financial incentives to encourage healthy behaviors. Such provisions help assuage the concerns of conservative lawmakers that Medicaid promotes dependence and the overuse of care. Waivers have thus proven to be politically expedient, allowing conservatives to remain critical of Medicaid and the ACA while pursuing federal funds for their states (Jones, Singer, and Ayanian 2014).

In summary, the Medicaid expansion's policy design lent itself to self-reinforcing feedback by virtue of the broad state flexibility afforded by waivers, the powerful financial incentives it created for state participation, and the political pressure it elicited from private interests within the states. This provision of the ACA also entailed relatively low administrative costs, given that it merely expanded a preexisting program that was already well-established in all fifty states. Notwithstanding heightened partisan polarization and the intense opposition of conservative interest groups, these aspects of the policy's design proved too compelling for many Republican leaders to resist. Although it is too soon to make definitive claims, the Medicaid expansion's policy design appears to be contributing to self-reinforcing feedback. The Congressional Budget Office initially estimated that an additional 17 million people would be covered as a result of the Medicaid expansion by the year 2022. It revised this number downward to 11 million following the Supreme Court's decision in *National Federation of Independent Businesses* v. *Sebelius*,[11] but – thanks in part to the unexpected reversal of many red state leaders – the expansion has already added 17 million people to the Medicaid rolls.[12]

HEALTH INSURANCE EXCHANGES

A second major feature of the Affordable Care Act that directly implicated the states was health insurance exchanges. The Center for Consumer Information and Insurance Oversight defines a health insurance exchange as "a mechanism for organizing the health insurance marketplace to help consumers and small businesses shop for coverage in a way that permits easy comparison of available plan options based on price, benefits and services, and quality."[13] The primary rationale for the exchanges – also known as "marketplaces" – was to pool uninsured individuals in larger numbers so as to spread risk, enhance purchasing power, and thus reduce the cost of insurance. To further defray the cost of purchasing insurance through the exchanges, the law made low-income individuals eligible for federal subsidies. The exchanges were designed as a "partial federal preemption," whereby federal and state governments share power; specifically, the ACA gave states the option of running exchanges or deferring this task to the federal government (Dinan 2014). The exchanges represented the primary mechanism through which the Affordable Care Act sought to expand access to coverage; policymakers

---

[11] Congressional Budget Office, "Estimates for the Insurance Coverage Provisions of the Affordable Care Act Updated for the Recent Supreme Court Decision," July 2012 (www.cbo.gov/sites/default/files/112th-congress-2011–2012/reports/43472–07-24–2012-coverageestimates.pdf).

[12] Kaiser Family Foundation, "Medicaid Expansion Enrollment: Timeframe FY 2017," accessed February 1, 2019 (www.kff.org/health-reform/state-indicator/medicaid-expansion-enrollment).

[13] Center for Consumer Information & Insurance Oversight, "Initial Guidance to States on Exchanges," accessed February 2, 2019 (www.cms.gov/CCIIO/Resources/Files/guidance_to_states_on_exchanges.html).

originally estimated that 24 million people would receive insurance through
the exchanges.[14]

The idea of health insurance exchanges predated the ACA by several decades.
A handful of states had experimented with small-business purchasing pools,
starting in the 1990s, albeit with limited success. But it was not until 2006, when
Massachusetts's Republican Governor, Mitt Romney, signed into law
a groundbreaking health care reform – featuring both a major expansion of
Medicaid eligibility and a health insurance "Connector" for uninsured
individuals and small businesses – that the idea began to feature prominently
in the national debate. This market-oriented reform model had long been
advocated by the conservative Heritage Foundation, and yet the reform also
enjoyed support among Massachusetts Democrats as well as Republicans;
indeed, the bill passed both chambers of the state legislature by a nearly
unanimous vote. Exchanges thus represented "a conservative means to
a liberal end" and came to be seen by Democrats in Washington as "a vehicle
to expand coverage that potentially has broad, bipartisan political appeal"
(Jones, Bradley, and Oberlander 2014).

Not surprisingly, therefore, health care exchanges were initially relatively
uncontroversial among policymakers during the national debate over health
care reform in 2009–2010. Whereas the individual mandate, the ill-fated public
option, and other Democratic proposals were the subject of scathing
conservative criticism, the idea of creating state-run insurance marketplaces
was widely accepted. Indeed, a prominent Republican alternative to the ACA
known as the Patients' Choice Act included a similar proposal for the creation
of state marketplaces for health insurance.

Health insurance exchanges also enjoyed bipartisan popular support. In
a June 2010 Kaiser Family Foundation survey, shortly after the ACA's
passage, fully 87 percent of all respondents – including 77 percent of
Republicans – reported having a somewhat or very favorable opinion of
exchanges. This broad support is especially striking because it occurred at
a time when only 48 percent of respondents favored the ACA overall and just
34 percent favored the individual mandate. The exchanges also had stronger
support than the Medicaid expansion, which 69 percent of all respondents and
54 percent of Republicans endorsed.[15] When faced with the choice between
a federally run or state-run exchange, the public strongly preferred the latter.
According to a November 2012 Associated Press Poll, 63 percent of all
respondents favored a state-run exchange. In keeping with conservatives'

---

[14] Douglas Elmendorf, "CBO's Analysis of the Major Health Care Legislation Enacted in
March 2010." Testimony before the House Subcommittee on Health, Committee on Energy and
Commerce, March 30, 2011 (www.cbo/gov/sites/default/files/03–30-healthcarelegislation.pdf).

[15] Kaiser Family Foundation, "Kaiser Health Tracking Poll: Public Opinion on Health Care Issues,
June 2010" accessed May 21, 2018 (www.kff.org/health-reform/poll-finding/kaiser-health-
tracking-poll-june-2010).

longstanding penchant for states' rights and the tailoring of public policies to local preferences, fully 81 percent of Republican respondents supported this option (Alonso-Zaldivar 2012).

Nor were health insurance exchanges initially controversial among state leaders, whose primary reaction during the legislative debate was to advocate for state-based exchanges with minimal federal regulation. In the summer of 2009, Raymond Scheppach, executive director of the National Governors Association, testified before Congress that "a properly designed health insurance exchange can help correct inefficiencies in the existing health insurance markets and should be considered in the context of other proposed reforms." However, Scheppach noted that the governors felt strongly that "exchange mechanisms should be established, operated, and regulated at the state-level," and that "state flexibility is needed to design the structure, specify the functions, and determine how insurance products operate within a marketplace that has an exchange."[16] Similarly, the National Association of Insurance Commissioners (NAIC) wrote to congressional leaders in early 2010 expressing support for the exchanges, which "could streamline the process of purchasing coverage and make meaningful comparisons of health insurance plans much easier." However, NAIC also urged Congress to "take advantage of state expertise, experience, and resources in implementing this legislation by ensuring that states retain primary responsibility for regulating the business of insurance and that health insurance exchanges be established and administered at the state level with the flexibility to meet the needs of our local markets and consumers."[17]

State officials ultimately succeeded in convincing Congress to give them the option to run their own exchanges. The House version of the law had called for a federally administered exchange, but in the Senate, where governors and state insurance commissioners wielded more influence in the drafting of the bill, state prerogatives prevailed (Dinan 2014). State officials also convinced Congress that states should retain substantial regulatory authority over insurance markets. And after passage, state negotiations with the US Department of Health and Human Services (HHS) yielded numerous concessions that afforded the states additional administrative flexibility – most notably the creation of alternative "partnership" models whereby federal and state governments could share responsibility in a variety of ways (Dinan 2014).

---

[16] Raymond Scheppach, "Testimony – Health Care Reform," testimony before the House Subcommittee on Health, House Committee on Energy and Commerce on comprehensive health reform, June 24, 2009 (www.nga.org/testimony/health-and-human-services-committee/testimony-health-care-reform-scheppach).

[17] National Association of Insurance Commissioners and the Center for Insurance Policy and Research, letter to Nancy Pelosi and Harry Reid, January 6, 2010 (www.naic.org/documents/testimony_100106_health_reform_letter_officers.pdf).

From Receptiveness to Rejection

After the ACA's passage, Republican governors and legislators faced a dilemma. On the one hand, if they established exchanges they risked being seen as traitors by conservative voters and interest groups; although the exchanges were not initially controversial, the ACA as a whole was. On the other hand, if they did not establish exchanges HHS would step in, resulting in greater federal intervention. Uncertainty over the looming Supreme Court ruling on the ACA's constitutionality further complicated matters. Should state leaders act as if the law would – and should – be struck down, or hedge their bets? Ultimately, most Republican-led states initially responded to the ACA's enactment by "simultaneously opposing it and laying the foundation for its implementation" (Jones, Bradley, and Oberlander 2014).

Throughout 2010 and 2011, dozens of Republican governors urged state lawmakers to introduce legislation to establish exchanges, albeit with varying degrees of enthusiasm and with mixed success. Moreover, nearly all governors accepted federal grants for the purpose of setting up exchanges. HHS offered states several types of grants to help defray the costs associated with planning and establishing an exchange. First, 48 states and Washington, DC applied for and received "exchange planning grants" of approximately $1 million each in 2010. Second, HHS made available "exchange establishment grants" to help states set up exchanges, and 37 states and Washington, DC accepted a total of approximately $4.7 billion in funding (Mach and Redhead 2014). More than a dozen Republican-led states were among the recipients. Finally, states could apply for "early innovator" grants to support the design and implementation of the information technology infrastructure needed to operate health insurance exchanges. Although only six states and a consortium of New England states received these grants – which totaled $249 million – in February 2011, the list included Republican-led Kansas, Oklahoma, and Wisconsin (Mach and Redhead 2014).

Outward signs of initial support notwithstanding, many governors harbored a variety of concerns about setting up state exchanges. These concerns crossed party lines, but Republicans felt them particularly acutely. Some worried about the highly uncertain administrative burdens and fiscal costs of establishing an exchange. Others doubted that the alleged benefits of exchanges, such as cost savings for consumers, would actually materialize. And despite the Obama administration's assurances, many doubted that the states would retain substantial autonomy in the operation of exchanges in practice (Jones and Greer 2013; Dinan 2014).

The political landscape began to shift following the 2010 midterm elections, as opposition to the ACA contributed to major Republican gains at both the national and state levels. The Republican Party gained 63 seats in the US House of Representatives, six seats in the US Senate, 6 governorships, and more than 650 seats in state legislatures. Perhaps most importantly, "the fortunes of state-based exchanges underwent cataclysmic changes as Tea Party opposition swept conservative states and exerted a particularly strong influence on members of state legislatures, vocally raising concerns about accepting any federal money or engaging in activities that could be interpreted as any form of cooperation with the Obama administration" (Haeder and Weimer 2013).

Following the midterm elections, conservative organizations escalated pressure on state leaders to reject all aspects of the ACA. Conservative opposition to the individual mandate – to which the exchanges were symbolically linked – was particularly fervent. In 2011, the American Legislative Exchange Council (ALEC) published a *State Legislator's Guide to Repealing Obamacare*, urging states not to apply for exchange grants and to return any that they had received. ALEC also invited Republican state lawmakers to their annual meetings and sent representatives to visit state capitals, where they advocated boycotting the exchanges (Jones, Bradley, and Oberlander 2014).

The lobbying of ALEC and other conservative organizations contributed to a notable shift in the behavior of Republican officials. In February 2011 Florida governor Rick Scott became the first state leader to return a $1 million planning grant, saying he did not "want to waste either federal money or state money on something that's unconstitutional" (Sack 2011). The governor of Louisiana soon followed suit, and New Hampshire also returned part of its planning grant. In April 2011, Oklahoma governor Mary Fallin became the first to return an early innovator grant. Although she had initially argued that "the exchange we are trying to build offers a positive, free-market alternative to the big government, tax-and-spend plan that is the PPACA," she succumbed to pressure from conservative groups and Republican lawmakers and claimed that returning the funds "accomplishes [her] goal from the very beginning: stopping implementation of the president's health care exchange in Oklahoma" (Jones, Bradley, and Oberlander 2014). The governors of Kansas and Wisconsin returned their early innovator grants shortly thereafter.

When the 2013 deadline by which states had to inform HHS of their exchange plans arrived, only four of the nation's thirty Republican governors announced that they would create an exchange; one chose the partnership model and the remaining twenty-five defaulted to a federal exchange (Jones and Greer 2013). By contrast, thirteen Democratic-led states elected to set up a state exchange, five opted for the partnership model, and two defaulted to a federal exchange. In three out of the four states with Republican governors that set up a state exchange (California, New Mexico, and Nevada), Democrats controlled the state legislature; only one state with unified Republican control of government (Idaho) set up its own exchange. Thus, while Republican resistance was by no means universal, the states' response was strikingly partisan in contrast to the bipartisan roots and initially widespread popularity of health insurance exchanges.

This seemingly surprising reversal begins to make sense when one considers how the exchanges' policy design did not lend itself to self-reinforcing feedback. First, the ACA provided little financial incentive for state participation in the exchanges. Although the law did offer the states grants for planning, implementation, and technological innovation, the amounts were quite modest compared to the money at stake in the Medicaid expansion. Nor did the law specify a clear penalty for states that did not set up their own exchanges. Thus, "the ACA provided little in the way of either fiscal inducements or regulatory punishments for not creating exchanges, which means no tempting fiscal 'carrot' or 'stick' is available to sway state officials who may dislike the ACA but face direct pressure to accept a 'good deal' offered by the federal government" (Béland, Rocco, and Waddan 2016, 91).

Second, the task of establishing a health care exchange posed a nontrivial administrative hurdle. Only two states – Massachusetts and Utah – had established insurance-purchasing pools prior to the ACA's enactment. In the remaining states, exchanges represented a brand new policy instrument, and a highly technical and costly one at that. In short, the exchanges had "thin policy legacies" (Béland, Rocco, and Waddan 2016, 64). Indeed, several states that set up exchanges subsequently shuttered them because they found them too cumbersome and costly to operate. According to Larry Levitt, senior vice president at the Kaiser Family Foundation, operating an exchange is "a really big hassle and it's really expensive" (Mangan 2015). By contrast, the Medicaid expansion merely required the states to expand an existing, well-established program to new populations – by no means an easy task, but certainly a simpler one administratively.

Third, and closely related, the exchanges had limited coalition potential as a result of their thin policy legacies. Due to the newness of this policy instrument, there were no preexisting "vested interests, or economic relationships that otherwise could have facilitated federal-state cooperation over the implementation of exchanges" (Béland, Rocco, and Waddan 2016, 73). For instance, hospitals and business leaders did not possess a coherent position on the exchanges; they pressured lawmakers to approve state-run exchanges in some states, such as Idaho, but opposed exchanges in other states, such as California (Jones, Bradley, and Oberlander 2014, 111). This incoherence is especially striking when it is compared to the coalition potential of the Medicaid expansion. Hospitals, nursing homes, and other medical providers had long received Medicaid funds, had a clear financial stake in securing additional federal funding, and were already highly organized and influential at the state level. Thus, whereas the Medicaid expansion elicited crosspressure from "two dueling factions within the Republican coalition: statewide business associations and cross-state networks of ideologically conservative organizations," the exchanges provoked a more lopsided interest-group response in which the opposition of Tea Party groups dominated (Hertel-Fernandez, Skocpol, and Lynch 2016).

In summary, the health insurance exchanges' impact on state officials has been widely – though not universally – characterized by self-undermining feedback. The rejection of exchanges in a majority of states has left the policy vulnerable to retrenchment. For example, states that defaulted to the federal exchange have been less successful in keeping insurance premiums low and retaining enrollees than states that run their own marketplaces, and have been less able to withstand the Trump administration's various efforts to undermine the ACA, such as cuts in federal outreach (Oberlander 2018). These forces have contributed to the exchanges' failure to live up to expectations; although it was originally estimated that 24 million people would receive insurance through an exchange, only 11.8 million people were enrolled as of 2018.[18]

CONCLUSION

State reactions to the Affordable Care Act present an intriguing set of puzzles. Why did so many red states successfully challenge the ACA's Medicaid expansion in court only to turn around and embrace this provision of the law? Why did so many Republican leaders express support for the ACA's widely popular health insurance exchange provision during the legislative debate only to sharply criticize the provision following enactment and refuse to establish state exchanges? And what are the implications of these state reactions for the policy's durability? This chapter has argued that key features of each provision's policy design, combined with the unique timing of the law's passage, can help explain the states' seemingly puzzling responses.

The ACA's timing made it vulnerable to retrenchment because the law "relied on states to implement core provisions at a time both of exceptional partisan polarization and of rising Republican electoral strength at the state level" (Patashnik and Oberlander 2018, 670). Inopportune timing notwithstanding, the Medicaid expansion has shown signs of greater policy durability than have the health insurance exchanges. This variation is largely due to key differences in the two provisions' financial incentives, administrative ease and flexibility, and coalition potential. Even at this relatively early stage, the diverse developmental trajectories of the Medicaid expansion and the exchanges demonstrate the importance of policy design and also seem to suggest that self-reinforcing and self-undermining feedback processes "will frequently flow simultaneously from the same set of policies" (Jacobs and Weaver 2015, 454). Multifaceted effects are especially likely when policies have a "patchwork design" (Patashnik and Oberlander 2018, 677), which certainly describes the ACA.

[18] Centers for Medicare and Medicaid Services, *Health Insurance Exchanges 2018 Open Enrollment Period Final Report*, April 3, 2018 (www.cms.gov/newsroom/fact-sheets/health-insurance-exchanges-2018-open-enrollment-period-final-report).

Conclusion

Responsive States

This book began by asking why state officials greet national policy initiatives with reactions that range from enthusiasm to indifference to hostility. Combining the insights of existing scholarship on American political development (APD), federalism, and policy feedback, it devised an analytical framework that accounts for these varied responses on the basis of policy design, timing, and the interaction of these two factors. The financial generosity of a policy, the level of administrative discretion it offers state officials, the duration for which it is authorized, and its potential to build or preserve a protective coalition all affect its developmental trajectory. Its trajectory is also shaped by the political, economic, and administrative context in which the policy is created and how those environmental conditions interact with its design. These factors help determine whether the policy will generate self-reinforcing, self-undermining, or negligible feedback effects among state government elites. The case studies presented in previous chapters amend the standard story about state officials' preferences, open up several potential avenues for future research on intergovernmental relations and policy feedback, offer lessons for government officials who want to design durable public policies, and illuminate broader trends in American governance. This concluding chapter addresses each of these topics in turn.

BEYOND MONEY AND AUTONOMY

Conventional wisdom holds that state officials want two things from their national counterparts: money and autonomy. In other words, they want programs to be well funded so as to alleviate the fiscal and competitive pressures that state governments face, and they want expansive control over how programs are implemented. By this logic, states should embrace policies that confer sizeable resources and flexibility on them, and reject those that do not. However, the cases presented in this book suggest that the conventional wisdom is insufficient to explain state officials' diverse reactions to intergovernmental policy initiatives.

To be sure, the financial generosity of some intergovernmental initiatives influenced how state officials reacted to them. After Congress created Medicaid in 1965, many states moved swiftly to establish Medicaid plans largely because of the law's generous open-ending matching grants; most states embraced the ACA's Medicaid expansion for similar reasons. State officials reacted less enthusiastically to the capped matching grant in the Sheppard–Towner Act, and they consistently described the No Child Left Behind Act (NCLB) as an "unfunded mandate" because it included a small and temporary increase in Title I funding that did not keep pace with inflation. The fiscal provisions of a federalism-related law certainly affect the incentives it offers and the response it receives.

Similarly, the level of administrative discretion that intergovernmental initiatives bestow on state governments helps shape how those initiatives are received by state officials. Medicaid generated self-reinforcing feedback partly because it delegated central decisions about eligibility and benefits to the states. Governors such as Nelson Rockefeller exploited their policymaking authority to design far-reaching state programs and then defended them from retrenchment. In contrast, state officials chafed under the highly centralized provisions of the Superfund program. They lobbied for major changes and, when the program was reauthorized in 1986, convinced Congress to guarantee the states a "substantial and meaningful role" in all aspects of Superfund implementation. This concession did not halt intergovernmental conflict over the law, however. The program continued to generate self-undermining feedback as state policymakers devoted considerable financial and administrative resources to state-level programs that competed with national efforts to clean up hazardous waste sites.

While fiscal and administrative concerns represent an appropriate starting point for understanding why state leaders' responses to national laws vary widely, they are not sufficient to explain them fully. The precise nature of the task at hand, and its relationship to existing state responsibilities, also matters a great deal. The nontrivial administrative challenge that creating a health care exchange posed is one example; it was one of the reasons why state officials resisted that particular component of the ACA. Similarly, some of the provisions of NCLB that the Bush administration depicted as decentralizing – such as the ability to design standardized tests and determine proficiency levels – required state agencies to take charge of tasks with which they had limited administrative experience. State officials grew increasingly frustrated with the law as it imposed increasingly demanding tasks that strained their capacity, which helps explain why NCLB generated self-undermining feedback effects. Understanding which responsibilities state governments are asked to perform and how those tasks relate to their current capacities is critical.

Of the intergovernmental policies profiled in the preceding chapters, however, general revenue sharing best illustrates the limitations of the conventional wisdom. State and local leaders were a driving force behind the enactment of this policy in 1972, primarily because it delivered large, unrestricted grants with virtually no strings attached. When the state portion of the program was terminated less than a decade later, however, state officials hardly put up a fight. The surprising demise of general revenue sharing implies that fiscal generosity and administrative discretion alone cannot account completely for whether and how state leaders react to national initiatives. Other elements of policy design, such as the duration for which a program is authorized, can be even more critical. Permanently authorized programs are less vulnerable to shifting political, economic, or administrative conditions than are policies that require periodic renewal. Showcasing the potential impact of the interactive relationship between policy design and timing, general revenue sharing was undone partly due to its establishment just before a period of party turnover, federal deficits, state surpluses, intergovernmental tensions over budget policy, and the emergence of a fiscal regime of austerity. It therefore came up for renewal in an environment that differed considerably from the one in which it was enacted. Similar interactions between policy design and timing help explain why the Sheppard–Towner Act, Superfund, and NCLB failed to take root and flourish.

The conventional focus on fiscal generosity and administrative discretion also overlooks the possible impact of an initiative's coalition potential. Policies that bring together disparate constituencies, particularly during their implementation, retain strong bases of political support that enhance their durability and protect them against retrenchment or outright elimination. The diffuse benefits of general revenue sharing, for instance, resulted in an absence of pressure from state-level special interest groups. This lack of political mobilization facilitated the elimination of the program. Other national laws became politically unstable because they sparked opposition from key stakeholders. Growing antagonism from medical professionals helped undermine the Sheppard–Towner Act, and the hostility of the business community contributed to the political instability of Superfund. In contrast, state officials worked with the business community to fight the nationalization of UI, and their efforts to protect and expand Medicaid were aided by support from hospitals, nursing homes, physicians, and insurers. The durability of an intergovernmental program can often be traced to its ability to generate a wide base of political support that extends beyond the government elites charged with its administration.

Finally, state responses to national policies are often much more complex than the conventional wisdom suggests, evolving over time as political actors accommodate themselves to a new policy regime. Indeed, one striking pattern across the cases profiled in this book is the frequency with which state officials' initial positions changed as programs were implemented. In the early twentieth century they weakly supported the adoption of UI and the Sheppard–Towner Act. Once both programs were enacted, however, their positions shifted dramatically. State officials and the business community fought to preserve the UI program, pushing back strongly against any changes that would have granted the national government a larger role. In contrast, their tepid support for the Sheppard–Towner Act shifted largely to indifference as that program faced elimination. State officials' shifting positions also affected the developmental trajectories of Medicaid and general revenue sharing. Their mild opposition to Medicaid evaporated remarkably quickly, and state leaders fought retrenchment efforts in the late 1960s. In contrast, their meek response to the termination of general revenue sharing constitutes a surprising about-face given their initial enthusiasm. These shifts only become apparent through careful analyses of the policy decisions that state officials make in their home jurisdictions and their lobbying efforts in the nation's capital.

In summary, the preceding case studies illustrate several potential ways that policy design, timing, and their interaction help shape whether a new government initiative generates self-reinforcing, self-undermining, or negligible feedback. Design features like financial generosity, duration of authorization, administrative control, and coalition potential affect programs' developmental trajectories. In a similar vein, short-term fluctuations and long-term shifts in the political or economic environment can help or hinder a policy's ability to take root, and long-term changes in governance structures and the American state can determine whether the public officials with jurisdiction over a policy have the resources and capacity to engage in policy development. This framework helps explain why national policy initiatives generate responses from state officials that range from enthusiastic support to indifference to vociferous opposition. These responses depend on much more than money and autonomy.

AVENUES FOR FUTURE RESEARCH

Intergovernmental programs constitute a significant percentage of the policy activity that occurs in the United States. Understanding why, and how, state officials react to national policy initiatives is therefore critical to the study of American public policy. While existing scholarship on federalism and APD illuminates the issues that motivated this book, the preceding case studies suggest that standard portrayals of the relationship between the national government and the states are underdeveloped in several important ways. Viewing this intergovernmental relationship through the lens of policy feedback and reframing how we think about state governments both enhances scholars' understanding of a key element of the policy process and offers multiple avenues for future research.

The analytical framework developed here demonstrates the necessity of viewing the states as much more than a site of important policy decisions.

While the famous portrayal of the American states as "laboratories of democracy" accurately alludes to the policy innovation and experimentation that occurs at the subnational level in the United States and draws attention to an element of the policy process that is sometimes overlooked, it does not do justice to the states' potential impact. State officials are not passive recipients of resources and authority who defer to their national counterparts. Instead, they are major players in national politics. Decision-makers in their own right, their actions can influence the fate of major domestic policy initiatives. The divergent trajectories of programs like UI and the Sheppard–Towner Act, or like Medicaid and general revenue sharing, can be traced partly to the actions that state officials took, or failed to take, in response. In short, state officials must be recognized as stakeholders in national programs. Like other stakeholders, including program beneficiaries and interest groups, they mobilize to defend what they perceive to be their interests. Thus intergovernmental policy initiatives, by transforming the administrative and financial resources of state government elites, generate feedback effects that influence their development over the medium to long term.

Moreover, state officials who mobilize to shape national policy can draw upon resources that other political actors lack. The American constitutional system grants them a key role in the selection and composition of the national government. These political safeguards of federalism help them gain access to their counterparts in the nation's capital, either individually or through the professional organizations that represent their collective interests. This "intergovernmental lobby" is a powerful force in national politics, testifying at congressional hearings and lobbying the executive branch in an effort to shape, or reshape, public policy. Existing federalism scholarship isolates the origins of the intergovernmental lobby and offers numerous illustrations of its influence (Cammisa 1995; Haider 1974; Herian 2011; Marbach and Leckrone 2002). These studies possess considerable merits, but their general focus on the adoption of specific policies renders them incomplete. It is absolutely essential to look beyond the dramatic moment of adoption and to assess whether and how public policies reshape politics. The case studies presented in this book illustrate how postenactment policy feedback effects and the shifting positions of state officials can shape the long-term durability and sustainability of national initiatives.

The combined impact of policy design, timing, and their interaction help explain state officials' varied responses to national policies, and this analytical framework offers a broader set of lessons for the study of intergovernmental relations in the United States. The most important lesson is to approach sweeping generalizations about the nature of American federalism with considerable skepticism. For example, efforts to define the relationship between the national government and the states have led scholars to identify different historical eras in which this relationship was either autonomous, cooperative, or uncooperative. As previous chapters make clear, however, timing alone offers an insufficient explanation. Indeed, this book has identified cases of state cooperation, conflict, and indifference throughout the past century, contradicting the notion of a chronological evolution among discrete periods of "dual," "cooperative," and "uncooperative" federalism.

The divergent postenactment development of the Medicaid expansion and the exchanges showcase how state officials' responses to national policy initiatives are shaped by the design of those programs. The two provisions of the ACA were established at precisely the same moment, implying that this variation cannot be attributed to the differences that characterize different eras of American federalism. The broad temporal conceptualizations that emerge from the scholarly literature on intergovernmental relations in the United States cannot explain why state officials greet some national initiatives with enthusiasm and others with either indifference or hostility.

At the same time, however, intergovernmental relations in the United States are not simply an endogenous matter of policy design. The conjuncture between temporal dynamics and the design of a policy helps explain why similar intergovernmental policies that were enacted at different historical moments evolve in distinct ways. Their developmental paths differ because policy designs that are conducive to self-reinforcing feedback effects at a given moment in time will have different implications once the political, economic, and administrative context changes. Neither policy design nor timing alone is sufficient to explain these differences.

With its emphasis on conjunctures, this book's analytical framework integrates a recent trend in APD scholarship into the study of federalism. The study of APD has moved away from efforts to describe the broad contours of the "American state" in recent years, instead adopting a nuanced approach that recognizes the complexity and layered nature of the American political system. Karen Orren and Stephen Skowronek (2004, 113) use the terms "multiple-orders-in-action" and "intercurrence" to highlight how policy development in the United States follows a range of paths. The existence of multiple orders is also apparent in the evolution of American public policy, which is characterized by a striking range of policy tools and regimes. Existing programs vary in the level of authority they grant to bureaucrats. And as federalism scholars have long recognized, some public policies are highly centralized while others devolve more responsibility to the states (McCann 2016). These differences are not limited to policies established at different historical moments. As the preceding case studies reveal, policies may represent different logics or employ different approaches even if they are created at around the same time. Importantly, these logics and approaches interact with broader contextual changes in ways that shape their long-term political fortunes (Finegold and Skocpol 1995; Mettler 1998; Lieberman 1998). The analytical framework outlined here therefore opens up a valuable line of communication between APD scholarship and the study of federalism, two distinct areas of the American politics subfield that have evolved largely along separate lines.

At the same time, the book's focus on federalism offers several lessons for the study of policy feedback. The first is a reminder of the varied forms that feedback effects can take. Many canonical examples of programs that generated self-reinforcing feedback, such as Social Security, expanded dramatically. Medicaid is a good example of this standard dynamic. It is important to acknowledge, however, that self-reinforcing feedback does not necessarily imply programmatic expansion. It simply means that the status quo becomes entrenched because of its ability to "produce social effects that reinforce [its] own stability" (Pierson 2005, 37). Stability and the foreclosure of potential alternatives that once were viable are the hallmarks of a self-reinforcing process. The UI case study, which illustrates how state officials and the business community worked to limit the generosity of the program, provides an example of this dynamic.

More broadly, the preceding case studies demonstrate that scholars of policy feedback must examine a wider range of outcomes. Early studies offered many persuasive illustrations of self-reinforcing feedback effects, which developed and validated a concept that is now central to the study of the policy process. Following the advice of several scholars (Patashnik and Zelizer 2013; Campbell 2012; Patashnik 2008; Jacobs and Weaver 2015; Weaver 2010), this book cast a wider net. In addition to examining policies that reshaped politics in ways that contributed to their long-term stability, it investigated other policies that sowed the seeds of their own demise or that generated negligible feedback effects. This variation allowed it to address a longstanding gap in existing research, namely, an inability to outline the conditions that are conducive to the generation of policy feedback (Pierson 2006). Just as individuals' political beliefs and behaviors may or may not be influenced by their interactions with a particular program, government elites may or may not mobilize to preserve, eliminate, expand, or retrench a given policy. The previous chapters suggest that their calculus will be affected by specific dimensions of policy design and timing. As national policies implicate the states across a growing range of policy arenas, the framework offered here can help identify which of them are likely to endure and flourish.

Indeed, the wide range of contemporary intergovernmental policy initiatives provides a dizzying array of possibilities for future research on feedback effects among state government officials. As Chapter 1 explained, the policies investigated in this book were chosen because they vary in theoretically significant ways. Extending the analysis presented here to the study of new policy arenas represents a potentially fruitful direction for future research. The relationship between the national government and the states has influenced the evolution of abortion policy, marijuana regulation, immigration policy, gun control, and many other issues. Developments in these fields offer new permutations of the design and temporal factors highlighted by our analytical framework, permitting an extension of the analysis advanced here. Moreover, they also represent an analytical opportunity to extend our framework to a broader range of policy tools. Virtually all of the intergovernmental initiatives that appeared in previous chapters incorporated some sort of financial incentive to induce state government activity. While this shared design feature facilitated comparability across our cases, intergovernmental policies rely on many other approaches. For instance, the REAL ID Act of 2005 required states to adopt standardized procedures and formats for driver's licenses and other forms of identification. The prescriptive nature of these requirements provoked widespread opposition at the state level, and it appears that "social advocacy coalitions and state associations played important roles in facilitating and leading state resistance" (Regan and Deering 2009, 476). The gradual evaporation of this controversy as more state governments became complaint with the REAL ID Act reveals how stakeholders' initial reactions to intergovernmental policies can shift over time. Similarly, the Tax Cut and Jobs Act of 2017 placed an unprecedented cap on the state and local tax deduction – another policy tool not analyzed in this book. This tax policy change took place over the objections of many state officials, especially those in jurisdictions with high income and property taxes.

In addition, with its macro-level perspective and emphasis on the emergence and relative durability of federalism-related initiatives, the book demonstrates the analytical leverage that can be gained by reorienting policy feedback research. Politicians and program administrators initially played a central role in this line of study but have largely been superseded by a focus on mass publics. Reviving the study of elite feedback effects will provide a more balanced view of how policies remake politics. Moreover, it opens up additional potentially constructive avenues for future research. Most fundamentally, the state officials emphasized in this book represent a broader class of actors – government elites – who merit a more prominent place in the literature. Assessing whether and how public policies alter the resources, incentives, and perceptions of public officials need not be limited to governors, state legislators, state attorneys general, and other subnational actors. The American political system is unusually fragmented, distributing governing authority among a wide range of actors and institutional settings. As scholars move from the illustration of feedback effects to broader questions about the conditions that are conducive to their generation, returning to the study of political elites of various sorts has the potential to further their understanding of the many critical ways in which policies remake politics.

Another possibility is to examine the relationship between policy feedback effects at the elite and mass levels. The preceding case studies treated them independently, often using public opinion polls to buttress the argument that state officials' positions could be attributed to policy design rather than to the views of the constituents they represented. This general strategy makes it easier to identify the existence of elite feedback effects and to trace them to specific features of a policy. However, it overlooks possible interactions between elite and mass reactions to the same policy initiative. For instance, the Social Security program generated self-reinforcing feedback effects among government elites (Derthick 1979), mass publics (Campbell 2003a), and the interest group community (Walker 1991), which suggests the value of bridging this scholarly divide and granting these potential interactions a more prominent place in feedback-related work. Policies that directly implicate race, for instance, seem especially likely to generate feedback at both the mass and the elite level; investigating their development might reveal whether and how feedback effects differ for public and private actors (Gilens 1999; Soss 1999).

Other promising avenues for future research grow out of the specific institutional domain on which this book focuses, namely, American federalism. The case studies emphasize state officials' common tendencies in responding to national policies, examining their collective lobbying activities as well as the policy changes they adopted in their home jurisdictions. Even though this focus on commonalities is appropriate for identifying the existence and direction of feedback effects, it fails to leverage a central methodological advantage of studying state policy choices – interstate variation in policy adoption and design. The states represent a suitable venue in which to analyze diverse political phenomena because they offer a combination of underlying similarity and manageable variation that makes it possible to evaluate causal relationships in a valid way (Mooney 2001; Jewell 1982; Brace and Jewett 1995). When state officials' responses to national initiatives diverge, this variation may lead to different feedback dynamics across the states. At the individual level, for example, the geography of federalism seems to influence the impact of Medicaid enrollment on political participation patterns (Michener 2018; Clinton and Sances 2018). State-level policy variation can have a similar effect on the mobilization of both key stakeholder groups and the elites charged with administering existing programs. The relative entrenchment of a policy, and the ease with which it can be modified or eliminated, may depend on the state under consideration (Karch and Cravens 2014). In summary, diverse state responses to national laws represent an analytical opportunity to identify the conditions that are especially likely to produce self-reinforcing, self-undermining, or negligible feedback effects.

Comparative analysis represents another avenue for federalism-related feedback research. The United States differs from other federal systems, and certain institutional features may affect the bargaining power of subnational actors, making elite feedback effects more or less likely. In Germany, for example, the federal system concentrates lawmaking responsibilities at the national level and implementation responsibilities at the subnational level. In addition, the upper chamber of the German Parliament represents the subnational governments (rather than their electorates) and plays a critical role in the national legislative process (Baldi 1997). Canadian federalism also differs from its American counterpart, most fundamentally in its relative centralization of power. The original Canadian system specifically defined and limited provincial powers while granting most residual powers to the national government. This arrangement is the converse of the federal system in the United States. These and other institutional differences may affect the relative ease with which subnational officials mobilize as well as the stage of the policy process during which they are most likely to be successful.

LESSONS FOR PRACTITIONERS

Although national leaders have enacted policies with profound intergovernmental implications for over a century (Johnson 2007; Clemens 2006), many of the most significant national policy initiatives of recent years implicate the states in critical ways. Indeed, federalism plays a central role in contemporary policies, addressing everything from education and health care to immigration and the environment. Intergovernmental policy instruments like grants-in-aid hold special appeal in a political environment, like that of recent decades, characterized by strong resistance to higher national taxation. They also appeal to national lawmakers because representation in the United States is based on geography; the political safeguards of federalism give the president and members of Congress an electoral incentive to be responsive to the states (Wechsler 1954). As a result, subnational officials are frequently given at least some authority to customize policy templates to the specific needs and preferences of their jurisdictions.

The adoption of a policy does not guarantee that it will endure over the medium to long term, however, and the way that state officials react to an intergovernmental policy initiative can profoundly shape its developmental trajectory. Thus the case studies in the previous chapters add to a growing scholarly literature that offers lessons for lawmakers who want to craft durable and sustainable policies (Jenkins and Patashnik 2012; Patashnik 2008; Jordan and Matt 2014).[1] If programs that implicate the states are to endure, then the national lawmakers who endorse them must be attentive to the policy design issues that play a central role in our analytical framework.

Perhaps the most critical decision is whether to grant the new policy a permanent or a temporary authorization. The ability to revisit a policy offers substantial advantages, such as an opportunity to adjust its operations based on new information (Adler and Wilkerson 2012, 207–208). However, subjecting a policy to renewal renders it inherently unstable and makes it vulnerable to shifts in the political, economic, and administrative environment. The demises of the Sheppard–Towner Act and general revenue sharing, as well as the legislative limbo experienced by the Superfund program in recent decades, all testify to the immense importance of the duration of authorization. Policies with permanent authorizations

---

[1] In addition to designing programs that take root and flourish, strategic lawmakers can also design public policies to structure future politics to their own advantage (Anzia and Moe 2016; Hertel-Fernandez 2018). Political strategies of that sort lie beyond the scope of the present discussion.

will not be invulnerable to environmental shifts, but they will be better able to withstand them. The impact of a permanent authorization calls to mind Kent Weaver's (1988, 2) observation about indexation, the automatic adjustment of public policy outputs for inflation: "Once federal programs get indexed, they generally stay indexed." The typical stability of indexation does not necessarily forestall minor changes to the formula used to calculate changes, just as permanent authorization does not imply that a program will not change at all over the medium to long term. Yet both indexation and permanent authorization seem to place programs on a more stable, durable footing.

In designing intergovernmental policies, national officials must also be attentive to their impact both on state officials and on private interests. This book's focus on governmental elites highlights the potential impact of the structural politics of public administration. Programs that establish a new bureaucratic apparatus without fully supplanting existing ones or that facilitate the formation of competing bases of authority are unlikely to remake politics. Dislodging the existing order is a prerequisite to establishing a new order, and this type of competition extends to private-sector actors (Patashnik 2008). When government programs produce or prioritize goods and services that already are available in the private marketplace, then the affected groups are likely to mobilize against it. In contrast, policies that subsidize private actors can facilitate the emergence of a powerful supporting coalition that straddles the public and private sectors. The divergent developmental trajectories of the Sheppard–Towner Act and Medicaid, which can be traced in part to their respective coalition potential, illustrate the importance of anticipating such impacts.

Policy design is critical, yet the preceding case studies should not be taken to imply that there is a single formula for program durability. National lawmakers cannot emulate past designs and expect the results to be identical. Intergovernmental policies that generated self-reinforcing feedback effects, such as UI and Medicaid, did so in part because of the interaction between their key features and the environment in which they were established. The rise of skilled and policy-oriented governors, for instance, facilitated the expansion of Medicaid. Had the program been created in a different administrative, political, and economic context, its developmental trajectory probably would have been different. Similarly, the long-term prospects of the UI program were buttressed, in part, by the alacrity with which state officials joined forces with business leaders to prevent any steps toward nationalization. Thus the political context in which UI was created contributed to the emergence of its supporting coalition. Policies with similar design features will be more or less likely to remake politics when certain background conditions are met. This book, therefore, will close by turning to distinctive features of the contemporary United States and what they herald for the making of intergovernmental policies.

FEDERALISM AND FEEDBACK IN THE CONTEMPORARY
UNITED STATES

The states' prominent role in contemporary American policymaking illustrates broader trends in American governance. According to Hugh Heclo (2000, 28), "a pervasive presence of public policy expectations" has characterized the United States since the late twentieth century. This evocative phrase captures the high stakes involved in activist government with its panoply of taxing, spending, and regulatory activities; it also invokes the notion that "conceptions of who [Americans] are as a people [are] increasingly translated into arguments about what Washington should do or should stop doing." Acknowledging that the scope of national government activity has expanded, however, does not adequately capture the complexity and layering that currently characterize contemporary public policy. The proliferation of new pathways to policy is equally significant. Decisions about the appropriate scope of government activity are not made solely in the halls of Congress or exclusively in the nation's capital. State officials in various posts – governors, legislators, bureaucrats, attorneys general – can and do stake claims to policymaking authority. Indeed, national laws often depend on the actions of these subnational officeholders or on decisions taken in other institutional venues.

In the contemporary United States, more issues are subject to policy discretion and more actors are claiming jurisdiction over those issues than ever before. When new lawmakers come into power, they rarely have the opportunity to work on a blank canvas. Instead, they inherit a dense thicket of existing programs, each with their own set of stakeholders with varying levels of commitment to the status quo. Policy scholars have described these dynamics as "the increased crowding of the policy space" and as "institutional thickening" (Hogwood and Peters 1982; Clemens and Cook 1999). One implication of this state of affairs is that it has become increasingly difficult either to launch new policy initiatives or to move existing programs in a new direction.

The challenge of launching new policy initiatives is matched, or possibly even exceeded, by the difficulty of preserving them. Although the recent proliferation of policy pathways "opens government to a wider range of options, it also makes it less likely that government can be tied down to any one of them" (Orren and Skowronek 2017, 35). Policymaking is increasingly fluid, characterized by a constant churning that prevents new programs from taking root and becoming entrenched. The trajectories of the most recent intergovernmental initiatives profiled in this book are illustrative. Under Superfund, the task of cleaning up hazardous waste sites remains in limbo, with the national government and the states offering competing jurisdictional claims. Similarly, the rejection of NCLB and Common Core led to the recalibration of accountability-based school reform but not its demise.

Finally, when most states rejected the option to establish a health insurance exchange under the Affordable Care Act, the national government stepped into the breach. Developments in these three policy areas showcase the complexity that is a hallmark of the contemporary era, with multiple actors making claims of policymaking authority. The national initiatives at the center of these contests remain in existence but their footing is anything but solid.

Even our most recent case of self-reinforcing feedback, the Medicaid expansion that is a central component of the ACA, highlights the current volatility of policymaking. It built upon a well-established program, offered the states unprecedentedly generous financial terms, and had the political backing of powerful economic interests. Nevertheless, it came within a hair's breadth (or, more precisely, a dramatic thumbs-down from Senator John McCain [R-AZ]) of repeal less than a decade after its enactment. The story of the Medicaid expansion suggests that new policies will be durable only if they can overcome intense partisan polarization as well as an increasingly complex institutional environment characterized by competing jurisdictional claims. Thus the challenge of remaking politics by generating self-reinforcing feedback effects seems particularly formidable in the early twenty-first century (Patashnik and Zelizer 2013). The emergence of the contemporary policy state, combined with the vast chasm that separates Republicans and Democrats, "makes achievements provisional, protections unreliable, and commitments dependent on who is next in charge" (Orren and Skowronek 2017, 6). As this book has illustrated, the relationship between the national government and the states has long been critical to the substantive impact of public policies and the likelihood that they will be politically sustainable over the long term. Federalism is very likely to retain this central role for the foreseeable future, even as the obstacles to policy durability continue to grow.

Bibliography

Abbott, Grace. 1930. The Federal Government in Relation to Maternity and Infancy. *The Annals of the American Academy of Political and Social Science* 151:92–101.

Adler, E. Scott, and John D. Wilkerson. 2012. *Congress and the Politics of Problem Solving*. Cambridge, UK: Cambridge University Press.

Advisory Commission on Intergovernmental Relations (ACIR). 1970. *Revenue Sharing – An Idea Whose Time Has Come*. Washington, DC: ACIR.

Advisory Commission on Intergovernmental Relations (ACIR). 1974. *General Revenue Sharing: An ACIR Reevaluation*. Washington, DC: ACIR.

"All States Oppose Job Insurance Federalization." 1945. *Los Angeles Times*, September 1.

Alonso-Zaldivar, Ricardo. 2012. "States Reveal Their Choices on Obama's Health Law." *Yahoo! News*, November 16.

Altmeyer, Arthur J. 1966. *The Formative Years of Social Security*. Madison, WI: University of Wisconsin Press.

Amenta, Edwin, Elisabeth S. Clemens, Jefren Olsen, Sunita Parikh, and Theda Skocpol. 1987. The Political Origins of Unemployment Insurance in Five American States. *Studies in American Political Development* 2:137–182.

Anzia, Sarah F., and Terry M. Moe. 2016. Do Politicians Use Policy to Make Politics? The Case of Public-Sector Labor Laws. *American Political Science Review* 110:763–777.

"Appeal on Medicaid Is Sent to Johnson." 1967. *New York Times*, December 13, 39.

Applebome, Peter. 1989. "3 Governors in the South Join to Lift Their States." *New York Times*, February 12.

"Assails Medicaid Cut." 1967. *New York Times*, November 18, 23.

Ayres, Drummond, Jr. 1979. "Budget Balancers Warned by Muskie." *New York Times*, February 14, A17.

Ayers, B. Drummond. 1981. "Reagan Plans Welfare Shift to States." *New York Times*, August 13, A8.

Babich, Adam. 1995. Our Federalism, Our Hazardous Waste, and Our Good Fortune. *Maryland Law Review* 54:1516–1551.

Bacon, Perry. 2015. "In Rebuke of Tennessee Governor, Koch Group Shows Its Power." *NBC News*, February 6.

Baicker, Katherine, Claudia Goldin, and Lawrence F. Katz. 1998. A Distinctive System: Origins and Impact of U.S. Unemployment Compensation. In *The Defining Moment: The Great Depression and the American Economy in the Twentieth Century*, eds. Michael D. Bordo, Claudia Goldin, and Eugene N. White. Chicago: University of Chicago Press, 227–264.

Bailey, Michael A., and Mark Carl Rom. 2004. A Wider Race? Interstate Competition across Health and Welfare Programs. *Journal of Politics* 66:326–347.

Baldi, Brunetta. 1997. *Federalism and Public Policy: A Comparative View*. Berkeley, CA: Institute of Governmental Studies. Working Paper 97–2.

Barber, Michael, and Nolan McCarty. 2015. The Causes and Consequences of Polarization. In *Political Negotiation: A Handbook*, eds. Cathie Jo Martin and Jane Mansbridge. Washington, DC: Brookings Institution Press, 19–53.

Barrilleaux, Charles J., and Mark E. Miller. 1988. The Political Economy of State Medicaid Policy. *American Political Science Review* 82:1089–1107.

Barrilleaux, Charles, and Carlisle Rainey. 2014. The Politics of Need: Examining Governors' Decisions to Oppose the "Obamacare" Medicaid Expansion. *State Politics and Policy Quarterly* 14:437–460.

Baumgartner, Frank R., and Bryan D. Jones. 1993. *Agendas and Instability in American Politics*. Chicago: University of Chicago Press.

Bearden, David M. 2012. *Comprehensive Environmental Response, Compensation and Liability Act: A Summary of Superfund Cleanup Authorities and Related Provisions of the Act*. Washington, DC: Congressional Research Service.

Beer, Samuel H. 1976. The Adoption of General Revenue Sharing: A Case Study in Public Sector Politics. *Public Policy* 24:127–196.

Beins, Kaley, and Stephen Lester. 2015. *Superfund: Polluters Pay So Children Can Play*. Falls Church, VA: Center for Health, Environment & Justice.

Béland, Daniel, Philip Rocco, and Alex Waddan. 2016. *Obamacare Wars: Federalism, State Politics, and the Affordable Care Act*. Lawrence, KS: University Press of Kansas.

Berger, Pamela Marie. 1986. "Superfund: An Analysis of Implementation Failure." Unpublished PhD diss., University of Texas Health Science Center at Houston, School of Public Health.

Berry, Christopher R., Barry C. Burden, and William G. Howell. 2010. After Enactment: The Lives and Deaths of Federal Programs. *American Journal of Political Science* 54:1–17.

Besley, Timothy, and Anne Case. 1995. Incumbent Behavior: Vote-Seeking, Tax-Setting, and Yardstick Competition. *American Economic Review* 85:25–45.

Bickers, Kenneth N., and Robert M. Stein. 1996. The Electoral Dynamics of the Federal Pork Barrel. *American Journal of Political Science* 40:1300–1326.

Blaustein, Saul J. 1993. *Unemployment Insurance in the United States: The First Half Century*. Kalamazoo, MI: Upjohn Institute.

Blaustein, Saul J., Christopher J. O'Leary, and Stephen A. Wandner. 1997. Policy Issues: An Overview. In *Employment Insurance in the United States: Analysis of Policy Issues*, eds. Christopher J. O'Leary and Stephen A. Wandner. Kalamazoo, MI: Upjohn Institute, 1–49.

Bowling, Cynthia J., and J. Mitchell Pickerill. 2013. Fragmented Federalism: The State of American Federalism 2012–13. *Publius: The Journal of Federalism* 43:315–346.

Bowman, Ann O'M. 1985. Hazardous Waste Management: An Emerging Policy Area within an Emerging Federalism. *Publius: The Journal of Federalism* 15:131–144.

Bowman, Ann O'M., and Richard C. Kearney. 1986. *The Resurgence of the States.* Englewood Cliffs, NJ: Prentice Hall.

Brace, Paul, and Aubrey Jewett. 1995. The State of State Politics Research. *Political Research Quarterly* 48:643–681.

Break, George F. 1980. *Financing Government in a Federal System.* Washington, DC: Brookings Institution.

Brooks, Glenn E. 1961. *When Governors Convene: The Governors' Conference and National Politics.* Baltimore, MD: Johns Hopkins Press.

Brown, Lawrence D., and Michael S. Sparer. 2003. Poor Program's Progress: The Unanticipated Politics of Medicaid Policy. *Health Affairs* 22:31–44.

Bulman-Pozen, Jessica. 2014. Partisan Federalism. *Harvard Law Review* 127:1077–1146.

Bulman-Pozen, Jessica, and Heather Gerken. 2009. Uncooperative Federalism. *Yale Law Journal* 118:1256–1310.

Burford, Anne. 1986. *Are You Tough Enough?* New York: McGraw-Hill Book Company. With John Greenya.

Burrow, James G. 1963. *AMA: Voice of American Medicine.* Baltimore, MD: Johns Hopkins Press.

Cammisa, Anne Marie. 1995. *Governments as Interest Groups: Intergovernmental Lobbying and the Federal System.* Westport, CT: Praeger.

Camobreco, John F. 1996. Medicaid and Collective Action. *Social Science Quarterly* 77: 860–876.

Campbell, Andrea Louise. 2002. Self-Interest, Social Security, and the Distinctive Participation Patterns of Senior Citizens. *American Political Science Review* 96:565–574.

Campbell, Andrea Louise. 2003a. *How Policies Make Citizens: Senior Citizen Activism and the American Welfare State.* Princeton, NJ: Princeton University Press.

Campbell, Andrea Louise. 2003b. Participatory Reactions to Policy Threats: Senior Citizens and the Defense of Social Security and Medicare. *Political Behavior* 25:29–49.

Campbell, Andrea Louise. 2012. Policy Makes Mass Politics. *Annual Review of Political Science* 15:333–351.

Cannon, James M. 1986. "Federal Revenue Sharing: Born 1972. Died 1986. R.I.P." *New York Times*, October 10, A39.

Chambers, John C., Jr., and Peter L. Gray. 1989. EPA and State Roles in RCRA and CERCLA. *Natural Resources and Environment* 4:7–10, 43–44.

Chapman, William. 1971. "Governors Split on Nixon's Revenue Sharing." *Washington Post*, February 24, A2.

Chepaitis, Joseph B. 1972. Federal Social Welfare Progressivism in the 1920s. *Social Service Review* 46:213–229.

Church, Thomas W., and Robert T. Nakamura. 1993. *Cleaning Up the Mess: Implementation Strategies in Superfund.* Washington, DC: The Brookings Institution.

Clarity, James F. 1969. "Governor Plans Talk with Nixon on Aid to States." *New York Times*, February 8, 1.

Clark, Jill, and Thomas H. Little. 2002. National Organizations as Sources of Information for State Legislative Leaders. *State and Local Government Review* 34:38–44.

Clemens, Elisabeth S. 2006. Lineages of the Rube Goldberg State: Building and Blurring Public Programs, 1900–1940. In *Rethinking Political Institutions: The Art of the*

State, eds. Ian Shapiro, Stephen Skowronek, and Daniel Galvin. New York: New York University Press, 187–215.

Clemens, Elisabeth S., and James M. Cook. 1999. Politics and Institutionalism: Explaining Durability and Change. *Annual Review of Sociology* 25:441–466.

Cline, Kurt. 2003. Influences on Intergovernmental Implementation: The States and the Superfund. *State Politics and Policy Quarterly* 3:66–83.

Cline, Kurt. 2010. Working Relationships in the National Superfund Program: The State Administrators' Perspective. *Journal of Public Administration Research and Theory* 20:117–135.

Clinton, Joshua D., and Michael W. Sances. 2018. The Politics of Policy: The Initial Mass Political Effects of Medicaid Expansion in the States. *American Political Science Review* 112:167–185.

Cohen, Steven, and Marc Tipermas. 1983. Superfund: Preimplementation Planning and Bureaucratic Politics. In *The Politics of Hazardous Waste Management*, eds. James P. Lester and Ann O'M. Bowman. Durham, NC: Duke University Press, 43–59.

Cohen, Wilbur J. 1983. Reflections on the Enactment of Medicare and Medicaid. *Health Care Financing Review*, 1983 Annual Supplement:3–11.

Cohen, Wilbur J., and Robert M. Ball. 1965. Social Security Amendments of 1965: Summary and Legislative History. *Social Security Bulletin* 28(9):3–21.

Cohn, Jonathan. 2017. "Bipartisan Group of Governors Warns Senate Not to Pass 'Skinny' Obamacare Repeal Bill." *Huffington Post*, July 26.

Coming, Peter A. 1966. Interview #2 with Arthur Altmeyer. Washington, DC: March 23. www.ssa.gov/history/ajaoral.html.

Committee on Economic Security. 1935. *Report to the President*. Washington, DC: Government Printing Office.

Congressional Budget Office (CBO). 1985. Superfund Cost-Sharing Policy and the Efficiency of Cleanup. Staff Memorandum. September.

Congressional Research Service (CRS). 2007. *Superfund: Implementation and Selected Issues*. Washington, DC: Congressional Research Service.

Conlan, Timothy. 1991. And the Beat Goes On: Intergovernmental Mandates and Preemption in an Era of Deregulation. *Publius: The Journal of Federalism* 21:43–57.

Conlan, Timothy. 1998. *From New Federalism to Devolution: Twenty-Five Years of Intergovernmental Reform*. Washington, DC: Brookings.

Connolly, Ceci. 2003. "Governors' Efforts to Revise Medicaid Stalls; GOP Group Looks to White House." *Washington Post*, June 13, A4.

Cooke, Gary E., III. 1987. Superfund and the Preemption of State Hazardous Waste Cleanup: *Exxon Corporation v. Hunt. Washington University Journal of Urban and Contemporary Law* 31:243–257.

Corwin, Edward S. 1950. The Passing of Dual Federalism. *Virginia Law Review* 36:1–24.

Davis, Susan M., and Steven Puro. 1999. Patterns of Intergovernmental Relations in Environmental Cleanup at Federal Facilities. *Publius: The Journal of Federalism* 29:33–53.

DeBray, Elizabeth H., Kathryn A. McDermott, and Priscilla Wohlstetter. 2005. Introduction to the Special Issue on Federalism Reconsidered: The Case of the No Child Left Behind Act. *Peabody Journal of Education* 80:1–18.

deLeon, Peter. 1978. Public Policy Termination: An End and a Beginning. *Policy Analysis* 4:369–392.

Derthick, Martha. 1970. *The Influence of Federal Grants: Public Assistance in Massachusetts.* Cambridge, MA: Harvard University Press.

Derthick, Martha. 1979. *Policymaking for Social Security.* Washington, DC: Brookings.

Derthick, Martha. 2001. *Keeping the Compound Republic: Essays on American Federalism.* Washington, DC: Brookings Institution.

Dinan, John. 2011a. Contemporary Assertions of State Sovereignty and the Safeguards of American Federalism. *Albany Law Review* 74:1637–1669.

Dinan, John. 2011b. Shaping Health Reform: State Government Influence in the Patient Protection and Affordable Care Act. *Publius: The Journal of Federalism* 41:395–420.

Dinan, John. 2014. Implementing Health Reform: Intergovernmental Bargaining and the Affordable Care Act. *Publius: The Journal of Federalism* 44:399–425.

Dommel, Paul R. 1974. *The Politics of Revenue Sharing.* Bloomington: Indiana University Press.

Dorn, Stan, Megan McGrath, and John Holahan. 2014. *What Is the Result of States Not Expanding Medicaid?* Washington, DC: Urban Institute.

Douglas, Paul H. 1936. *Social Security in the United States.* New York: Whittlesey House.

Drew, Elizabeth. 1997. *Showdown: The Struggle between the Gingrich Congress and the Clinton White House.* New York: Touchstone.

DuVal, Barry E. 2013. "Health Insurance Coverage Keeps State Competitive in Business." *Richmond Times-Dispatch*, February 8.

Edstrom, Eve. 1966. "U.S. Medicaid Bill Tops Billion." *Washington Post*, November 16, A16.

Edstrom, Eve. 1968. "Cut in Medicaid Funds Shocks Welfare Chiefs." *Washington Post*, September 26, A2.

Elazar, Daniel J. 1962. *The American Partnership: Intergovernmental Cooperation in the Nineteenth-Century United States.* Chicago, IL: University of Chicago Press.

Eliot, Thomas H. 1992. *Recollections of the New Deal: When the People Mattered.* Boston, MA: Northeastern University.

Elmore, Richard F., and Susan Fuhrman. 1990. The National Interest and the Federal Role in Education. *Publius: The Journal of Federalism* 20:149–162.

Engel, Jonathan. 2006. *Poor People's Medicine: Medicaid and American Charity Care Since 1965.* Durham, NC: Duke University Press.

Erikson, Robert S., Gerald C. Wright, and John P. McIver. 1993. *Statehouse Democracy: Public Opinion and Policy in the American States.* Cambridge, UK: Cambridge University Press.

Fernandez, Juan J., and Antonio M. Jaime-Castillo. 2013. Positive or Negative Policy Feedbacks? Explaining Popular Attitudes towards Pragmatic Pension Policy Reforms. *European Sociological Review* 29:803–815.

Finch, Robert H., and Roger O. Egeberg. 1969. *The Health of the Nation's Health Care System.* Washington, DC: Department of Health, Education, and Welfare.

Finegold, Kenneth, and Theda Skocpol. 1995. *State and Party in America's New Deal.* Madison, WI: University of Wisconsin Press.

Florini, Karen L. 1982. Issues of Federalism in Hazardous Waste Control: Cooperation or Confusion? *Harvard Environmental Law Review* 6:307–337.

Fraser, Irene. 1991. Health Policy and Access to Care. In *Health Politics and Policy*, eds. Theodor J. Litman and Leonard S. Robins. New York: Delmar, 302–319.

Freeman, Robert A. 1986. CERCLA Reauthorization: The Wise Demise of §114(c) and *Exxon v. Hunt. Environmental Law Reporter* 16:10286–10291.

Fuhrman, Susan H. 1994. Clinton's Education Policy and Intergovernmental Relations in the 1990s. *Publius: The Journal of Federalism* 24:83–97.

"Fund Sharing Cutoff Backed by Governors." 1980. *Los Angeles Times*, April 9, B2.

Fusarelli, Lance D. 2005. Gubernatorial Reactions to No Child Left Behind: Politics, Pressure, and Education Reform. *Peabody Journal of Education* 80:120–136.

Gamkhar, Shama, and J. Mitchell Pickerill. 2012. The State of American Federalism 2011–2012: A Fend for Yourself and Activist Form of Bottom-Up Federalism. *Publius: The Journal of Federalism* 42:357–386.

George, Alexander L., and Andrew Bennett. 2005. *Case Studies and Theory Development in the Social Sciences.* Cambridge, MA: MIT Press.

Gilens, Martin. 1999. *Why Americans Hate Welfare.* Chicago, IL: University of Chicago Press.

Goelzhauser, Greg, and Shanna Rose. 2017. The State of American Federalism 2016–2017: Policy Reversals and Partisan Perspectives on Intergovernmental Relations. *Publius: The Journal of Federalism* 47:285–313.

Goertz, Margaret E. 2005. Implementing the No Child Left Behind Act: Challenges for the States. *Peabody Journal of Education* 80:73–89.

"GOP Governors Letter to Sebelius: 'Flexibility on Exchanges.'" 2011. *Kaiser Health News*, February 10.

Goss, Kristin A. 2013. *The Paradox of Gender Equality: How American Women's Groups Gained and Lost Their Public Voice.* Ann Arbor, MI: University of Michigan Press.

Graetz, Michael J., and Jerry L. Mashaw. 1999. *True Security: Rethinking American Social Insurance.* New Haven, CT: Yale University Press.

Greenough, Peter B. 1966. "Hottest Potato in Labor Law." *Boston Globe*, January 9, B52.

Greif, Avner, and David D. Laitin. 2004. A Theory of Endogenous Institutional Change. *American Political Science Review* 98:633–652.

Grodzins, Morton. 1966. *The American System: A New View of Government in the United States.* Chicago, IL: Rand McNally.

Grogan, Colleen. 1994. Political-Economic Factors Influencing State Medicaid Policy. *Political Research Quarterly* 47:589–622. See also "Correction Note." 49:673–675.

Grogan, Colleen, and Eric Patashnik. 2003. Between Welfare Medicine and Mainstream Entitlement: Medicaid at the Political Crossroads. *Journal of Health Politics, Policy and Law* 28:821–858.

Grogan, Colleen, and Vernon Smith. 2008. From Charity Care to Medicaid: Governors, States, and the Transformation of American Health Care. In *A Legacy of Innovation: Governors and Public Policy*, ed. Ethan Sribnick. Philadelphia: University of Pennsylvania Press, 204–230.

Haber, William, and Merrill G. Murray. 1966. *Unemployment Insurance in the American Economy.* Homewood, IL: Richard D. Irwin.

Haberkorn, Jennifer, and Rachana Pradham. 2017. "Heller Comes Out against Senate GOP Health Care Bill." *Politico*, June 23.

Hacker, Jacob S. 2002. *The Divided Welfare State: The Battle over Public and Private Social Benefits in the United States.* Cambridge, UK: Cambridge University Press.

Haeder, Simon F., and David L. Weimer. 2013. You Can't Make Me Do It: State Implementation of Insurance Exchanges under the Affordable Care Act. *Public Administration Review* 73:S34–S47.

Haggerty, Mark, and Stephanie A. Welcomer. 2003. Superfund: The Ascendance of Enabling Myths. *Journal of Economic Issues* 37:451–459.

Haider, Donald H. 1974. *When Governments Come to Washington: Governors, Mayors, and Intergovernmental Lobbying.* Washington, DC: Free Press.

Hall, Peter A. 1993. Policy Paradigms, Social Learning, and the State: The Case of Economic Policymaking in Britain. *Comparative Politics* 25:275–296.

Harpham, Edward J. 1986. Federalism, Keynesianism, and the Transformation of the Unemployment Insurance System in the United States. In *Nationalizing Social Security in Europe and America*, eds. Douglas E. Ashford and E. W. Kelley. Greenwich, CT: JAI Press, 155–179.

Harvard Law Review. 2006. No Child Left Behind and the Political Safeguards of Federalism. *Harvard Law Review* 119:885–906.

Heclo, Hugh. 1974. *Modern Social Politics in Britain and Sweden.* New Haven, CT: Yale University Press.

Heclo, Hugh. 2000. Campaigning and Governing: A Conspectus. In *The Permanent Campaign and Its Future*, eds. Norman Ornstein and Thomas Mann. Washington, DC: Brookings Institution Press, 1–37.

Herbers, John. 1971. "Mayors Oppose Aid Cuts to Fund Revenue Sharing." *New York Times*, January 22, 1.

Herbers, John. 1980. "States, Facing Revenue-Sharing Loss, Planning Cuts." *New York Times*, August 4, A8.

Herian, Mitchel N. 2011. *Governing the States and the Nation: The Intergovernmental Policy Influence of the National Governors Association.* Amherst, NY: Cambria Press.

Hertel-Fernandez, Alexander. 2018. Policy Feedback as Political Weapon: Conservative Advocacy and the Demobilization of the Public Sector Labor Movement. *Perspectives on Politics* 16:364–379.

Hertel-Fernandez, Alexander, and Theda Skocpol. 2015. Asymmetric Interest Group Mobilization and Party Coalitions in U.S. Tax Politics. *Studies in American Political Development* 29:235–249.

Hertel-Fernandez, Alexander, Theda Skocpol, and Daniel Lynch. 2016. Business Associations, Conservative Networks, and the Ongoing Republican War over Medicaid Expansion. *Journal of Health Politics, Policy and Law* 41:239–286.

Hight, Joseph E. 1982. Unemployment Insurance: Changes in the Federal-State Balance. *University of Detroit Journal of Urban Law* 59:615–629.

Hird, John A. 1994. *Superfund: The Political Economy of Environmental Risk.* Baltimore, MD: The Johns Hopkins University Press.

Hoff, David J. 2004. "Chiefs Sense a New Attitude in Meeting with Bush." *Education Week*, March 31.

Hofstadter, Richard. 1955. *The Age of Reform: From Bryan to F. D. R.* New York: Vintage Books.

Hogwood, Brian W., and B. Guy Peters. 1982. The Dynamics of Policy Change: Policy Succession. *Policy Sciences* 14:225–245.

Howard, Christopher. 1997. *The Hidden Welfare State: Tax Expenditures and Social Policy in the United States.* Princeton, NJ: Princeton University Press.

Howard, Christopher. 1999. Field Essay: The American Welfare State, or States? *Political Research Quarterly* 52:421–442.

Howard, Christopher. 2002. Workers' Compensation, Federalism, and the Heavy Hand of History. *Studies in American Political Development* 16:28–47.

Howard, Christopher. 2007. *The Welfare State Nobody Knows: Debunking Myths about U.S. Social Policy.* Princeton, NJ: Princeton University Press.

Howell, William, and Asya Magazinnik. 2017. Presidential Prescriptions for State Policy: Obama's Race to the Top Initiative. *Journal of Policy Analysis and Management* 36:502–531.

Hula, Richard C. 2001. Changing Priorities and Programs in Toxic Waste Policy: The Emergence of Economic Development as a Policy Tool. *Economic Development Quarterly* 15:181–199.

Hyatt, James C. 1974. "Updating Jobless Aid." *Wall Street Journal*, April 22.

Ikenberry, G. John. 1988. *Reasons of State: Oil Politics and the Capacities of American Government.* Ithaca, NY: Cornell University Press.

Ikenberry, G. John, and Theda Skocpol. 1987. Expanding Social Benefits: The Role of Social Security. *Political Science Quarterly* 102:389–416.

Illson, Murray. 1968. "Governor Scores Medicaid Attack." *New York Times*, September 29, 36.

Ingram, Helen. 1977. Policy Implementation through Bargaining: The Case of Federal Grants-in-Aid. *Public Policy* 25:499–526.

Jacobs, Alan M., and R. Kent Weaver. 2015. When Policies Undo Themselves: Self-Undermining Feedback as a Source of Policy Change. *Governance* 28:441–457.

Jacobs, Lawrence R., and Timothy Callaghan. 2013. Why States Expand Medicaid: Party, Resources, and History. *Journal of Health Politics, Policy and Law* 38:1023–1050.

Jacobs, Lawrence R., and Theda Skocpol. 2010. *Health Care Reform and American Politics: What Everyone Needs to Know.* New York: Oxford University Press.

Jaffe, Natalie. 1966. "State Is Called Medicaid Leader." *New York Times*, August 7, 83.

Jenkins, Jeffery A., and Eric M. Patashnik, eds. 2012. *Living Legislation: Durability, Change, and the Politics of American Lawmaking.* Chicago and London: University of Chicago Press.

Jewell, Malcolm. 1982. The Neglected World of State Politics. *The Journal of Politics* 44:638–657.

Jochim, Ashley, and Lesley Lavery. 2015. The Evolving Politics of Common Core: Policy Implementation and Conflict Expansion. *Publius: The Journal of Federalism* 45:380–404.

Johnson, Kimberley S. 2007. *Governing the American State: Congress and the New Federalism, 1877–1929.* Princeton, NJ: Princeton University Press.

Jones, David K., Katharine W. V. Bradley, and Jonathan Oberlander. 2014. Pascal's Wager: Health Insurance Exchanges, Obamacare, and the Republican Dilemma. *Journal of Health Politics, Policy and Law* 39:97–137.

Jones, David K., and Scott L. Greer. 2013. State Politics and the Creation of Health Insurance Exchanges. *American Journal of Public Health* 103:e8–e10.

Jones, David K., Phillip M. Singer, and John Z. Ayanian. 2014. The Changing Landscape of Medicaid: Practical and Political Considerations for Expansion. *Journal of the American Medical Association* 311:1965–1966.

Jordan, Andrew, and Elah Matt. 2014. Designing Policies that Intentionally Stick: Policy Feedback in a Changing Climate. *Policy Sciences* 47:227–247.

Karch, Andrew. 2007. *Democratic Laboratories: Policy Diffusion among the American States*. Ann Arbor, MI: University of Michigan Press.

Karch, Andrew. 2013. *Early Start: Preschool Politics in the United States*. Ann Arbor, MI: University of Michigan Press.

Karch, Andrew, and Matthew Cravens. 2014. Rapid Diffusion and Policy Reform: The Adoption and Modification of Three Strikes Laws. *State Politics and Policy Quarterly* 14:461–491.

Karch, Andrew, and Shanna Rose. 2017. States as Stakeholders: Federalism, Policy Feedback, and Government Elites. *Studies in American Political Development* 31:47–67.

Keller, Bess. 2005. "NEA Files 'No Child Left Behind' Lawsuit." *Education Week*, April 20.

Keller, Robert R. 1987. The Role of the State in the U.S. Economy during the 1920s. *Journal of Economic Issues* 21:877–884.

Key, V. O., Jr. 1984 edn. *Southern Politics in State and Nation*. Knoxville, TN: University of Tennessee Press.

Khazan, Olga. 2013. "The State Where Obamacare Is Working." *The Atlantic*, November 13.

Kilpatrick, Carroll. 1970. "$2.5 Billion Spending Cut Proposed by Nixon." *Los Angeles Times*, February 27, 22.

Kincaid, John. 1987. The State of American Federalism – 1986. *Publius: The Journal of Federalism* 17:1–33.

Kincaid, John. 1990. From Cooperative to Coercive Federalism. *Annals of the American Academy of Political and Social Science* 509:139–152.

Kingdon, John W. 1995. *Agendas, Alternatives, and Public Policies*. 2nd ed. New York: HarperCollins College.

Kooijman, Jaap. 1999. *And the Pursuit of National Health: The Incremental Strategy toward National Health Insurance in the United States of America*. Amsterdam: Rodopi.

Koppich, Julia E. 2005. A Tale of Two Approaches: The AFT, the NEA, and NCLB. *Peabody Journal of Education* 80:137–155.

Kotulak, Ronald. 1966. "Title 19 – The Sleeper Provision of the Medicare Act." *Chicago Tribune*, July 24, 12.

Kousser, J. Morgan. 1974. *The Shaping of Southern Politics: Suffrage Restriction and the Establishment of the One-Party South, 1880–1910*. New Haven, CT: Yale University Press.

Kousser, Thad. 2002. The Politics of Discretionary Medicaid Spending, 1980–1993. *Journal of Health Politics, Policy and Law* 27:639–671.

Kraft, Michael E., and Denise Scheberle. 1998. Environmental Federalism at Decade's End: New Approaches and Strategies. *Publius: The Journal of Federalism* 28:131–146.

Kriner, Douglas L., and Andrew Reeves. 2015. *The Particularistic President: Executive Branch Politics and Political Inequality*. New York: Cambridge University Press.

Landy, Marc K., Marc J. Roberts, and Stephen R. Thomas. 1990. *The Environmental Protection Agency: Asking the Wrong Questions*. New York: Oxford University Press.

Large, Arlen. 1965. "Mills and Medicine." *Wall Street Journal*, August 2, 10.

Lecher, Colin. 2018. "Dozens of States Are Now Considering Rules to Keep Net Neutrality." *The Verge*, March 17.

Lemons, J. Stanley. 1990. *The Woman Citizen: Social Feminism in the 1920s.* Charlottesville and London: University Press of Virginia. First published 1973 University of Illinois Press.

Lieber, Harvey. 1983. Federalism and Hazardous Waste Policy. In *The Politics of Hazardous Waste Management*, eds. James P. Lester and Ann O'M. Bowman. Durham, NC: Duke University Press, 60–72.

Lieberman, Robert C. 1998. *Shifting the Color Line: Race and the American Welfare State*. Cambridge, MA: Harvard University Press.

Light, Alfred R. 1987. Federal Preemption, Federal Conscription under the New Superfund Act. *Mercer Law Review* 38:643–663.

Lindblom, Charles E. 1965. *The Intelligence of Democracy: Decision Making through Mutual Adjustment*. New York: Free Press.

Lindenmeyer, Kriste. 1997. *"A Right to Childhood": The U.S. Children's Bureau and Child Welfare, 1912–46*. Urbana and Chicago: University of Illinois Press.

Link, Arthur S. 1959. What Happened to the Progressive Movement in the 1920s? *The American Historical Review* 64:833–851.

Lowande, Kenneth S., Jeffery A. Jenkins, and Andrew J. Clarke. 2018. Presidential Particularism and US Trade Politics. *Political Science Research and Methods* 6:265–281.

Lukens, Gideon. 2014. State Variation in Health Care Spending and the Politics of State Medicaid Policy. *Journal of Health Politics, Policy and Law* 39:1213–1251.

Mach, Annie L., and C. Stephen Redhead. 2014. *Federal Funding for Health Insurance Exchanges*. Washington, DC: Congressional Research Service.

Madden, Richard L. 1968a. "State's Medicaid Program Faces Cut of up to $90 Million in Federal Funds." *New York Times*, September 26, 1.

Madden, Richard L. 1968b. "Javits and Goodell Stop Medicaid Cut with a 'Minibuster.'" *New York Times*, October 12, 1.

Maltzman, Forrest, and Charles R. Shipan. 2008. Change, Continuity, and the Evolution of the Law. *American Journal of Political Science* 52:252–267.

Mangan, Dan. 2015. "States Shuttering Obamacare Exchanges, But Should They?" *CNBC*, July 15.

Manna, Paul. 2006. *School's In: Federalism and the National Education Agenda*. Washington, DC: Georgetown University Press.

Manna, Paul. 2011. *Collision Course: Federal Education Policy Meets State and Local Realities*. Washington, DC: CQ Press.

Marbach, Joseph R., and J. Wesley Leckrone. 2002. Intergovernmental Lobbying for the Passage of TEA-21. *Publius: The Journal of Federalism* 32:45–64.

March, James G. 1994. *A Primer on Decision Making: How Decisions Happen*. New York: Free Press.

Markell, David L. 1993. The Federal Superfund Program: Proposals for Strengthening the Federal/State Relationship. *William and Mary Journal of Environmental Law* 18:1–82.

Marmor, Theodor. 1970. *The Politics of Medicare*. New York: Aldine de Gruyter.

Mason, Liliana. 2018. *Uncivil Agreement: How Politics Became Our Identity*. Chicago, IL: University of Chicago Press.

May, Henry F. 1956. Shifting Perspectives on the 1920s. *The Mississippi Valley Historical Review* 43:405–427.

Mayhew, David R. 1974. *Congress: The Electoral Connection.* New Haven, CT: Yale University Press.

Mayhew, David R. 1986. *Placing Parties in American Politics.* Princeton, NJ: Princeton University Press.

Mazmanian, David, and David Morell. 1992. *Beyond Superfailure: America's Toxic Policy for the 1990s.* Boulder, CO: Westview Press.

McCann, Pamela J. Clouser. 2016. *The Federal Design Dilemma: Congress and Intergovernmental Delegation.* Cambridge, UK: Cambridge University Press.

McConnaughy, Corrine M. 2013. *The Woman Suffrage Movement in America: A Reassessment.* Cambridge, UK: Cambridge University Press.

McDermott, Kathryn A. 2011. *High-Stakes Reform: The Politics of Educational Accountability.* Washington, DC: Georgetown University Press.

McDermott, Kathryn A., and Laura S. Jensen. 2005. Dubious Sovereignty: Federal Conditions of Aid and the No Child Left Behind Act. *Peabody Journal of Education* 80:39–56.

McDonough, John E., Brian Rosman, Fawn Phelps, and Melissa Shannon. 2006. The Third Wave of Massachusetts Health Care Access Reform. *Health Affairs* 25: w420–w431.

McGuinn, Patrick J. 2005. The National Schoolmarm: No Child Left Behind and the New Educational Federalism. *Publius: The Journal of Federalism* 35:41–68.

McGuinn, Patrick J. 2006. *No Child Left Behind and the Transformation of Federal Education Policy, 1965–2005.* Lawrence, KS: University Press of Kansas.

McGuinn, Patrick J. 2016. From No Child Left Behind to the Every Student Succeeds Act: Federalism and the Education Legacy of the Obama Administration. *Publius: The Journal of Federalism* 46:392–415.

McKeown, Timothy J. 2004. Case Studies and the Limits of the Quantitative Worldview. In *Rethinking Social Inquiry: Diverse Tools, Shared Standards*, eds. Henry E. Brady and David Collier. Lanham, MD: Rowman & Littlefield, 139–167.

Meckel, Richard A. 1990. *Save the Babies: American Public Health Reform and the Prevention of Infant Mortality, 1850–1929.* Baltimore and London: Johns Hopkins University Press.

"Medical Economics Revolution." 1970. *New York Times*, May 4, 36.

"Medicare." 1966. *New York Times*, July 3, 87.

Messerly, Megan. 2017. "Sandoval, Other Governors Say ACA Repeal Bill 'Calls into Question' Health Care Coverage for Vulnerable Americans." *The Nevada Independent*, June 16.

Mettler, Suzanne. 1998. *Dividing Citizens: Gender and Federalism in New Deal Public Policy.* Ithaca, NY: Cornell University Press.

Mettler, Suzanne. 2002. Bringing the State Back In to Civic Engagement: Policy Feedback Effects of the G.I. Bill for World War II Veterans. *American Political Science Review* 96:351–365.

Mettler, Suzanne. 2005. *Soldiers to Citizens: The G.I. Bill and the Making of the Greatest Generation.* New York: Oxford University Press.

Mettler, Suzanne. 2011. *The Submerged State: How Invisible Government Policies Undermine American Democracy.* Chicago, IL: University of Chicago Press.

Mettler, Suzanne, and Joe Soss. 2004. The Consequences of Public Policy for Democratic Citizenship: Bridging Policy Studies and Mass Politics. *Perspectives on Politics* 2:55–73.

Mettler, Suzanne, and Jeffrey M. Stonecash. 2008. Government Program Usage and Political Voice. *Social Science Quarterly* 89:273–293.

Mettler, Suzanne, and Richard M. Valelly. 2016. Introduction: The Distinctiveness and Necessity of American Political Development. In *The Oxford Handbook of American Political Development*, eds. Richard M. Valelly, Suzanne Mettler, and Robert C. Lieberman. Oxford, UK: Oxford University Press, 1–23.

Mettler, Suzanne, and Eric W. Welch. 2004. Civic Generation: Policy Feedback Effects of the GI Bill on Political Involvement over the Life Course. *British Journal of Political Science* 34:497–518.

Michener, Jamila. 2018. *Fragmented Democracy: Medicaid, Federalism, and Unequal Politics*. Cambridge, UK: Cambridge University Press.

Miller, Norman. 1966. "Medicaid Mistake." *Wall Street Journal*, October 20, 18.

Moe, Terry M. 1989. The Politics of Bureaucratic Structure. In *Can the Government Govern?*, eds. John E. Chubb and Paul E. Peterson. Washington, DC: Brookings Institution, 267–329.

Mooney, Christopher Z. 2001. *State Politics and Policy Quarterly* and the Study of State Politics: The Editor's Introduction. *State Politics and Policy Quarterly* 1:1–4.

Moore, Judith D., and David G. Smith. 2005. Legislating Medicaid: Considering Medicaid and Its Origins. *Health Care Financing Review* 27:45–52.

Morgan, Kimberly J., and Andrea Louise Campbell. 2011. *The Delegated Welfare State: Medicare, Markets, and the Governance of Social Policy*. Oxford, UK: Oxford University Press.

Morris, John. 1967. "Senate Affirms Medicaid Reductions in Federal Payments to States." *New York Times*, November 21, 35.

Nathan, Richard P., Fred C. Doolittle, and Associates. 1983. *The Consequences of Cuts*. Princeton, NJ: Princeton University Press.

Nathan, Richard P., Fred C. Doolittle, and Associates. 1987. *Reagan and the States*. Princeton, NJ: Princeton University Press.

National Conference of State Legislatures. 2015. *Summary of the Every Student Succeeds Act, Reauthorizing the Elementary and Secondary Education Act*. Denver, CO: National Conference of State Legislatures.

Nilsen, Ella. 2018. "Democrat Jacky Rosen Beats Endangered Republican Sen. Dean Heller in Nevada." *Vox*, November 7.

Nugent, John D. 2009. *Safeguarding Federalism: How States Protect Their Interests in National Policymaking*. Norman, OK: University of Oklahoma Press.

Oberlander, Jonathan. 2008. The Politics of Paying for Health Care Reform: Zombies, Payroll Taxes, and the Holy Grail. *Health Affairs* 27:w544–w555.

Oberlander, Jonathan. 2018. The Republican War on Obamacare – What Has It Achieved? *New England Journal of Medicine* 379:703–705.

Oberlander, Jonathan, and R. Kent Weaver. 2015. Unraveling from Within? The Affordable Care Act and Self-Undermining Policy Feedbacks. *The Forum* 13:37–62.

O'Leary, Rosemary. 1990. Will Hazardous Waste Cleanup Costs Cripple Our State and Local Governments? *State and Local Government Review* 22:84–89.

Olson, Laura Katz. 2010. *The Politics of Medicaid*. New York: Columbia University Press.

Omenn, Gilbert. 1985. "Let Federalism Work in Medicaid." *Wall Street Journal*, April 26, 28.

"Oppose Job Federalization." 1941. *New York Times*, November 20.

Orloff, Ann Shola, and Theda Skocpol. 1984. Why Not Equal Protection? Explaining the Politics of Social Spending in Britain, 1900–1911, and the United States, 1880s–1920. *American Sociological Review* 49:725–750.

Orren, Karen, and Stephen Skowronek. 2004. *The Search for American Political Development*. Cambridge, UK: Cambridge University Press.

Orren, Karen, and Stephen Skowronek. 2017. *The Policy State: An American Predicament*. Cambridge, MA: Harvard University Press.

Palley, Marian L. 1997. Intergovernmentalization of Health Care Reform: The Limits of the Devolution Revolution. *Journal of Politics* 59:657–679.

Patashnik, Eric M. 2000. *Putting Trust in the US Budget: Federal Trust Funds and the Politics of Commitment*. Cambridge, UK: Cambridge University Press.

Patashnik, Eric. 2003. After the Public Interest Prevails: The Political Sustainability of Policy Reform. *Governance* 16:203–234.

Patashnik, Eric M. 2008. *Reforms at Risk: What Happens after Major Policy Changes Are Enacted*. Princeton, NJ: Princeton University Press.

Patashnik, Eric M., and Jonathan Oberlander. 2018. After Defeat: Conservative Postenactment Opposition to the ACA in Historical-Institutional Perspective. *Journal of Health Politics, Policy and Law* 43:651–682.

Patashnik, Eric M., and Julian E. Zelizer. 2013. The Struggle to Remake Politics: Liberal Reform and the Limits of Policy Feedback in the Contemporary American State. *Perspectives on Politics* 11:1071–1087.

Patterson, James T. 1994. *America's Struggle against Poverty, 1900–1994*. Cambridge, MA: Harvard University Press.

Pear, Robert. 2003. "Governors Resist Bush Plan to Slow Costs of Medicaid." *New York Times*, May 25, A1.

Peirce, Neil R. 1980. "Moving Off the Easy Street Paved with Revenue Sharing." *New York Times*, April 15, F5.

Perkins, Frances. 1946. *The Roosevelt I Knew*. New York: Penguin.

Persico, Joseph E. 1982. *The Imperial Rockefeller*. New York: Pocket Books.

Peterson, Paul E. 1995. *The Price of Federalism*. Washington, DC: Brookings Institution Press.

Pierson, Paul. 1993. When Effect Becomes Cause: Policy Feedback and Political Change. *World Politics* 45:595–628.

Pierson, Paul. 1995a. Fragmented Welfare States: Federal Institutions and the Development of Social Policy. *Governance* 8:449–478.

Pierson, Paul. 1995b. The Creeping Nationalization of Income Transfers in the United States, 1935–94. In *European Social Policy: Between Fragmentation and Integration*, eds. Stephan Liebfried and Paul Pierson. Washington, DC: Brookings Institution, 301–328.

Pierson, Paul. 2000a. Increasing Returns, Path Dependence, and the Study of Politics. *American Political Science Review* 94:251–267.

Pierson, Paul. 2000b. Not Just What But When: Timing and Sequence in Political Processes. *Studies in American Political Development* 14:72–92.

Pierson, Paul. 2001. From Expansion to Austerity: The New Politics of Taxing and Spending. In *Seeking the Center: Politics and Policymaking at the New Century*, eds.

Martin A. Levin, Marc K. Landy, and Martin Shapiro. Washington, DC: Georgetown University Press, 54–80.

Pierson, Paul. 2004. *Politics in Time: History, Institutions, and Social Analysis.* Princeton, NJ: Princeton University Press.

Pierson, Paul. 2005. The Study of Policy Development. *Journal of Policy History* 17:34–51.

Pierson, Paul. 2006. Public Policies as Institutions. In *Rethinking Political Institutions: The Art of the State,* eds. Ian Shapiro, Stephen Skowronek, and Daniel Galvin. New York: New York University Press, 114–131.

Posner, Paul L. 1998. *Politics of Unfunded Mandates: Whither Federalism?* Washington, DC: Georgetown University Press.

Pracht, Etienne E., and William J. Moore. 2003. Interest Groups and State Medicaid Drug Programs. *Journal of Health Politics, Policy and Law* 28:9–40.

Prial, Frank. 1966. "And Now 'Medicaid.'" *Wall Street Journal*, July 11, 1.

Price, Daniel N. 1985. Unemployment Insurance, Then and Now, 1935–1985. *Social Security Bulletin* 48(10):22–32.

Ragin, Charles C. 2004. Turning the Tables: How Case-Oriented Research Challenges Variable-Oriented Research. In *Rethinking Social Inquiry: Diverse Tools, Shared Standards*, eds. Henry E. Brady and David Collier. Lanham, MD: Rowman & Littlefield, 123–138.

Ragusa, Jordan Michael. 2010. The Lifecycle of Public Policy: An Event History Analysis of Repeals to Landmark Legislative Enactments, 1951–2006. *American Politics Research* 38:1015–1051.

Rahm, Dianne. 1998a. Controversial Cleanup: Superfund and the Implementation of U.S. Hazardous Waste Policy. *Policy Studies Journal* 26:719–734.

Rahm, Dianne. 1998b. Superfund and the Politics of US Hazardous Waste Policy. *Environmental Policy* 7:75–91.

Ravitch, Diane. 1995. *National Standards in American Education: A Citizen's Guide.* Washington, DC: Brookings Institution Press.

Reeves, Richard. 1966. "Travia, in Reversal, to Ask Tightening of Medicaid Rules." *New York Times*, July 1, 1.

Regan, Priscilla M., and Christopher J. Deering. 2009. State Opposition to REAL ID. *Publius: The Journal of Federalism* 39:476–505.

Regas, Diane. 1986. Federal Preemption of State Hazardous Waste Funds: *Exxon Corp. v. Hunt. Ecology Law Quarterly* 13:535–553.

Reitz, Stephanie. 2011. "Connecticut Loses 'No Child Left Behind' Legal Challenge." *Associated Press*, February 22.

Reston, James. 1962. "Big Problems and Little Men in State Capitals." *New York Times*, October 5, 32.

Reticker, Ruth. 1945. State Unemployment Compensation Laws of 1945. *Social Security Bulletin* 8(7):9–26.

Rigby, Elizabeth. 2012. State Resistance to "Obamacare." *The Forum: A Journal of Applied Research in Contemporary Politics* 10:1–16.

Robertson, David Brian. 2012. *Federalism and the Making of America.* New York: Routledge.

Robertson, David Brian. 2016. Federalism and American Political Development. In *The Oxford Handbook of American Political Development*, eds. Richard M. Valelly,

Suzanne Mettler, and Robert C. Lieberman. Oxford, UK: Oxford University Press, 345–363.

Robinson, Nan. 1966. "Senate Puts Off Early Increase in Social Security." *New York Times*, October 15, 1.

Roosevelt, Franklin D. 1938. *The Public Papers and Addresses of Franklin D. Roosevelt*, vol. 3, comp. Samuel I. Rosenman. New York: Random House.

Rose, Shanna. 2013. *Financing Medicaid: Federalism and the Growth of America's Health Care Safety Net.* Ann Arbor, MI: University of Michigan Press.

Rose, Shanna. 2015. Opting In, Opting Out: The Politics of State Medicaid Expansion. *The Forum: A Journal of Applied Research in Contemporary Politics* 13:63–82.

Rosenbaum, Sara. 1993. Medicaid Expansions and Access to Health Care. In *Medicaid Financing Crisis: Balancing Responsibilities, Priorities, and Dollars*, eds. Diane Rowland, Judith Feder, and Alina Salganicoff. Washington, DC: American Association for the Advancement of Science, 45–81.

Rosenbaum, Sara. 2009. Medicaid and National Health Care Reform. *New England Journal of Medicine* 361:2009–2012.

Rosenthal, Alan. 1996. State Legislative Development: Observations from Three Perspectives. *Legislative Studies Quarterly* 21:169–198.

Rossiter, Clinton, ed. 1961. *The Federalist Papers*. New York: Mentor.

Rothman, Robert. 2012. How We Got Here: The Emergence of the Common Core State Standards. *The State Education Standard* 12:4–8.

Rothman, Sheila M. 1978. *Woman's Proper Place: A History of Changing Ideals and Practices, 1870 to the Present*. New York: Basic Books.

Rubin, Murray. 1983. *Federal-State Relations in Unemployment Insurance: A Balance of Power*. Kalamazoo, Michigan: W. E. Upjohn Institute for Employment Research.

"Rush-Hour Lawmaking." 1966. *New York Times*, May 21, 23.

Sabato, Larry. 1983. *Goodbye to Goodtime Charlie: The American Governorship Transformed*. 2nd ed. Washington, DC: CQ Press.

Sack, Joetta L. 2005. "Utah Lawmakers Pass Bill Flouting NCLB." *Education Week*, April 20.

Sack, Kevin. 2011. "Opposing the Health Law, Florida Refuses Millions." *New York Times*, July 31.

Sanford, Terry. 1967. *Storm over the States*. New York: McGraw-Hill.

Saultz, Andrew, Lance D. Fusarelli, and Andrew McEachin. 2017. The Every Student Succeeds Act, the Decline of the Federal Role in Education Policy, and the Curbing of Executive Authority. *Publius: The Journal of Federalism* 47:426–444.

Schanberg, Sydney. 1966. "House Committee Agrees on New Plan to Cut U.S. Funds for Medicaid." *New York Times*, October 6, 25.

Schattschneider, E. E. 1935. *Politics, Pressures, and the Tariff*. New York: Prentice-Hall.

Schickler, Eric. 2001. *Disjointed Pluralism: Institutional Innovation and the Development of the U.S. Congress*. Princeton, NJ: Princeton University Press.

Schickler, Eric. 2016. *Racial Realignment: The Transformation of American Liberalism, 1932–1965*. Princeton, NJ: Princeton University Press.

Schmidt, William M. 1973. The Development of Health Services for Mothers and Children in the United States. *American Journal of Public Health* 63:419–427.

Scott, Dylan. 2017. "Nevada's Governor Is the Most Important Person in the Senate Health Care Debate." *Vox*, July 14.

Sebelius, Steve. 2012. "Sandoval Does the Right Thing in Expanding Medicaid." *Las Vegas Review-Journal*, December 14.

Severns, Maggie. 2015. "The Plot to Overhaul No Child Left Behind." *Politico*, January 2.

Shefter, Martin. 1983. Regional Receptivity to Reform: The Legacy of the Progressive Era. *Political Science Quarterly* 98:459–483.

Sher, Andy. 2009. "Governors Leery of Health Proposal." *Chattanooga Times Free Press*, July 21.

Shillinger, Kurt. 1995. "Welfare Reform Is Central as Clinton, Dole Jockey for '96." *Christian Science Monitor*, August 1.

Shipman, George A., and Harold J. Saum. 1936. Federal Grants and the Problem of Financing Public Assistance. *Law and Contemporary Problems* 3:289–297.

Sibley, John. 1966. "Medical Care Furor: The Confusion and Sudden Opposition Indicate Little Understanding of Plan." *New York Times*, May 21, 14.

Skelton, George. 1979. "Brown Calls for U.S. Budget Amendment." *Los Angeles Times*, January 9, A10.

Skinner, Rebecca R., Jeffrey J. Kuenzi, Cassandria Dortch, and Gail McCallion. 2013. *ESEA Reauthorization Proposals in the 113th Congress: Comparison of Major Features*. Washington, DC: Congressional Research Service.

Sklar, Martin J. 1992. *The United States as Developing Country: Studies in U.S. History in the Progressive Era and the 1920s*. Cambridge, UK: Cambridge University Press.

Skocpol, Theda. 1992. *Protecting Soldiers and Mothers: The Political Origins of Social Policy in the United States*. Cambridge, MA: Harvard University Press.

Skowronek, Stephen. 1993. *The Politics Presidents Make: Leadership from John Adams to George Bush*. Cambridge, MA: Harvard University Press.

Skowronek, Stephen. 2009. Taking Stock. In *The Unsustainable American State*, eds. Lawrence Jacobs and Desmond King. Oxford, UK: Oxford University Press, 330–338.

Smith, David G., and Judith D. Moore. 2008. *Medicaid Politics and Policy: 1965–2007*. New Brunswick, NJ: Transactions Publishers.

Snyder, Riley. 2017. "Sandoval Won't Support Rollback of ACA Medicaid Expansion." *The Nevada Independent*, March 9.

Social Security Administration. 1944. Unemployment Compensation in the Reconversion Period: Recommendations by the Social Security Board. *Social Security Bulletin* 7(10):3–8.

Social Security Administration. 1949. Unemployment Insurance: Recommendations of the Senate Advisory Council. *Social Security Bulletin* 12(1):12–20.

Sommers, Benjamin D., and Arnold M. Epstein. 2013. U.S. Governors and the Medicaid Expansion: No Quick Resolution in Sight. *New England Journal of Medicine* 368:496–499.

Soss, Joe. 1999. Lessons of Welfare: Policy Design, Political Learning, and Political Action. *American Political Science Review* 93:363–380.

Soss, Joe, and Sanford F. Schram. 2007. A Public Transformed? Welfare Reform as Policy Feedback. *American Political Science Review* 101:111–127.

Sparer, Michael S. 1996. *Medicaid and the Limits of State Health Reform*. Philadelphia, PA: Temple University Press.

Sparer, Michael S. 2009. Medicaid and the U.S. Path to National Health Insurance. *New England Journal of Medicine* 360:323–325.

Springer, Melanie Jean. 2012. State Electoral Institutions and Voter Turnout in Presidential Elections, 1920–2000. *State Politics and Policy Quarterly* 12:252–283.

Springer, Melanie Jean. 2014. *How the States Shaped the Nation: American Electoral Institutions and Voter Turnout, 1920–2000.* Chicago, IL: University of Chicago Press.

Squire, Peverill. 2012. *The Evolution of American Legislatures: Colonies, Territories, and States, 1619–2009.* Ann Arbor, MI: University of Michigan Press.

Stark, Louis. 1949. "Move to Federalize Jobless Benefits Meets Heavy Barrage of Criticism." *New York Times*, April 1.

Starr, Paul. 1982. *The Social Transformation of American Medicine: The Rise of a Sovereign Profession and the Making of a Vast Industry.* New York: Basic Books.

Steiner, Gilbert Y. 1965. *Social Insecurity: The Politics of Welfare.* Chicago, IL: Rand McNally & Company.

Stephens, G. Ross, and Nelson Wikstrom. 2007. *American Intergovernmental Relations: A Fragmented Federal Polity.* New York: Oxford University Press.

Stevens, Robert, and Rosemary Stevens. 2003. *Welfare Medicine in America: A Case Study of Medicaid.* New Brunswick, NJ: Transaction Publishers.

Stevens, Rosemary, and Robert Stevens. 1970. Medicaid: Anatomy of a Dilemma. *Law and Contemporary Problems* 35:348–425.

Stimson, James A. 1991. *Public Opinion in America: Moods, Cycles, and Swings.* Boulder, CO: Westview Press.

Stimson, James A. 1999. *Public Opinion in America: Moods, Cycles, and Swings.* 2nd ed. Boulder, CO: Westview Press.

Stimson, James A., Michael B. MacKuen, and Robert S. Erikson. 1995. Dynamic Representation. *American Political Science Review* 89:543–565.

Sullivan, Patricia. 2004. "Anne Gorsuch Burford, 62, Dies; Reagan EPA Director." *Washington Post*, July 22, B6.

Sullivan, Peter. 2017. "Fifth GOP Senator Announces Opposition to Healthcare Bill." *The Hill*, June 23.

Sullivan, Sean, Kelsey Snell, and Juliet Eilperin. 2017. "New Health-Care Plan Stumbles under Opposition from Governors." *Washington Post*, September 19.

Sunderman, Gail L., and Gary Orfield. 2006. Domesticating a Revolution: No Child Left Behind Reforms and State Administrative Response. *Harvard Education Review* 76:526–556.

Superfine, Benjamin Michael. 2005. The Politics of Accountability: The Rise and Fall of Goals 2000. *American Journal of Education* 112:10–43.

Swartz, Thomas R., and John E. Peck. 1990. Six Profiles of the Changing Face of Fiscal Federalism: An Overview. In *The Changing Face of Fiscal Federalism*, eds. Thomas R. Swartz and John E. Peck. Armonk, NY: M. E. Sharpe, 3–16.

Teaford, Jon C. 2002. *The Rise of the States: The Evolution of American State Government.* Baltimore, MD: Johns Hopkins University Press.

Theriault, Sean M. 2008. *Party Polarization in Congress.* Cambridge, UK: Cambridge University Press.

Thompson, Frank J. 2012. *Medicaid Politics: Federalism, Policy Durability, and Health Reform.* Washington, DC: Georgetown University Press.

Thompson, Richard E. 1973. *Revenue Sharing: A New Era in Federalism?* Washington, DC: Revenue Sharing Advisory Service.

Tolchin, Martin. 1966. "Javits, Governor Split on Medicaid." *New York Times*, September 3, 19.

Trussell, C. P. 1959. "Senate Approves 389 Million in Aid to Jobless Areas." *New York Times*, March 24.

US Census Bureau. 1961. *Current Population Survey*. Washington, DC: US Census Bureau.

US Environmental Protection Agency (EPA). 1984. *State Participation in the Superfund Program: CERCLA Section 301 (a) (I) (E) Study*. Washington, DC: US Environmental Protection Agency.

US Environmental Protection Agency (EPA). 1989. *An Analysis of State Superfund Programs: 50-State Study*. Washington, DC: US Environmental Protection Agency.

US Government Accountability Office (GAO). 1974. Letter from US Comptroller General to Honorable John Brademas. May 30. www.gao.gov/assets/210/202684.pdf.

US Government Accountability Office (GAO). 1975. Statement of Elmer B. Staats, Comptroller General of the United States, before the Senate Subcommittee on Revenue Sharing on the Revenue Sharing Program. April 17. www.gao.gov/assets/100/98156.pdf.

US Government Accountability Office (GAO). 1980. Impact of Eliminating the States from the General Revenue Sharing Program – A Nine-State Assessment. Report by the Comptroller General to the Congress. June 27. www.gao.gov/assets/130/129812.pdf.

US Government Accountability Office (GAO). 2015. Superfund: Trends in Federal Funding and Cleanup of EPA's Nonfederal National Priorities List Sites. Report to Congressional Requesters. September. www.gao.gov/products/GAO-15-812.

Vogel, Ed. 2012. "Groups Urge Sandoval to Support Medicaid Expansion." *Las Vegas Review-Journal*, November 15.

Volden, Craig. 2002. The Politics of Competitive Federalism: A Race to the Bottom in Welfare Benefits? *American Journal of Political Science* 46:352–363.

"Volpe Protests to Conferees on Proposed Medicaid Cuts." 1967. *New York Times*, December 10, 48.

Wagenet, R. Gordon. 1960. Twenty-Five Years of Unemployment Insurance in the United States. *Social Security Bulletin* 23(8):50–59.

Walker, Jack L., Jr. 1991. *Mobilizing Interest Groups in America: Patrons, Professions, and Social Movements*. Ann Arbor, MI: University of Michigan Press.

Wallin, Bruce A. 1998. *From Revenue Sharing to Deficit Sharing*. Washington, DC: Georgetown University Press.

Wanker, William Paul, and Kathy Christie. 2005. State Implementation of the No Child Left Behind Act. *Peabody Journal of Education* 80:57–72.

Weaver, R. Kent. 1988. *Automatic Government: The Politics of Indexation*. Washington, DC: Brookings Institution.

Weaver, R. Kent. 2010. Paths and Forks or Chutes and Ladders? Negative Feedbacks and Policy Regime Change. *Journal of Public Policy* 30:137–162.

Weaver, R. Kent. 2015. Policy Feedbacks and Pension Policy Change. In *Challenges of Aging: Pensions, Retirement and Generational Justice*, ed. Cornelius Torp. London: Palgrave Macmillan, 61–82.

Wechsler, Herbert. 1954. The Political Safeguards of Federalism: The Role of the States in the Composition and Selection of the National Government. *Columbia Law Review* 54:543–560.

Wehrwein, Austin. 1964. "A.M.A. Consults State Societies." *New York Times*, December 14, 72.

Weir, Margaret. 1992. *Politics and Jobs: The Boundaries of Employment Policy in the United States*. Princeton, NJ: Princeton University Press.

Weir, Margaret. 2005. States, Race, and the Decline of New Deal Liberalism. *Studies in American Political Development* 19:157–172.

Weir, Margaret, and Theda Skocpol. 1985. State Structures and the Possibilities for "Keynesian" Responses to the Great Depression in Sweden, Britain, and the United States. In *Bringing the State Back In*, eds. Peter B. Evans, Dietrich Rueschemeyer, and Theda Skocpol. Cambridge, UK: Cambridge University Press, 107–163.

Welch, Susan, and Kay Thompson. 1980. The Impact of Federal Incentives on State Policy Innovation. *American Political Science Review* 24:715–729.

Whittaker, Julie M., and Katelin P. Isaacs. 2014. *Unemployment Insurance: Programs and Benefits*. Washington, DC: Congressional Research Service.

Wilgoren, Jodi. 2001. "State School Chiefs Fret Over U.S. Plan to Require Testing." *New York Times*, July 17.

Wilson, Jan Doolittle. 2007. *The Women's Joint Congressional Committee and the Politics of Maternalism, 1920–30*. Urbana and Chicago: University of Illinois Press.

Witte, Edwin E. 1936. An Historical Account of Unemployment Insurance in the Social Security Act. *Law and Contemporary Problems* 3:157–169.

Witte, Edwin E. 1942. "Federalization" of Unemployment Compensation? *American Labor Legislation Review* 32:41–48.

Wong, Kenneth K. 2015. Federal ESEA Waivers as Reform Leverage: Politics and Variation in State Implementation. *Publius: The Journal of Federalism* 45:405–426.

Wong, Kenneth, and Gail Sunderman. 2007. Education Accountability as Presidential Priority: No Child Left Behind and the Bush Presidency. *Publius: The Journal of Federalism* 37:333–350.

"Wrong Approach." 1942. *Washington Post*, February 22, B6.

Young, James P. 1990. Expanding State Initiation and Enforcement under Superfund. *University of Chicago Law Review* 57:985–1007.

Young, Jeffrey. 2009. "Medicaid Costs Fueling Dispute between States, Senate." *The Hill*, August 6, 49.

Zackin, Emily. 2010. To Change the Fundamental Law of the State: Protective Labor Provisions in U.S. Constitutions. *Studies in American Political Development* 24:1–23.

Zelizer, Julian E. 1998. *Taxing America: Wilbur D. Mills, Congress, and the State, 1945–1975*. New York: Cambridge University Press.

Zimmerman, Joseph F. 2005. *Congressional Preemption: Regulatory Federalism*. Albany, NY: State University of New York Press.

Zimmerman, Joseph F. 2007. Congressional Preemption during the George W. Bush Administration. *Publius: The Journal of Federalism* 37:432–452.

Index